THE REAL ESTATE TURNAROUND:
Craig Hall's Investment Formula That Makes Millions

Craig Hall

Prentice-Hall, Inc.   **Englewood Cliffs, New Jersey**

Prentice-Hall International, Inc., *London*
Prentice-Hall of Australia, Pty., Ltd., *Sydney*
Prentice-Hall of Canada, Ltd., *Toronto*
Prentice-Hall of India Private Ltd., *New Delhi*
Prentice-Hall of Japan, Inc., *Tokyo*
Prentice-Hall of Southeast Asia, Pte., Ltd., *Singapore*
Whitehall Books, Ltd., *Wellington, New Zealand*

© 1978, *by*

PRENTICE-HALL, INC.

Englewood Cliffs, N.J.

Reward Edition . . . . . . September 1980

Library of Congress Cataloging in Publication Data

Hall, Craig,
    The real estate turnaround.

    Includes index.
    1. Real estate business. I. Title.
HD1375.H28   332.6'324   77-17191

Printed in the United States of America

Dedication

This book is dedicated to all of you who dare to take "The Hard Road" — those of you who seek to meet challenge and realize your individual potential in spite of the pressures we all sometimes face when we try to do what we really want.

This book is intended to offer you constructive, practical ideas on how you can make money. Further, it is my hope that this book may in some way encourage and inspire you to try harder at realizing all of your personal goals. The fruits of your courage and hard work will be well rewarded.

FOREWORD

Real estate is a field of great challenge. In real estate, an individual entrepreneur starting with little capital can still make millions of dollars in a short time. It is one of the few fields in which major corporations have found it difficult to profit, but individuals working within localized conditions are making very substantial profits. In real estate, as in any other field, the greater the challenge the greater the potential profit. Therefore, it is not surprising that the turnaround process involving problem properties is probably the most profitable area in real estate today. Turning around problem real estate involves virtually all areas of expertise, including management, marketing, legal and financial problems, physical and developmental problems, negotiating strategy, and many others.

In this book, Craig Hall shows you how to enter the turnaround real estate business and how to proceed on a step-by-step basis. He details every aspect of the business, from finding and evaluating the properties to management techniques, financing, and ultimate resale at substantial profits. This is not a book based on theory, but consists of actual experiences which enabled the author to make millions of dollars starting with just a few thousand in a period of six years.

In my own career, I have been involved in hundreds of millions of dollars of real estate transactions. I have come in contact with hundreds of the leading people in the real estate industry. In the past few years, I have been privileged to come to know Mr. Hall and have grown to respect him as one

7

of the finest real estate professionals in the United States. His success today will undoubtedly be eclipsed by his future success as he is rapidly becoming a major power in the American business community. This book is the first of its kind to actually detail the turnaround process and will, undoubtedly, stand as the finest. It can be a major source of knowledge and profit for all people who are involved in real estate or who are contemplating such an involvement.

M. Martin Rom

M. Martin Rom is President of The Martin Rom Company, Inc. which is involved primarily in finance and real estate.

Mr. Rom was the 1975 President of the Real Estate Securities and Syndication Institute, a Director of the National Association of Realtors, and a member of the National Association of Securities Dealers Committee on Real Estate Securities. Mr. Rom has been involved in over 250 million dollars' worth of real estate transactions.

What This Book Can Do for You

Why This Book Was Written

This book is a down payment on a debt I owe to the real estate business, and to the many fine people who have helped in my career. I doubt any other business would have allowed me to start at age 18 with a $4000 investment, and to achieve a net worth of $6,000,000 in my first six years of full-time work. Now I want to share the ideas and techniques which made this success possible.

Of course, there is much more than money involved in success. As others have discovered before me, making a lot of money is not in itself very satisfying. However, my work has also allowed me to perform a service by conserving and improving distressed properties. Along the way, I have had the opportunity to help dozens of associates achieve their own financial success. My personal reason for writing this book is the hope that I can share with a wider audience the knowledge that has given me so much satisfaction in these areas.

Turnaround Opportunities — What Are They, Where Are They?

The world of real estate is full of opportunities. Perhaps because there are so many, some investors find it difficult to establish a focus or strategy. Circumstances pushed me into a specific and somewhat unique direction. My career has been concentrated on an activity I have labeled "Turnaround." Simply stated, this is the art of taking distressed, under-productive real estate and dramatically improving its value through a special process of problem solving described fully in this book.

Turnaround opportunities exist everywhere. As I explain in Chapter 2, they are created by well-established attitudes and activities which are an integral part of the real estate business. Therefore, wherever you live, you will be able to find opportunities to apply the techniques detailed in this book. My own experience indicates that there is probably not a good-sized town in the U.S. that does not offer exciting opportunity to the turn-around investor! While this book is based on my personal experience, it is important to understand that many others are pursuing similar activities in salvaging distressed properties: The opportunity is here for anyone with the knowledge and motivation.

"How To" Information Included in This Book

You will have the opportunity to learn many things from this book. For example, I will show you how to spot properties which are in trouble, how to analyze their potential for turnaround, and how to always buy in a buyer's market. You will discover the three vital requirements for turn-around success, and the three bonus conditions that can bring you super profits. You will learn why distressed real estate should be less risky than so-called conservative investments.

Here is a sampling of the specific "how to" information available to guide you in your real estate investment activities:

- How to completely eliminate personal liability in your purchase con-tracts to provide a substantially risk-free way to make and keep your real estate fortune.
- How to buy valuable, large properties with little or no money down.
- How small investors can use home improvement loans to pyramid their investment capital and get off to a fast start.
- How to consistently buy real estate for far less than its true value based on your turnaround plans.
- How dramatic increases in occupancy can be achieved at the same time as rental rates are materially increased.
- How to take a situation that has creditors in default mortgage fore-closures and general financial chaos, and make huge profits from financial disaster.
- How you can minimize the tax bite when you sell.
- How to know when to sell and what is the best way to sell.
- How you can use what I call the "magic of paper" to get the highest sales price for your property.

Virtually all of the techniques and principles involved can be applied *to investments of any size.*

Why Turnarounds Work

The turnaround process is basic. It is equally appropriate for invest-ments of any size. The secret of success is the ability to analyze and meet the needs of tenants, lenders, and investors and profiting by providing needed services. Tenants, even in a soft market, will pay more for a place to live that best meets their needs. Lenders will give a turnaround expert who is really improving a property far greater modification of terms on their loan than an average owner who is not helping to solve the lender's problems. Finally, by meeting investors' needs in structuring deals properly, you can profit by having investors put up the risk capital. How you analyze and meet the needs of the players in the real estate game and end up profiting from your service is the essence of what I will cover in this book.

Case Histories

In describing how you too can turn around financially distressed real estate, I use many case histories to illustrate practical examples. The case histories are all based on actual experiences I have had in the turnaround business. Chapters 15 and 18 present complete case histories including the real names of the properties involved. In all other cases, names and the exact size of properties have been fictionalized out of respect to third parties involved in those transactions. However, the essential actions and results are actual facts in all cases. Some examples of case histories discussed include:

- *A $25,000,000 transaction* that involved 1145 apartment units, marina facilities, a public golf course, and vacant land. The property was losing $173,000 per month when it was purchased. It had unpaid construction bills of $1,200,000 and unpaid operating expenses of over $350,000. The six mortgages involved were in default in excess of $2,000,000.

  In just 17 months, occupancy was increased from 58% to 97% while four rent increases were instituted. Many complex financial problems were worked out and the project put on a sound basis.

- *How a $7000 investment* in a property on total rent strike was turned into a 20-year annuity.

- *How a no-money-down purchase* of a 144-unit apartment complex resulting from the "right of first refusal" in a property management contract was accomplished.

- *The 90-day wonder turnaround*, purchased for $3,769,240, with nothing down, from a virtually bankrupt partnership, and unexpectedly resold exactly three months later for a net profit of $430,760!

- A typical older 72-unit apartment project that appeared to have stalled out. When the turnaround techniques were applied, they produced a $230,000 profit on the $80,000 original investment in two years and two months!

A Word of Thanks

Because this book is biographical, much of it is written in the first person. Don't let this mislead you. From the earliest days of my full-time activities in real estate, I recognized that an expanded operation could not be handled by one man. I have been fortunate to have a unique group of intelligent, loyal, and hard-working men and women share my experiences and progress throughout the years. Everything described in this book was made possible because these people were working with me. Each of them is an integral part of the successes described throughout the book.

How the Book Is Organized

This book is organized to provide a logical understanding of the total turnaround process if you read it thoroughly from cover to cover. I urge you to do this because the subject is too big to approach on a random basis.

On the other hand, the book can also be used as an action reference as you go along in your real estate career. For this purpose, it is divided into six parts to help you quickly locate the information you need.

I   Basics of the Turnaround Process
II   Getting Ready to Buy
III   Buying
IV   Making Your Turnaround Work
V   Selling
VI   Putting It All Together

There is no guarantee that you will make millions from real estate investment, but personal experience proves that it is possible. The methods that have worked for me are honestly and completely described in this book. While not everyone can make a million dollars, many, many more people can than do. With the basic background that this book provides, it is my sincere hope that these experiences may help give you a sound foundation to reach your goals and maximize your personal potential. The rest will be up to you; your desire, your energy, and your determination.

Craig Hall

ACKNOWLEDGMENTS

I would like to thank the many people who have had an influence on my career and in particular on the writing of this book. I would like to express my deep appreciation to the following individuals whose guidance, wisdom, and friendship have been a source of inspiration and influence to me in my personal and professional life:

Ron Berlin — *J. David Mackstaller*
Tom Connellan — *Elizabeth McGlinnen*
Larry Deitch. — *Allan Nachman*
Mark Doepker — *Bill Poore*
David Goldman — *Marty Rom*
Colleen Hall — *Kathy Sageman*
Marti Heman — *Dougie Stewart*
Bob Hobbs

And last, but not least, my parents, Herbert and Eleanor Hall.

C. H.

Table of Contents

III
Buying

Contents

IV
Making Your Turnaround Work

VI
Putting It All Together

I

BASICS OF THE
TURNAROUND PROCESS

Chapter 1

Perspective

Through the window of my temporary office, I could see that only a few lights remained on in the hotel that towered above the now lonely highway. Gas stations on two corners across the street had long since closed. The clock on my desk told me it was 3:32 a.m. I was well aware that the date was December 29.

I lay back in my chair, put my feet on the desk, and let my mind wander. I still had $1,848,000 to raise by December 31 in order to complete the $3,300,000 syndication of our latest and largest real estate acquisition. My eyelids felt heavy and I fought the urge to sleep. It had been a couple of nights since I had more than two hours sleep. By day I was out with the security salesmen trying to raise money. By night I was planning strategy and keeping up with some of my other work.

My selling approach had been one of emphasizing the risks the prospective investor would be taking on in this transaction. Perhaps that was the problem. In any event, the investors were reluctant and anyone with any sense would have given up. I truly believed that with a lot of work, my company could make the apartment project involved a viable investment, a real turnaround. I had always believed, however, that investors should know all the negatives before they enter into an investment. Even though at this time I was desperate for funds, I stuck to my position.

With everyone I met, I emphasized the risks and problems at least as much as the benefits and potential rewards. I wanted to be sure no investor could ever feel we had misrepresented the situation.

During one of my calls on the previous day, a prospect was so taken by my negative presentation he simply couldn't pass up the deal. He said he had never heard anyone emphasize the risks of a transaction as much as I did and things couldn't be all that bad. On that reverse logic, he wrote out a check and became a $66,000 investor for one unit of the 50-unit partnership! We had moved one step closer to making this dream a reality.

My body was weary and aching. A slight sweat came over my unshaven face. I truly was wondering whether it could be done. $1,848,000 to go. Again, I went through the list of all the prospects: who was most likely, who was possible, and what needed to be done to try to make the deal work.

Outside, the cold, snowy night was giving way to dawn. It was now a little after 7:00 a.m. and my secretary had arrived. She probably arrived early because she knew I needed someone to talk with during these trying times. While I couldn't let my guard down and show any doubt with other employees, it was different with my secretary. She and I had been through many problems and many moments of great success since I entered the real estate investment business just six years earlier.

She made coffee and we talked for an hour. As we reminisced about the old days and other tough situations, the confidence returned. After all, in six years I had moved from a $4000 down ramshackle boarding house that was losing a little money, to my concern now with a $25,000,000 property that was losing $173,000 a month. That's progress! My first purchase had been turned around and became a good investment. Why should I doubt that this latest challenge wouldn't be successful as well?

That was the kind of thinking I needed to get back on the track. Before the new year arrived just three days later, I did finish the money raising requirement, and our largest turnaround to date was over one major hurdle. That story is told in Chapter 18, *How We Turned a Lemon into Pure Gold.*

To really understand how I came to be in that sleepless situation, we have to take a look at the whole area of turnaround real estate investments — the activity that allowed me to turn $4000 into $6,000,000 in just six years.

What Is a "Turnaround"?

Turnarounds are investments which follow a planned process of selecting and buying under-performing real estate, improving it, and reselling it at a substantial profit.

"Under-performing real estate" is property which is not achieving its economic potential. Most often, turnarounds involve "distressed" rental properties which are in serious financial difficulty ranging from negative cash flow to default and mortgage foreclosure. Properties which fit into the turnaround formula must meet certain vital requirements and they may possess bonus characteristics which make them very profitable turnaround candidates.

Turnaround opportunities can be found in all kinds of markets and in all parts of the country. These opportunities may involve small or large properties. Because the properties selected for turnaround operations are usually in serious distress, opportunities exist for dramatic results. Consider these actual examples:

A two-family rental, bought for $27,250 with $4000 down payment. A $2500 improvement allowed rents to be raised by $3280, and this in turn led to a resale of the property within two years for $49,000!

A 432-unit apartment project which had occupancy of about 65% through its first four years of existence. After turnaround techniques were in operation for 18 months, occupancy was stabilized at 94% with rents increased almost 10%.

As a part of the process of selecting and buying under-performing real estate, a carefully planned action program is put together. This program uses proven turnaround techniques which meet identified needs in the areas of finance, operation, physical improvement, and marketing. After implementing the necessary programs and maximizing the potential of the property, the final step is to sell the improved investment at a profit.

The turnaround process discussed in this book does not ignore the conventional values of real estate investment. It builds on them. Tax advantages, inflation power, and leverage power are all fully employed in turnarounds. However, the additional impact of planned actions to create improvement achieves a far greater economic value for the property than conventional growth factors alone.

Why Distressed Properties Are not Speculative

At first consideration, most conservative investors shy away from the idea of deliberately buying a property that is in trouble — especially serious trouble. But when that purchase is made under the turnaround principle, every test of a conservative investment *can* be met.

"Speculative" usually refers to an investment with an unknown or uncertain future, but a hope of large potential profit. "Conservative" usually describes a known situation with a reasonably reliable anticipation of future results. But, there is no law that says a conservative investment cannot carry a projected profit that is larger than a speculative hope. My experience has been that carefully selected turnaround projects are the most conservative, as well as the most profitable, of all real estate investments.

With those working definitions in mind, consider the special advantages available to the skilled turnaround investor who actively seeks financially troubled property.

The "White Knight" Syndrome

The new owner or manager comes in and starts to do things. There are so many problems that when he starts to correct them, people immediately start to look at him as a white knight — a good guy. The proper turnaround program, carefully implemented, quickly gains amazing credibility. As a white knight, you will be amazed at what people will do for you.

Tenants who were upset with the last landlord will be very coopera-tive to the white knight who fixes a leaky roof and cleans their hallway, even though he then raises their rent to pay for both, plus adding extra profit to the bottom line.

The lender wants to cooperate with the white knight since he sees the property being improved and the gross rent potential increased. You are either working him out of a spot or helping to avoid the trouble which was seen as probable. The lender will often make financial concessions to a new white knight once the turnaround is underway and success seems assured.

Local government officials who were hassling the former landlord for code violations and zoning problems do an about-face. They become very friendly supporters of the white knight because the turnaround owner makes their job easier. For one thing, he works hard to make the tenants happy, and therefore they don't call the code inspector or their city council representative with complaints.

When you are a turnaround investor, you are doing something the community, the lender, and the tenants can be proud of. They will all be anxious to help you make more money from your investment because you will be truly providing a needed service in conserving and improving distressed property.

A wonderful example of the cooperation phenomenon is unfolding right now, as this book is being written. About ten weeks ago, I purchased a large mobile home park in a community where I had never worked be-fore. At the time of purchase, local officials indicated they had no inten-tion of issuing any more move-in permits because the development was only partially built and there had been a long history of broken promises from previous owners.

I moved ahead with our program of proper funding, active work on the unfinished construction, and property management of the portion of the park already in use. Last week a building inspector was on site to o.k. some of the new work. Strangely, he excused himself and left for a half hour in the middle of the inspection. He returned with the mayor of the community because he was so enthused about the way a former eyesore was turning into a community asset!

The mayor not only announced that move-in permits were available again, he also suggested the entire city council would appreciate invita-tions to the Grand Opening. Once again, the white knight won.

How Turnarounds Became My "Thing" in Real Estate

I had one great advantage when I started my real estate investment career during the summer before entering college: I knew almost nothing about conventional approaches to the business.

My mind was open. I was filled with boundless curiosity, and a desire to learn what made this gigantic business tick. I had read a few books about real estate investment and talked to a few brokers. I was convinced that real estate offered abundant opportunity for an ambitious young person.

At that time, I only had $4000 to invest, but I had a burning desire to do big things.

Certainly, my lack of apprenticeship or formal real estate education left me without basic information which would have been helpful. On the other hand, I was not burdened with the conventional ideas which might have doomed me to conventional results. In my blissful ignorance, I felt that real estate was a field where logic, common sense, and perhaps a little imagination might open the door to more than average success. Now, after more than $100,000,000 worth of real estate transactions, I am firmly convinced that this business does offer a unique opportunity to newcomers who are willing to think things through for themselves instead of merely following the accepted paths. It was that attitude that led to the development of my turnaround formula.

My plan to break into the real estate investment field was not very original. I decided to look for a "fix-it-up rental special" which I could buy cheaply and then improve with cosmetic refurbishing.

To protect my $4000 nest-egg—the result of spare-time work since the age of 12 — I carefully examined and analyzed almost 100 seemingly suitable listings. Detailed notes concerning location, condition, operating costs, income, an estimate of fix-up costs, and an estimate of the value of the refurbishing were included.

Following the Crowd Can Be Costly

As my notebook became heavier, so did my spirits. I couldn't find the kind of opportunity I had been led to believe awaited me in real estate. The difference between the asking prices and my best estimate of what I could gain through appearance or cosmetic improvements seemed mighty slim.

It took me a while to realize what was happening. The idea of building a fortune through cosmetic improvement had been highly publicized and the market was full of would-be investors looking for fix-up opportunities with low down payments. The market had reacted in its normal way. Prices had gone up because of high demand, and if I wanted to follow the crowd I would have to pay the price.

The Birth of the Turnaround Technique

I decided to look for another kind of opportunity. I remembered one listing that had seemed so negative I had not even inspected it the first time around. So I took another look and ended up buying my first property.

The full story of that investment, the Glendaloch Place Story is told in Chapter 13. For now, just let me say that this property had been a total disaster for the previous owner. His 2½ year investment had cost him out-of-pocket money almost every month! He had purchased it as a fix-up investment, but he never got around to carrying out his plans because he was unable to cope with unexpected vacancies, non-payment of rents, mismanagement, poor utilization of space, and numerous other problems. Of course, I didn't think of this as a "turnaround" at the time, merely as a bigger challenge than a cosmetic improvement and a bigger opportunity. I was sure I was on the right track when I sold the property two years later and realized a net profit of $18,750 on my $4000 investment!

Key Requirements of Turnaround Properties

1. The property must be producing substantially less income than would be warranted by its cost, size, or other characteristics.
2. The current owner must be ready to admit the financial difficulty at least to himself. While he may not say it directly, it is important that he really welcomes the opportunity to sell.
3. The location must be fundamentally good. The area may have been premature in development or may be temporarily over-developed, but the long term potential must be good.
4. The construction quality must be basically sound. While cosmetic improvements may often be required and some structural changes may be necessary, it is essential that the basic physical plant be solid and structurally sound. Any product defects must be of a type which can be corrected. The cost of the planned work must be accounted for in the capitalization of the project.

Bonus Conditions

1. *Over-built* — Oftentimes, the best potential turnaround situations are over-built projects. These usually are created when the developer-owner satisfied his ego by putting more quality into the project than renters are prepared to pay for. At a discounted price, this quality can be of benefit to the turnaround buyer. Since you are not really paying for the extra quality, having it is a definite bonus.
2. *Tired owner* — If the owner has been emotionally drained by tenant problems and financial stress, he may be ready to sell at your price. The owner may be a builder-developer, subsequent owner, or even a financial institution which has foreclosed on the property. The point remains the same — the owner is psychologically sick of the property, he is ready to give you the kind of price and terms that will help you make a super turnaround profit.

3. *Improving market* — Timing is important in buying turnaround properties. Oftentimes, I buy the property that has just come through a very severe downturn in the marketplace. If I time the purchase with the early stages of market recovery, I will not only benefit from the turnaround technique improvements I will make, but as the market strengthens, the property will achieve an additional boost in profitability.

Stages of the Turnaround Process

The Turnaround process involves three separate stages: problem analysis, remedy, and result. Each of these stages requires active commitment and involvement on the part of the turnaround investor or qualified manager. The only way to successfully turn around a development or a property is to carefully identify and attack every problem area completely on a carefully planned basis. This three-stage process must be applied to all problems.

Problem Analysis

During this stage, the property is carefully studied to determine what items are causing it to under-perform. In these cases, it is necessary to look far beyond superficial problems and perform an in-depth analysis.

For example, if a property has a high vacancy, identifying the complete reason why is essential to determine the correct remedy. I remember once our company took over a 50-unit apartment development which had continually operated with 15-20 units vacant since it had been built. Several good management companies had tried unsuccessfully to improve the high vacancy primarily through cutting the rent.

When my company came into the situation, the first activity was to analyze the problem. Everyone had written off the vacancy problem as being one of excess competition in the area. Competition seemed to be the problem, but my people dug below the surface. By talking to residents who lived in the project and interviewing prospects who decided not to rent, they quickly found the real reason. The project was a fine physical facility offered at a fair price, but it wasn't delivering the services and snob appeal some prospects expected at the existing rent structure!

Remedy

Once a property has been properly analyzed and the problems are known, the next step is to map out a plan for solving each and every need. I emphasize that we must not forget any part of the problem, so the problem analysis and proposed remedies are put in writing. This forces careful consideration of a total program instead of trying surface solutions on a helter-skelter basis.

The remedy which was used in the above example included expanding services and, in fact, raising rents. The existing rent schedule was too high for a low income market and services were too low for a higher income market. The property fell into a void. By adding and upgrading services to include social programs and superior maintenance, I was able to very quickly achieve a better resident selection. This was coupled with advertising and rental attitudes that helped the project generally take on an air of exclusivity in the marketplace.

In short, there was a complete psychological face-lift and a changeabout in the community's image of the project. This did not occur overnight. It required numerous planned actions, but in less than one year, the property which for five years had maintained a 30% to 40% vacancy rate, became 100% occupied and had a waiting list.

Result

For many property managers, establishing the required result as part of the turnaround program seems to be the most difficult part of the process. They want to "try the remedy and see what happens." That approach invites financial trouble and seriously reduces the value of a planned turnaround.

Only by planning *specific* results for each identified problem can you identify the remedies and budgets which will be required. Only with specific anticipated results can you monitor performance and make necessary adjustments as you go along. While the obvious result of a total program is improved profitability, much more specific goals must be established in each prime area. I work on a goal orientation system covering each part of the total plan. Whenever possible, these goals or results are quantified in a range of acceptable levels.

The three-stage process of the turnaround program is carefully reviewed and monitored on an ongoing basis throughout the actual implementation. It is important to realize that the remedy may have to be changed several times in order to produce the desired result. In fact, problem re-analysis may be required if results are not being obtained. The key is that these three stages are always viewed in a common context during planning and implementation. Review and ongoing change is an expected part of the program.

Four Ways to Look at a Turnaround Property

Experience has indicated that the problems of distressed properties tend to clump around four vital areas: physical, finance, marketing, and operation. When considering a purchase or when planning a turnaround program, I give each of these areas separate consideration. Depending on the size and complexity of the property, the specific elements which must be examined will vary. More detail is provided in Chapters 11, 12, 13, 14, and 15 as to the ways of applying turnaround techniques in each of the vital areas.

No matter how small or how large your turnaround may be, the key is planning to cover every base. Take nothing for granted. Look for every possible need or problem as these are your raw materials to effect profitable change. The famous industrialist, Henry Kaiser, frequently pointed out to his executives, "There are no problems in our business, only opportunities for improvement." This philosophy also applies to real estate, and it will provide big dividends if you put it to work.

Final Step — Cashing in

Turnaround real estate is for selling! A fundamental part of the turnaround principle is selling the property for profit after the economic value has been maximized. Knowing when and how to sell is all-important because the real profit from turnarounds is made from the sale, not operation and ownership. It is important not to be afraid to take your profit and go on to your next challenge.

Unfortunately, too many people become too emotionally attached to real estate. This is particularly true when a lot of sweat and hard work has been put into turning an under-performing property into a success. If your objective is continued capital appreciation and growth, remember, there is always a larger turnaround opportunity available. The profit in moving on is much greater than simply operating a producing property.

Chapter 2

The Turnaround Process
Crystallized

Success starts with opportunity, so it is important to know how and why your opportunities are created. The truth is that real estate is a very individualistic people business. It is the last stronghold of entrepreneurs where a small man with the leverage of readily available financing can literally move mountains.

This individual power in a high-velocity money business is both the strength and the weakness of real estate. It allows individuals to start from scratch and make fortunes. It also allows individuals to make the kinds of errors which create turnaround opportunities. If you are going to seek turnaround opportunities, it is well to recognize the individuals who may create them for you.

Builder-Developers are the creators of most investment properties. By and large, they are capable entrepreneurs who play a vital role in supplying housing for our growing population. However, developers are also human beings, and as such they are subject to foibles which from time to time create problem properties.

Every once in a while a developer will subconsciously decide to build a monument to himself — a superior project that will be admired by everyone. This is an admirable objective, but usually it results in a high cost property that simply cannot be supported by the market. Everyone admires this kind of property, but few are willing to pay the rent required to support the mortgages and maintenance. Frequently such projects get into serious financial difficulty, and turnaround opportunities are born.

Lenders are another vital part of the housing industry. Somehow, we fail to realize that lenders are businessmen, supplying their product (money) at costs that are controlled by supply and demand. As a result, there are times when the lender cannot provide the builder-developer with all the funds requested for a project. Furthermore, when money is in short supply, the cost to the builder-developer will increase in the form of loan points and higher interest rates.

If the builder-developer is not willing to postpone his new venture, he may simply adjust his economic projections to make the figures for the development fit the money that is available.

The problem is that projections are not reality. If future rent projections are set higher to meet the debt service created by high money costs, that does not mean those rents will be accepted by the market. On the other hand, if the projected cost of a new development is reduced to fit the loan money available, that does not assure the quality and features which will attract sufficient renters to financially support the development.

Naturally, no lender or developer would purposely establish a financial structure that would lead to operating deficits. But no one has a crystal ball. As a result, the fact is that many turnaround opportunities are created by financial imbalances built into projects at the time of original financing.

Owners, too, are a source of some of the basic problems which create the need for turnarounds. Certainly owners are interested in maintaining sound, profit-producing operations. Most do, but some make serious errors.

For example, there are owners of seasoned properties who have the benefit of lower original construction costs and interest rates. Instead of keeping their rents up with the market, they cautiously avoid increases on the premise that they can keep their projects 100% full with low rents reflecting their original costs. They forget that other costs are going up dramatically: security, landscaping, appliances, carpet replacement, roof repairs, painting, management, and on and on. This type of owner fails to watch the bottom line until one day he suddenly finds his gold mine has run out.

Another owner who creates turnaround opportunities is the individual who feels that management of rental real estate is simply a necessary evil. He relegates the job to a lightweight and provides minimum financial support. The property may not suffer in an expanding market, but as soon as things tighten even slightly, poor management will create serious problems.

Errors Create Turnaround Opportunities

Essentially, potential turnarounds are created by one or a combination of errors: errors in construction, errors in financing, errors in calculating market demand, errors in management. As you examine properties, it is well to keep these major areas in mind.

Frequently you will see indications of major errors in one area or another, and yet the project may seem to be doing very well. This doesn't mean the error wasn't made, it simply indicates the project is temporarily operating within the "margin of error" allowed by the marketplace at the moment. A slight shift in the economy or the competitive situation can trigger the inherent error into action which will eventually lead to a turn-around opportunity.

The Downward Cycle

Many properties that get into serious financial difficulty and make particularly good turnaround prospects have first undergone a downward cycle. I have seen this cycle occur time after time. It may affect either a new property that never really gets on its feet or an existing property that has apparently been successful.

It frequently starts when a project is in marginal financial condition, just making expenses and debt service, and then other financial pressures crop up. Suppose you have a ten-unit apartment building with a cash flow of $2500 per year and suddenly you have a major boiler expense. Your entire cash flow can be wiped out.

If shortly after your cash flow is wiped out something else occurs that causes you to be $1000 in deficit, it makes you a very nervous owner. In addition to being upset about their financial loss position, some owners simply do not have the money to continue supporting the property.

The next step in the downward cycle is usually that the owner must decide how to balance his budget so he looks for the areas in which he can cut expenses and save money.

So, let's assume your tenant in apartment #3 complains about the condition of his carpet and wants to have it replaced. You take a look at the carpet and realize that indeed it is fairly old. If you have just had two or three serious problems and you are in a money-losing position for the year, you might decide to tell the tenant he is going to have to wait. You put off the capital improvement because you simply can't afford it. If, on the other hand, you had been in a good cash flow year, you probably would have replaced the tenant's carpet.

We now have a situation where you have just told one tenant that he cannot have new carpet, and you are still looking for places to save money and balance the budget. You get an idea. Instead of paying someone to cut the lawn once a week, you will have it cut every ten days. Instead of having the building hallway cleaned weekly, you will have that done every other week. On and on it goes, and all of a sudden, the appearance of your property has changed noticeably.

Meanwhile, back to the tenant who lives in apartment #3 of our hypothetical ten-unit building. At this point he is unhappy about not getting new carpet. He sees the hallway a little dirtier than previously and the lawn a little higher, and he becomes more and more irritated. Mr. Tenant is doing a slow burn, but at this point is still keeping it to himself.

Next, you find you still haven't saved enough money, so you decide to lag bills a bit. You realize you must pay the lender and must pay the utilities. You decide to simply be a little slower with payment to the painter, lawn service, and the local hardware store. Slower becomes even slower over a period of time and the hardware store cuts off credit, the lawn service becomes angry, and Mr. Landlord must find two or three new vendors.

At the same time, you are turning down other tenants who request carpet replacement. When an appliance goes bad, you replace it with a less attractive, used appliance. You are simply doing everything possible to save money.

Tenant Reaction Speeds the Cycle

You then decide you must raise the rents to make ends meet. You give everyone notice, and their rent goes up. Mr. Tenant in #3 is now going from a slow burn to a firecracker rage. He sees his neighbor, Mr. Jones in #7, who just had a refrigerator replaced with a less expensive model than the one he previously had. They talk about what a bad guy the landlord is. Knowing that Mr. Landlord is, of course, ripping them off for unconscionable profit, they decide they will not pay the raise. In fact, they are not going to pay rent at all until the services that have been slowly cut down are restored.

About this time you notice there aren't as many prospective tenants dropping by as there were formerly. Matter of fact, it's getting hard to fill a vacancy, and you wonder why. The reason, of course, is that tenants and vendors are part of the community. When they are unhappy they talk, and word spreads fast.

With the hardware store mad at you, the lawn service not cutting the lawn because of non-payment, the tenants talking about a rent strike, and another utility bill due, you must do something. Frequently, at this stage, the next logical step seems to be to delay paying the mortgage by one month. The cycle goes on, and the one month becomes two, and Mr. Landlord is in deep trouble. The property is looking worse and worse. Good tenants are moving out and you have trouble re-renting. You have a real mess on your hands because you have been caught in the downward cycle.

In rental management, it is so easy to be penny-wise and dollar-foolish. Our Mr. Landlord vainly tried to save his way into prosperity, only to make matters worse and worse. You may think that this story is an exception, yet it is a common situation in large and small rental properties and in new and old rental properties. Landlord-managers often react 180 degrees opposite to their best interests when they begin to get into financial difficulty. This downward cycle often leads to opportunity for the turnaround expert.

The entrepreneurial nature of the real estate industry lays the groundwork for turnaround opportunities. Individual foibles create errors, and the very human reactions of those involved compound these errors into a downward cycle that leads to disasters begging for rescue.

A Creative Management Approach

The turnaround investor does have a fertile field, but that alone is not enough to assure success. The turnaround specialist must have a searching, creative mind. He or she must enjoy going down uncharted paths instead of following the mob. This requires a high level of self-confidence backed by effective analytical and problem-solving abilities.

Even the small turnaround investor should have management knowledge and ability. You must know how to plan a step-by-step approach to achieve identified goals. You must know how to monitor results and evaluate constantly changing needs. You must know how to work with and through people: employees, vendors, and tenants.

I emphasize these basic requirements because turnaround properties will not turn around by themselves. If you are not prepared to manage your investment, it will surely manage you. And the results will not be happy. If you do not feel qualified in this area, face up to it before you try to invest in a turnaround opportunity. You have several options.

Investing Through Others

The investor without time for personal planning and management can use the knowledge available in this book as a guide to seeking out and evaluating qualified management services, or limited partnership investment groups who may be specializing in turnarounds. The secret of success in utilizing the turnaround method is to prepare.

Prepare yourself to fully examine the actual operation of any group you intend to use as an investment vehicle. Talk is cheap. But actual operational results count. Be prepared to look beneath the surface before you count on others to make your investments work.

Active Investment Requires Specialized Knowledge

If you are going to handle your own turnaround investments, be sure you are properly prepared. Theoretical knowledge isn't essential, but it does help. This might include college or junior college courses in property management, real estate finance, general business management, problem-solving, etc.

The one absolute requirement for turnaround is the ability to manage the property on a day-to-day basis, or to effectively plan and supervise this activity. Some personal experience in this area is highly desirable, almost essential, for the active personal turnaround investor.

If you don't have experience, consider a full-time, low-level job with a large property management company. If this is not practical, another approach is to invest in a small rental property in a stable situation, not a turnaround. Manage it for a year or so as a sideline to your normal work as you observe and study the turnaround field. In either event, you'll be exposed to the realities of property management, and will be preparing yourself for more complex challenges.

Property Management as a Springboard to Investment

If your circumstances will allow it, I recommend active property management service for other investors as an excellent springboard for your own turnaround investment. The management business is easy to enter, requires little capital, and allows for fast growth in both size and experience.

While you are gaining knowledge, you will also be gaining credibility which will pay off handsomely when dealing with sellers, lenders, and potential investors.

One of my early growth jumps as an investor came about entirely because I was in the property management business. It allowed me to intelligently buy a $1,000,000 property with almost no money down at a time when I had no money to put down. In fact, I walked out of the closing with a $17,000 check from the seller!

The Sunshine Terrace Project

Sunshine Terrace was a 140-unit apartment complex that had all the earmarks of a perfect turnaround. It was owned by a lender who had foreclosed during the construction of the building. The property had not been properly launched due to many delays in construction and significant cost over-runs. In fact, the bank had to hire contractors to finish the construction during a time of significant construction trade union strike problems. The actual labor which finished the project did so with armed guard protection against union threats.

The bank continued to have difficulties. Properties tend to suffer from getting off to a wrong start or having a bad reputation, and this particular property was a classic example. When I heard about the property I contacted the bank, but we were unable to work out a price and terms which would be mutually satisfactory. At that particular time, which was about five years ago, I did not have the capital base to offer the bank a sizable down payment or commitment to the project. In our discussions it became apparent that I was financially out of my ball park and did not have enough money to buy the property, but I had established my credibility in being able to deliver the specialized turnaround management the property needed.

Since the bank had always worked by hiring outside property management companies, and since they were impressed with my ability to handle this type of property, they asked if my company would be interested in managing it. I, of course, was delighted, since at that time I was most interested in anything that would add to my cash flow survival level. In that particular year, the sole income from my business was only $5900. This management contract could produce an additional $15,000 to $20,000, so of course it was most welcome.

Naturally, I did not tell the bank how much their contract would help our business, and I negotiated from a position of strength because I was convinced my company could provide the necessary energy and direction to the project.

As a result, I obtained rent-up fees in addition to the property management fee, and the bank-owner agreed to put up the money necessary to turn around the image of the property.

In addition to the much needed fees, we were able to negotiate a right of first refusal on future purchase of the property. At the time, this seemed harmless to all of us. Basically, the right of first refusal stated that if at any time the bank had a bona fide offer to acquire the property they were willing to accept, they were first to offer it to my company on the same terms and conditions. About one and a half years after the management contract commenced, with the property doing much better, the bank received such a bona fide offer, and presented the offer to me for review.

The offer was from a good, financially strong customer of the bank. It represented a no down payment deal for the new buyer. It was a favorable transaction for the bank at the time based on internal needs since the bank had held the property in excess of five years. Based on recent sale of bank stock and additional capitalization, they were ready to take the substantial loss necessary to sell the property.

I immediately agreed to meet the terms and conditions of the offer and acquired the property. That transaction later worked out to be very profitable. Just a short time after acquiring the property, a little over 18 months, we sold the project for a profit of $525,000. I must add, this was not cash, but was in the form of a secured receivable. This form of sale is more fully discussed in Chapter 17, *The Magic of Paper.*

In the end, the bank got what they needed and wanted in the transaction. I was, of course, very pleased and the owners who purchased from me received a substantially stronger, proven product than I originally bought.

Turnaround Pitfalls to Avoid

There are several pitfalls to avoid. Here are some of the more common ones to keep in mind:

- *Don't chase rainbows* — Analyze your deal, make your offer, be thorough, but don't spend time with an unreasonable seller who is just playing games. Too often, the seller or the lender may not really be financially capable of selling, or desirous of selling on a reasonable basis. Size up the situation quickly and don't chase rainbows.
- *Beware of properties that won't turn* — Don't be so anxious to buy that you buy the wrong type of property. Not every property can be a turnaround. Some properties that are in financial trouble have problems which cannot be solved. A key part of the buying process must be a reasonable analysis of the problems to see whether or not adequate remedies do, in fact, exist.
- *Don't buy something just because it is cheap* — Sometimes cheap properties are really expensive in the long run. I remember spending a great deal of time analyzing a development that could be bought for $4000 per unit. To rebuild it would have cost $12,000 to $16,000 per unit! I couldn't believe that you couldn't make a lot of money on a property that could be bought for so little.
  The truth was that after really looking over the numbers, the property was selling for exactly what it was worth. Its chance of improving was slim to zero. The inner city location was poor and the area was getting worse and worse. While per unit prices may seem very low, they may, in fact, be expensive prices in the long run.
- *The double turnaround* — Once you have turned your property around and it is profitable, get out. Don't wait for the property to to get into new trouble. Sell when you are at the top. Too often, we fall in love with the property when it is doing well, but the essence of turnaround is to improve and sell, to buy near the bottom and sell near the top.
- *Don't lose your credibility* — Don't announce a turnaround program until you are completely organized. Start doing things for people before you tell them what you are going to do. People are interested in results, not hot air. Credibility and the white knight image can help you achieve turnaround success, but lost credibility can kill you faster than anything else.

II

GETTING READY
TO BUY

Chapter 3

Defining Your
Turnaround Objectives

How to Avoid One of the Biggest Real Estate Investor Costs

The real estate investment field is filled with a tremendous variety of opportunities. Once you start looking, you will have one broker after another calling you about deals. Sooner or later, if you look at all the deals that are offered, you will find some exceptionally interesting properties. Shopping opportunities can work out, but there is a hidden cost in this approach.

In real estate, everything you touch takes time, effort, and energy, a "transaction cost." Any new area you enter requires special skills and it takes time to learn those skills, an "education cost." Finally, any area about which you are not familiar and knowledgeable, has a potentially high degree of risk. This does not mean that you should avoid new kinds of opportunities, but it does suggest caution against going in too many directions at once. Anyone who is doing too many things can easily lose control and find himself in financial difficulty.

The best approach is to work out a list of your investment objectives. Think thoroughly, realistically, and creatively about your investment goals. Then sit down and consciously write up a description of the type of property you will be seeking. This should be in a detailed form but with sufficient flexibility to allow you to stick to the program. Periodically, you must review your activities and progress toward your goals. Be absolutely honest with yourself. Adjust activities as necessary or you can even change your objectives, but always do so with a conscious reason and purpose in mind and do it in writing.

The value of a written set of objectives to limit and direct real estate investment activity is illustrated by one of my friends in the business. Let's call him Sam. He can't seem to say no. Sam is the type of person who has a good mind for real estate and is very successful in some of his ventures. But Sam has strayed from one investment to another without any rhyme

43

or reason. Sam owns some rooming houses, a couple of smaller apartment buildings, some land, two grocery stores, one warehouse, and three down-town office and shopping buildings. Sam is always broke and just barely keeps going.

Sam is much older than I and has been in the business for a long time, but he never seems to save himself from one or two big loss deals a year. This sets back all his profitable ventures. It is ironic how people like Sam constantly move ahead three steps and back two.

Yet, Sam is typical of many real estate people I know. They grab at the brass ring everytime the merry-go-round goes by. If Sam would only apply his energy in a straight line and choose one direction — grocery stores, office buildings, or whatever — and master that, he could stabilize his portfolio instead of trying to be all things to all people. Sam could be a very successful and wealthy real estate entrepreneur. Unfortunately, he has probably never heard of, or chooses to ignore, the idea of organizing his activities to meet a specified set of personal objectives.

Setting Realistic Objectives

In setting realistic objectives, there are several things you should consider. The following is a brief checklist of some of the items which will help you decide on the type and size of property you should be looking for:

- *Your commitment* — Is real estate investment to be the most important activity in your life, or is it a part-time hobby?
- *Your personality* — Are you ready and able to continuously deal with tenants personally? Will you do better negotiating with businessmen and corporations? Are you mechanically oriented, or more at home with numbers?
- *Time available* — How much time and energy do you realistically have to devote to achieving your objectives? If you can't handle everything properly, who will? What will this help cost? Can you afford it?
- *Cash available* — How much cash are you willing and reasonably able to dedicate to the program of meeting your objectives?
- *Credit available* — From what sources and to what extent can you obtain credit?
- *Experience* — Do you have any special knowledge or skill which might prove valuable in a particular type of real estate investment? What experience will be required to reach your objectives?
- *Property Management skills* — What level of management skill do you really have as it relates to your proposed objective? If you lack the necessary skills, do you have a real plan to bring someone into the picture who can provide what you lack?

Obviously, everyone must start somewhere and if you are interested in a type or size of property in which you have not been previously involved, that is fine. In fact, I personally have found that the best way to learn anything is to do

Nevertheless, you need to consider the above points to be sure you have commitment, time, energy, experience, cash, and credit available in line with the objectives you are setting. You must look at these considerations on balance and decide what is a reasonable objective for your type of investment program. If you ignore the real facts at this stage, you are just flirting with disaster. Be completely honest with yourself

Review Your Plans Frequently

In my own case, I evaluate my business activities every six months. I seek to become involved with new investment activities I think I will find exciting and challenging. But I only do so after first evaluating my ability to properly handle the new activity.

In thinking about time or cash availability, I must look at our current activities and whether or not they are under good control. It is only after careful consideration on a six-month basis that I set up our company's written objectives for each type of business activity. This program has served well over the years, and every time I have deviated from it I have found it costly.

Economic Signals

In establishing your acquisition objectives, you must consider more than just your own inclinations and ability. One major element is the status of the national and local economy. For years, real estate investors felt the economy was stable enough that if they ran their own business properly, that was enough. That is not always true, however, and you can easily find yourself doing all the right things at the wrong time if you are not aware of economic swings.

While you cannot expect to be an economist yourself, you must be aware of what the economists are predicting. Educate yourself as to what the experts say about the local market in which you are interested and about the national economy. Short term movements are not as important as anticipating basic trends one to two years in advance. See what predictions are being made and consider their effect on your plans before moving forward.

Your Marketplace

Check into the market demand for the type of property you are interested in acquiring. For instance, if you are interested in acquiring a rental apartment property in your home town, check into how other rental apartment projects are doing. Consider whether population has increased or decreased in recent years. Is the industry diversified, or is this a one-industry town subject to wild employment swings?

The most important thing in checking out market demands is not how the market is doing, but what the trend is. Often when you are buying a turnaround, the best acquisitions are available during a bad rental market. The point is to qualify *why* the rental market is bad. If the market is soft and there are a high number of vacancies because several new apartment projects recently came on stream at the same time, or because there is a temporary recession in the local economy, that is one thing. If it's soft because people and businesses are moving out of the area to the extent that population is being reduced, that is a completely different story.

The key thing to determine is why the market is doing poorly, and how long the trend is likely to continue. Then dig hard to decide what the future trend will be. Remember, turnarounds are bought for the future market, not for current demand.

The "Swim Against the Stream" Theory

In setting your objectives as to the type, size, and nature of the property you will seek, if you come up with a program that other real estate investors think is crazy, you may well be on the right track!

In the turnaround business, you will often be buying when everyone else is selling, and selling when everyone else is buying. You must have confidence in the recovery of markets in the overall cycles that affect real estate and the economy in general. When most people in the marketplace are panicky, that is the time to keep a cool head and quietly pick and choose the best buys in the market.

I can remember giving speeches on my optimism and bullishness on real estate during 1974 and 1975. Many real estate professionals listened to me with interest but few, if any, followed my advice. Many felt "this guy Hall has to be a crazy man." I was saying "buy" when daily they were losing more and more money on apartments.

During that particular time, vacancies in many markets were high and expenses were increasing much faster than rents. Equally important, however, was the fact that new family formations were on the rise at record levels. This was anticipated in my plans, based on birth records of 18 to 20 years earlier. Most important, new construction starts were at their lowest levels in years. Applying those national trends to particular local markets, it wasn't difficult to see that we were in a pendulum situation which had swung temporarily to a disadvantage for apartment owners. I emphasize "temporarily." By the acquisition of properties from lenders or owners who were in trouble, properly capitalizing the ownership of the property, and applying turnaround techniques, the property value could be maximized and improved. Furthermore, I knew the bonus condition of an improving market would be right behind, be it by six months or one year or even 18 months, simply based on the economics of supply and demand which seemed so obvious.

During that time, I did a great deal of buying and only regret that I didn't buy more. Unfortunately for most of my colleagues, they were doing the selling, only to be on the outside looking in when the market began to improve. It is usually true that when you swim against the stream, with good reason, you will find the biggest profits. The important thing is not to just buy right, but, when everyone else in the flock starts buying again, to sell the properties back at big profits.

Deciding on Your Investment Vehicle

There are a number of types of entities to use as your investment vehicle in buying turnaround properties. The right investment vehicle for your objectives depends on the exact facts of the situation. Here are the major possibilities and the advantages and disadvantages you should consider. For details that apply in your state, be sure to seek the advice of an attorney with specific real estate investment knowledge.

- *On your own* — Buying property in your own name and holding it in your name is often the best way if you can handle the investment without partners. The advantages are that it is simple and keeps the profit and tax advantages in your personal financial position. The major disadvantage is that if title is held in your name, you are personally accountable to creditors. Additionally, you may not want to have the fact that you own the property be public knowledge, and of course this information is available to anyone if you take title in your name.

- *General and co-partnership* — This vehicle is frequently used by active business partners. It has the advantage of holding the property in the partnership according to the agreement of the principals Further, the tax losses can be passed through to the individuals in proportion to their percentage ownership, and the profits from cash distribution also passed through according to the terms of the partnership agreement. The disadvantages are that you may be liable for the debts incurred or the decisions made by your partner or partners.

- *Private limited partnership* — This is a vehicle which can be very effective if you are interested in getting a small number of other investors to put money into your transaction I have used limited partnership to purchase and operate many properties and find it to be an excellent vehicle. Basically, the limited partners are the investors who put up capital and have no active say in management decisions of the partnership. They are "limited" in that each limited partner's liability cannot exceed the capital he has invested. The limited partnership must have one or more individuals designated as the general partner. The general partner is the active operating partner who has full control of all management decisions and accepts unlimited liability for the debts of the partnership. Frequently, the general partner invests little or no money, but receives a portion of the partnership interest in return for his work. This is a very effective way for a turnaround property to be capitalized with other people's money.

- *Public limited partnership* — This is a vehicle similar to the private limited partnership, but it must be registered with Securities Bureaus and generally is subject to a number of regulatory laws which must be carefully obeyed. Public limited partnerships are useful when you desire to raise sums of money requiring more investors than state regulations allow in a limited partnership. They are, however, cumbersome, and you usually end up with many investors with whom you have little rapport and even less control. Sometimes, this can cause difficulties in the operation of the partnership business.

- *Real estate investment trust* — This is similar to the public limited partnership in that it usually contains many investors. It is a vehicle that is generally not particularly favorable for the turnaround developer, but it can be useful if you are raising large sums of money. An advantage of a real estate investment trust over public limited partnership is that the investor's ownership is more liquid because it is usually traded in a manner similar to stock on the stock exchange. This will attract a broader group of potential investors. However, in recent years many real estate investment trusts have performed poorly, so they have a bad name in the marketplace and investor interest is limited.

- *Corporation* — I strongly urge against buying property in a corporation vehicle. The tax advantages of property ownership would remain in the corporation rather than going to the individual investors. Cash flow would have to be taken out in the form of salary and dividends. The corporate form does provide some degree of protection from liability and creditors, but it is not very profitable for real estate turnaround programs. Since there are other techniques to provide protection against your biggest liabilities, there is no real advantage to a corporation for the purpose of limiting real estate investor liability.

The only time it would pay to buy property as a corporation would be if you have an existing corporation, already making profits, which can supply the capital to buy the property and can use the tax advantage.

Chapter 4

Finding Your
Turnaround Deal

There are two basic ways of finding good turnaround opportunities: personal observation and working with third party sources. Both are important, and a successful investor will actively pursue both methods constantly, even when not actively in the market for new property. Complete knowledge of what is available in the marketplace is vital to turnaround success, so the search for opportunities should not be an off-and-on activity.

Personal Observation and Fact Gathering

The first step in finding prize properties is to develop a searching attitude which will help you spot signals that a particular property may become a candidate for turnaround investment. You will probably also work with brokers, lenders, and other sources, but never stop your own personal effort. Here are three personal observation techniques you should pursue automatically every week:

- *Counting cars and draperies* — Spot properties which are having vacancy problems. In those rentals where the tenant usually supplies the drapes, you can actually count the vacancies as you drive by. Also take a look at parking lots. Are they full or empty? To double-check, look at mailboxes and count the ones without names. These are all signs of properties with high vacancy which may be suffering financially and which may fit into the categories we are looking for.

- *Watch for the "save yourself into prosperity" syndrome* — It is obvious when an owner is in the downward cycle and is trying the route of deferring maintenance in hopes of saving himself back into cash flow balance. He probably is not paying his bills on time, so one or more of your contractor or vendor friends may be able to lead you to these types of properties.

As you drive around, look for deterioration in the maintenance and normal services, such as cutting the lawn and cleaning the hallways. When you become convinced that a property is suffering from an effort to "save yourself into prosperity," it is time to contact the owner or representatives and follow through on possible acquisition.

- *Foreclosures* — Regularly check the legal notices advertised in newspapers in your market area to keep advised of foreclosure procedures as well as actual foreclosures. Check out the properties involved, and if they seem to meet your objectives, check with the lender and owner (in that order) to get more information.

After looking at a number of properties and becoming familiar with the signs of the downward cycle, you will develop a feeling for which properties may become available. My interest in a number of the properties which I have bought started with physically seeing the property, noting its condition, and believing that it was rapidly heading for serious trouble which might make a favorable acquisition possible. Then I would look at the market and other key factors and decide whether the property could be turned around.

That's really all I need to know to start to pursue a particular property in terms of making an initial contact. But you must keep in mind that it is a long way from initial contact to actual purchase. For each turn-around investment I have made in six years of full-time work, I estimate I have made some effort on at least 100 opportunities which did not come to fruition.

You should hold your initial contacts down by staying within the confines established by your property objectives. Before any contact, you should partially qualify prospective properties by observing specific signs of distress. But within these limitations, it just doesn't pay to try to guess which opportunities will blossom into deals, and which will not. You simply have to step forward and take the initiative to find out.

An initial contact is a small investment of time. Even though nothing may develop immediately, you will establish a position which may pay off later. I have acquired a number of properties two or three years after my initial interest and contact. Because I saw the downward cycle developing, and expressed interest, I was able to keep in touch, and was in position to buy favorably when the owner finally decided to give up.

The first large project I ever bought offers a good illustration of the value of developing a high level of automatic personal observation and follow-through.

In 1970, I was a student at Eastern Michigan University. I had had two years of part-time real estate investment activity resulting in the ownership of several small campus rental properties. I had financed these on large land contracts with small down payments. Fortunately, the owners hadn't questioned my age as I was only 20, and the age of legal majority at the time was 21. I had very little in the way of liquid assets.

I was not actively in the market for any investment at the moment, and certainly not for a large project. But I had developed the habit of constantly observing properties. That led me to one of the turning points of my real estate career.

Most of the student rental developments around the campus were doing moderately well, but one 128-unit project caught my attention because it had a significant number of vacancies. Actually only 20 units were rented when school started in the fall of 1970. So I decided to check further.

The project was located on the outskirts of the campus area, and this seemed to be one of the problems. Even more important, the property was suffering from a poor reputation stemming from lack of aggressive interest in management. The owners seemed to have no interest in operating the project properly.

Eventually, I found out the owners had tried to convert the property into a condominium development. They had tried to get students' parents to buy an apartment and rent out the extra spaces to their children's friends. The idea had failed miserably, and now the property was in default with neither owners nor lenders sure of what to do next.

It probably was ridiculous for an under-age, under-financed young fellow to even dream of acquiring this property. But once I had the facts of the situation in hand, I couldn't help thinking through the solution to the problem. I formulated ideas which I felt would lead to a quick turnaround, and I couldn't help wanting to buy.

In July 1970, I found two co-general partners who were able to provide the modest capital necessary to put the deal together. My major contribution was the identification of the opportunity and the plan for a turnaround. In August, somewhat to my amazement, I was a partial owner of my first million dollar-plus property! The detailed story of this turnaround is told in Chapter 14. This would never have happened except for the habit of personal observation of everything in the marketplace. There is no better use of time and mental energy for the real estate investor.

How to Broaden Your Exposure to Opportunities

Because I believe in personal involvement in the search for investment opportunities, I have devoted quite a bit of space to that activity. However, personal observation should not be the sole method of finding deals, it should be the extra activity added to all of the traditional methods. These include working through brokers, lenders, attorneys, accountants, and using classified newspaper ads.

Keep in mind that this aspect of real estate is very people oriented. Your success in establishing credibility and good working relationships with the right people will make all the difference. I suggest an honest, open rapport with clear and complete communication. Ethical and fair treatment as it relates to fee agreements will pay you back manyfold. It is important to realize that the real estate community is in fact a very small, tight-knit group of people. You have to earn acceptance.

Be specific and open about your objectives and desires. There is no need to hide your plans or be coy about the kind of opportunity you want. Don't worry about somebody running out and stealing your ideas. There is plenty of room for competition. The more specific you can be in giving your sources an idea of the type of property you are looking for, the more effective they will be in assisting you.

Be aggressive, but be fair. You are ethically free to work with more than one source at a time, and you should. However, make sure that any conflicts in terms of more than one person showing you the same property are immediately resolved. You should give any credit for fees to the first source who showed any given property. Particularly when you are working with different types of sources, be as organized and persistent as reasonably possible in your follow-through on all available leads which might meet your needs. Even when the transaction does not work out, make sure that your source for the lead is kept abreast of the situation so he will feel comfortable in continuing to generate potential property leads for you.

Using Real Estate Brokers

A key to success in dealing with a real estate broker is that you select the right broker for you. His or her personality must be acceptable and agreeable to you. The broker must be willing to work at the pace you are setting for yourself. In other words, the "chemistry" must be right.

Brokers usually work in one of two ways. They often represent the seller of a property and list for sale a given property or properties. In addition, they have various clients who are looking for specific properties, in which event the broker assists them.

If you do not know any real estate brokers in the immediate area, start phoning in response to broker newspaper ads which list specific properties that seem interesting to you. By calling about specific listings, you will begin to meet a number of brokers. They will all likely ask you what type of property you are looking for if it turns out you are not interested in the specific listing that you have inquired about. Feel free to convey your thoughts and desires, but explain that you are going to continue to look through various sources.

If you meet an aggressive real estate broker or salesperson who begins to call you about possible properties on a frequent basis, feel free to work closely with the individual and confide all you can about your desires.

Business Arrangements with the Real Estate Broker

If you start to work regularly with a real estate broker, it is a good idea to discuss your relationship. Set tighter ground rules as to types of property you want to see as well as your obligation to the real estate broker. A certain sense of loyalty to a real estate broker who has worked hard in showing you a number of properties is ethically appropriate. These ethics are unwritten business practices that vary widely from market to market. Therefore, it is important to discuss, in the open, what your thoughts are and what the broker's thoughts are relative to financial arrangements on an ultimate purchase.

In considering financial arrangements, keep in mind that on all listed properties the seller pays the commission. It is normal for the broker to obtain a cooperative spread of the commission with other brokers on properties that are listed through local real estate boards. Even properties that are not listed through the real estate board, if listed by another real estate broker, can usually be a source of compensation to your broker at no additional cost to you.

My suggestion would be to concentrate your efforts with one broker if he or she is doing a thorough and competent job. You should not, in any sense, however, be obligated to pay anything in addition to the normal real estate sales commission paid by the seller. You should not be obligated to pay a commission on any property you buy. Even while working with one broker, you should continue to look for properties which are not listed with anyone, in which event there would be no brokerage commission involved. It is my experience that most real estate brokers are well worth the commission they receive. Do not begrudge the dollars the real estate broker will make. He can perform many valuable services for you. Rather than worrying about how much he is making, make sure that he does everything he can to assist you and therefore earn his money.

When you begin to acquire properties with values in excess of $500,000, you will find the brokerage commissions can become quite significant if they are based on the normally accepted percentage figures for smaller transactions. Make sure your understanding in this area is discussed in front. I have seen unsophisticated brokers kill a deal because they were unwilling to compromise a commission that was so large as to make the transaction between seller and buyer truly "a commission apart." Most brokers, however, are willing to cut their fees on larger transactions from the customary percentages in order to make the transaction workable for both parties and to more fairly reflect the work and contribution of the brokerage firm.

What the Broker Can and Cannot Do for You

The broker obviously can be very helpful in saving your time and keeping you from having to look at properties that would otherwise be dead-end opportunities. When you are at the point of making an offer, you can effectively use the broker as a middleman negotiating tool. By being a middleman and a foil for effective negotiation, he can often earn his fee by helping create a better deal than you might be able to get on your own. I will discuss this in more detail in a later chapter.

In addition, the broker can provide expertise in assisting you in evaluating the property, in obtaining financing, and selecting contractors.

The main thing the broker cannot or will not be able to do is to make your decisions. You must make the final decision as to whether or not to buy and what the property is worth to you. Keep in mind that value in the turnaround analysis may not be the same as customary appraisal value. The key is what you can make on the property by turning it around, and what your downside risk is if the turnaround does not succeed. Most brokers are not able to contribute to this kind of thinking, and it is unfair to expect them to help you make your decisions.

Using "By Owner" Ads

One source of finding turnaround properties is searching "by owner" advertising of properties for sale. This can be extremely time-consuming if you don't have a technique to sift out the totally unworkable properties. The best method is to check through the paper and first eliminate ads you have already looked at on previous days. Next, eliminate all properties that don't fit your objectives in terms of price or size or are of a different type or nature than you are seeking. Take the balance of the ads that fall into the size and scope of property you seek, and call the owners.

When you call, be prepared to ask as many specific questions as possible. Get the current gross rental income, the size of the property, the asking price and terms, the location, the age, and as much general information as you can. If the property seems to be one which you might be interested in, set up an appointment to look at it. If it is questionable, tell the owner you will think about it and call back. If it is one which you obviously are going to eliminate, thank the individual for the time and immediately proceed to your next call.

Review all of your notes on marginal properties on which you have not obtained appointments. Eliminate those which upon reflection do not offer a strong possibility of meeting your needs. Then call and obtain appointments to look at the balance.

Using "Property Wanted" Ads

Another way to use advertising in the real estate section of the newspaper is to put in your own ad. An ad such as the following might be effective in catching the attention of an appropriate seller:

Property Challenge Wanted: Financially distressed apartment project, ten to 30 units, must be structurally sound and well located. We will tackle all other types of problems. If you have a property to sell which meets these qualifications, call Craig Hall at 389-6289.

The above ad qualifies your caller and indicates, without being too specific, the type of property and size range you are looking for. It is not a good idea in an ad of this nature to be overly specific since you may cut out some good prospective properties.

There are certain dangers or disadvantages to using property wanted ads. You may find, even though you have qualified the type of property you are looking for, that you will get calls from people who will simply waste your time. Some people will have something they wish to sell which may not fit your qualifications in the least. In addition it is difficult to get your message across in an ad, and you may in fact turn off some possible prospects. On balance, however, this is a method of finding properties which can be useful if you have the time to answer and screen the calls.

Using Accountants and Attorneys

Both attorneys and accountants are potential sources of influence in the community of real estate buyers and sellers. From time to time, they may have clients who are in need of selling a potential turnaround property. While attorneys and accountants are not primarily in the business of putting buyers and sellers of real estate together, they do so as a service to either one or both of the individuals in the transaction who may be clients of their firm. In fact, I know of at least one major accounting firm that has a formal referral program set up to assist some clients in finding acquisitions which meet their needs, and other clients in finding buyers who meet their needs.

Generally, referrals from attorneys or accountants are the result of personal rapport which does take time to develop. I personally have found it useful to spread my company's legal and accounting work among more than one professional. While I always seek the best advice in any specific area of legal or accounting need, I try overall to use more than one firm.

If you do business with a prestigious firm on a regular basis and have a personal relationship with the individuals handling your work, they will be interested in helping you even if you are a small client. However, you must encourage this interest by making your outside consultant aware of your business activities and plans. Make an extra effort to constantly sell your ability to handle the type of property you are seeking. If the attorney or accountant has confidence in you, he may be able to recommend deals or bring you together with other people who might be able to help you meet your objectives.

For example, one of the attorneys with whom I have done a modest amount of legal work recently recommended I talk to an individual who has a particular apartment development for sale. The attorney recommended this because he was well aware of my objectives, and he felt this property might fit our turnaround approach. My company is currently pursuing the deal. It involves a project of 800 apartment units and may turn out to be very profitable for us. Although it was listed by a broker, I doubt it would have come to our attention without the attorney's suggestion. Of course, we will use this particular attorney to handle all the legal work on the transaction, and we will show our gratitude by referring business to the attorney and assisting him in whatever manner possible.

Most attorneys and accountants are not looking for finder's fees when they put a potential buyer in touch with a potential seller. Their professional code of ethics prohibits such fees because conflicts of interest might develop when handling the professional aspects of a client's deal after having received a finder's fee.

In addition, attorneys and accountants want to be thought of as more than just high-priced technicians. They hope to be business confidants and counsellors to their clients. The opportunity to arrange valuable contacts for clients can therefore be very valuable.

An investor friend of mine decided to put this mutual interest to work by making calls on a number of selected attorneys and accountants. He did an excellent selling job, first of all getting in to see the attorneys and accountants, and secondly establishing himself as a credible purchaser. He found, to his delight, that this method was very successful. Even though he was never a client and paid no fees to these professionals, they did refer potential acquisitions to him. They referred clients of theirs whom they felt might benefit by selling property to my friend, because he had demonstrated that he had the expertise which was needed and was a capable buyer.

Using Financial Institutions

One of the best sources for buying turnaround properties is financial institutions. These include banks, savings and loan associations, and life insurance companies. Beyond this potential, it is a good idea to get to know the more important mortgage officers in your market area as a prelude to future mortgage applications. If they at least know who you are, you will be better off than a complete stranger coming in off the street to apply for a loan.

Although financial institutions do not like to admit it, they do usually have a number of loans they have either foreclosed or are maintaining in default. These loans are sources of potential turnaround acquisitions. Again, you must talk to the right person, which usually means the highest working officer in the mortgage department. By working officer, I am referring to the institution's officer, irrespective of title, who is in a position of authority with regard to administration and handling of delinquent loans or owned properties. Different banks, savings and loans, and life insurance companies have different internal ways of handling their financially distressed real estate portfolio. Get to know the internal structure as quickly as possible and who has what authority.

Your next step, when you know the right person to talk to, is to establish your credibility. If you are just starting, establish your desire, your aggressiveness, and your operating philosophy. Indicate why you think your buying a property from them can be a mutually advantageous transaction. If you have a track record, make sure that you get the right information to the key personnel in a position to help you find acquisitions. As previously stated, the more personal the relationship becomes, the better. This obviously will take time to develop, but it is well worth it. In addition to just selling properties which they may own, loan officers frequently know of properties which are in financial trouble and may recommend you to owners.

In my own experience I have bought directly from lenders, and from sellers with the assistance of lenders in making recommendations. In addition to recommendations alone, I have frequently been able to obtain new and better terms from the lender than those in their existing mortgage. They will make these concessions to you, the new "white knight" buyer, because it is in their best interest to be realistic about the particular property. In Chapter 11, I more specifically cover the nature and type of financial workouts you may obtain from lenders.

Chapter 5

Analyzing and Selecting
Turnaround Opportunities

Probably no step in the turnaround process is more important than the selection of properties you will attempt to buy. These are the most basic decisions, the moments of commitment. Your selection decisions will affect your financial success, your workload, your credibility in the community, and your confidence in yourself.

Be Prepared Mentally

Since selecting a prospective turnaround is a key event in the process, many investors get themselves into mental corners and go through a lot of fruitless effort.

Some investors over-analyze. They bury themselves in a sea of charts, graphs, and hypothetical views of the future. The more they work, the more they seem to cloud their considerations. My guess is they really haven't made the mental decision to get into the game. They haven't really decided to go, so they keep puttering and considering. They are bound to lose from the beginning.

Then, there are those who are so eager to buy, they take a look at one or two possibilities and start to act like a neophyte poker player who has just drawn two cards to an inside straight.

Selecting, and then buying, a large or a small turnaround is as much art as science, so the right mental attitude can be even more important than a big bankroll. I have found the best deals when my attitude has been, "I'm ready to buy, but only if it is my kind of property and it can be bought on my terms." The point is you should be ready for action, but never forget you are interested only in a very special kind of opportunity. When you find it, you will be in the driver's seat. You'll always be buying in a buyer's market.

Get Down to Basics Fast

When you have located a property that appears to offer turnaround opportunities, in that it is not producing to its economic potential, and it meets your objectives as to type and size, there are three critical areas to consider before you invest any further time and effort:

1. *Will the market get better?* Is the demand stable, in a downward trend, or will it improve? In addition, you should look at the type of market available. Many times, properties that are in financial difficulty are suffering from a lack of adequate demand in the market. They may also have missed their market; in other words, they may have been built for the wrong market in their particular location. You must evaluate whether over a period of time, these factors can change to your favor.

2. *Is the product basically sound?* You must evaluate the nature of the construction to be certain there are no latent defects. It is important to make sure that the major mechanical and structural aspects of the building are in good shape. It is further important to know what physical improvements will be needed so you can properly allocate funding in your overall capitalization plan.

3. *Is the location favorable?* There are, of course, many ways to judge location. The key thing to remember is the truth of the old real estate adage, "The three most important things in real estate are location, location, location." If your property is poorly located, for instance in an inner city, low income area, it doesn't matter what the price, you are probably better off avoiding it.

Since these are the basic, absolute considerations in evaluating turnaround opportunities, let's consider each of the three areas in more detail.

How to Analyze Long-Term Market Potential

To estimate the long-term market potential, you should put together information to reflect past and present developments and future expectations in the following areas:

1. Population.
2. Jobs, income, retail business activity, and other economic indicators.
3. Housing demand — multiple and single family.
4. Rent costs and land values.

A reliable estimate requires facts for the past ten years and planning indications for the next ten years. The key thing in addition to statistical information is to talk to the people in the area. Get the flavor of the local scene. Find out whether or not local people think the area is going to grow and if so, why? After all, people make up the market. Their feelings about the future of the market do count.

There are almost endless sources of information which will help you estimate demographics and factors in a marketplace. The precise sources may vary somewhat depending on your location, but the following chart will provide a helpful guide. The federal departments referred to have offices in most large cities. Check telephone books under "U.S. Government." Most public libraries have an amazing amount of published statistical data and the reference librarian will be pleased to help you locate what you need.

The following are some sources of market analysis information:

U.S. Bureau of Statistics	Employment statistics
Post Office	Vacancy studies
Department of Commerce	Business activity
H.U.D.	Housing supply and demand
State Government	Employment statistics
Department of Motor Vehicles	Number of car registrations (an important measure of economic activity)
County and/or City Governments	Various statistics including population, construction permits, etc.
Planning and Zoning Departments	Future plans for land use, types of building development, transportation development.

Miscellaneous:

Utility Companies — Research Dept.	Population and economic factors
Title Insurance Companies	Statistics for housing construction, sales, etc.
Chamber of Commerce	
Local colleges — Research Dept.	
Local newspaper reference library	

When it comes to market analysis, don't kid yourself into thinking that any amount of research will give you a guaranteed look into a crystal ball. The future depends on too many variables to be completely predictable. However, a good market study may reveal trends that will help you make exceptionally profitable decisions.

For example, when you are onto a good turnaround prospect, you may find a pattern along these lines:

• Four or five years ago, the area experienced a dramatic growth in employment and population. (That's when a number of developers decided to build apartments.)

- Two and three years ago, the rate of apartment expansion took a big surge. (The result of the developer planning four and five years ago.) Vacancy rates increased.
- One to two years ago, employment and population growth flattened out, but the trend has not turned down.
  During the same period, the apartment vacancy rate increased dramatically and rental rates went static instead of continuing the growth of previous years. Incentives to attract tenants suddenly became popular.

The implication to a turnaround investor is clear. The market was overbuilt, and the situation has been dramatized by a slow-down in population and employment growth.

The owners in the market probably do not study statistics and trends. They know from day-to-day experience that in fact there are more apartments in the area than there are tenants. The owners are hurting. Some of them are surely caught in the downward spiral. They see only the negative side of the market.

On the other hand, your study may show solid projections for more jobs and more population growth in the near future. With no new construction underway in the area, your analysis may indicate a strong possibility of movement from glut to scarcity in perhaps 12 to 18 months. At the same time, the owners' perception may be trouble, trouble, and more to come. This is one example of how market analysis can put you in the driver's seat.

Statistics are important, but don't fail to also seek out and talk to community leaders in business and government. These movers and shakers will be shaping future statistics and they can provide valuable insights.

For example, a few years ago we had an opportunity to acquire property in Kentucky. On the surface, the market was not favorable. However, when we contacted the personnel managers of major industries in the area, we discovered a great deal of plant and production expansion being planned for early implementation. Our entire perception of the market changed, and we moved ahead with a program which turned out to be very successful.

How to Analyze Construction Factors

In your initial qualification of a potential turnaround investment, it is not necessary to put a great deal of time and effort into detailed checking of structural and other physical aspects of the building. You will want to become aware of certain key items before you proceed, but it is not necessary to have a full professional examination until the deal moves closer to fruition. This can be covered with a contingency written into the sales agreement as detailed in Chapter 6.

However, there is no sense in wasting any time on a potential deal without knowing if there are major inherent defects that will create costs of such magnitude that they will materially change the value of the building. These include serious problems with heating, cooling, or plumbing systems, structural and foundation weakness, roof deterioration, and drainage difficulties.

For investors who are not construction experts, there are two important techniques for initial analysis of physical condition. One is visual inspection of key elements of the property looking for specific signs of trouble. The second method is to seek out the results of construction problems through conversations with a cross-section of tenants. It is important to use both techniques.

Serious, but curable, defects such as roof replacements need not rule out a purchase if you are able to capitalize the construction costs in your original plans. It is important, however, to avoid projects that have physical problems that cannot be corrected or which cannot be financially absorbed in your original capitalization.

The following guide is provided as a general reference of physical defects to be reviewed by you during a visual inspection of an apartment complex. You should be prepared in similar detail for your inspection of any other type of property. This kind of inspection will frequently point up several areas worthy of further consideration by experts.

GUIDE TO VISUAL INSPECTION OF APARTMENT PROJECT CONSTRUCTION

Where to Look	Trouble Signs	Potential Problem Indicated
Grounds:		
Roads	Cracked asphalt Chuck-holes	Resurfacing—if less than 3-4 years old, poor conditions may indicate bad sub-surface preparation or drainage, which can create constant repair needs.
	Receded manhole covers	Improper pitch of asphalt/cement
	Standing water	Drainage
Cement work		
Parking lots	Crowding	Repair or replacement — check for improper sub-surface preparation.
sidewalks	Cracking — holes	Check for weakened foundations.

Where to Look	Trouble Signs	Potential Problem Indicated
Lawns	Thatchy, sparse	Lack of water, lack of fertilizer, or disease.
	Standing water, mushy areas	Drainage problem.
Plantings	Scrubby, dry, sparse	Water, additional plantings needed.
Carports	Sagging roof, bent supports	Replacement
Lighting	Lack of lights	Installation of lights
	Non-function of lights	Possible electrical defects

Building Exterior:

Roof	Sagging, missing shingles	Structural defect, replacement
Gutters and Downspouts	Bent or broken	Replacement — may be vandalism
Masonry	Missing bricks, etc.	Repair
	Rusty stains	Defective downspouts or drainage
	Graffiti	Sandblast
Paint and Stain	Chipping, cracking, peeling	Repainting — cheap paint or bad resurfacing
Balcony decks	Sagging	Weakened structure — can be serious
Windows	Broken	Replacement — vandalism
	Fogged up	Broken seals
(lower level)	Standing water in sills	Drainage — flooding
Entrance doorways	Partially opened doors	Defective door closer
		Outside locks non-functional, check vandalism.
		Defective door jamb
Cement work	Cracked — unleveled	Repair or replacement — check for improper subsurface preparation.
		Check for weakened foundations.

Building Interior:

Hallways	Worn carpet	Carpet replacement
	Decayed wall surface	Paint or paper
	Holes in walls	Drywall repair — check for vandalism
Carpeting	Signs of wear and tear	Repair or replacement
Painting	Signs of wear and tear	Repair or replacement
Linoleum	Signs of wear and tear	Repair or replacement

Where to Look	Trouble Signs	Potential Problem Indicated
Appliances	Absence or age	Installation or replacement
Cabinetry and Carpentry	Signs of wear and tear	Repair or replacement
Walls	Warped	Foundation
Floors	Warped	Foundation
Mechanical Systems:		
Heating	Inadequacy of performance	Potential major repairs
Cooling	Inadequacy of performance	Potential major repairs
Plumbing	Flooding	Defective — potential major repairs
Common Areas:		
Swimming pool	Cracked	Major resurfacing
	Foggy, dirty	Filter system

Tenant Conversations

We sometimes forget that the real reason for the existence of most real estate is its use by tenants. That's what the whole business is all about. So doesn't it make sense to go right to the source when you want to know if the property has any serious problems?

Just go back to the property when you are not with the broker or seller and simply knock on a few of the resident's doors. Explain to them that you have an interest in possibly acquiring the property, or if you feel that would annoy the owners, just tell them you are doing a survey. Ask how long they have lived in the building and if they have had any physical problems. I do not like to use the indirect approach since later on you may be seeing the same residents after you have purchased the property and it can be a source of embarrassment. I have always found residents who have been living in a building for a number of years to be most helpful to a prospective new owner. They generally have no axe to grind and will give you the straight scoop on physical condition as well as other important aspects of living in the property.

How to Analyze Location

I have previously mentioned the old adage, "The three most important things in real estate are location, location, location." Certainly it was more than someone's stuttering that caused this to become a catch-phrase of the real estate business.

The fact is that location is the one thing you cannot change. It is as it is, and it will work to either make or break your turnaround. It is absolutely essential that you face up to the realities of the location before you move ahead on any turnaround opportunity.

As with market analysis, you must look at locations as they are, and as they will be in the near future. Often you will find that a troubled property is well-located, but simply a little ahead of its time. In fact, the indication that a particular location will be highly desirable in a year or two or three may be a key ingredient in turnaround of a troubled property. Of course the turnaround owner must buy in a way that will allow him to hold on financially during the period of location development.

The criteria of good location vary according to the type of property and the market area in general. A chart which follows shortly will give you a good point of view for medium-priced apartment rentals.

In reviewing these factors, remember that an emerging location may not have all of the desired attributes, but they may be coming. It is important to find out what changes are being planned for the near future to get the true picture. On the other hand, a location that has a prime reputation but has developed a scruffy look and signs of hard use may be heading for lower levels of desirability. Check the trend. The following chart of "Location Analysis Factors" describes things to look for in an apartment property, and how to go about your consideration of these factors.

LOCATION ANALYSIS
CHECKLIST OF FACTORS TO CONSIDER

Factors	*Notes*
1. Proximity to major arteries (drive time, convenience)	Apartment dwellers tend to be very mobile. Accessibility to major highways is a prime factor. If the project is visible from the highway, it is a location plus.
Ingress and Egress (visibility and accessibility to major arteries)	
2. Neighborhood characteristics 　Type of property 　Average age of buildings 　Price class 　New building activity 　Nuisance factors 　Access to property 　FHA-VA properties 　Condition and appearance	Any characteristics out of tune with the rest of the neighborhood are likely to be negative; i.e., if the prospective purchase is considerably older or newer than most others.

Factors   *Notes*

3. Community facilities   All of these items are important, but
       Employment   a complete shopping center within a
       Metropolitan area   few miles is the greatest of all facility
       Elementary school   factors. Apartment residents really
       Jr. High   appreciate one-stop shopping.
       Sr. High
       Recreation and playground
       Community shops
       Shopping center
       Churches
       Public transportation
       Fire protection
       Hospital
       Golf course
       Lake
4. Utilities and improvements   Adequacy of utilities is important to
       Gas   future growth of your market area. A
       Water   6" water main may be sufficient to-
       Fire hydrants   day, but will it provide sanitation, fire
       Telephone   protection, and so on when all ap-
       Electric   proved construction is built and oc-
       Street lights   cupied? Obviously, without ade-
       Sanitary sewers   quate utilities, commercial areas that
       Storm sewers   will provide for your residents' needs
       Culverts, etc.   as well as area employment will be
       Streets   built elsewhere.
       Curb and gutter
       Sidewalk
       Land reserves
5. Local ordinances and zoning   Check the potential results of ordi-
       Present zoning   nances and zoning on your turna-
       Future zoning   round plans. Marketing signs may be
       Property restrictions   affected. Surrounding area may be
       Affecting codes or ordinances changed.
         (i.e., sign)
       Future highway plans affecting
        property

How Low Can Value Go?

Hamilton Village was located in a suburban area of Detroit, in the outskirts of Ypsilanti, Michigan. This was a low income project. The entire development consisted of 52 townhouses on a 2-acre site.

My company became involved with the management after the lender had taken the project back with a deed in lieu of foreclosure. As the managers, we had a firsthand opportunity to view the property, and were to write a report for the lender on suggested methods of disposing of the property.

Prior to my firsthand involvement and analysis of the three critical areas, I had guessed that a townhouse project of this size had to be worth a minimum of $1,000,000, even in poor condition.

The amazing fact is that after analysis, I had to recommend to the lender that the buildings be demolished and the property sold as land only, or that the new buyer would have to be loaned more money than rents could justify in order to fix up the property. Accordingly, the mortgage would have to be subsidized.

The difference between a value of $1,000,000 and the actual $27,000 which was the "as is" final selling price, indicates the importance of the three critical areas of analysis in judging turnaround opportunities. You may find the basic facts of the Hamilton Village project enlightening.

To begin with, Hamilton Village was not only physically in terrible shape, but structurally and mechanically unsound. In fact, in looking at the project, one of the most obvious problems was the site plan itself. The units were crowded in and probably from day one were unpleasant to look at. The fact that the neighbors viewed other neighbors so closely along with the congested nature of the living arrangements was something that could not be overcome by merely improving the condition of the existing buildings.

At the time of our analysis, the project had a very poor reputation. Of the 52 units, there were only 14 units occupied. None of the residents had paid rent for over one year. The residents had free legal aid counselling them in defense against a lawsuit for eviction. The lender wanted to have the property completely boarded up for health and safety reasons. The residents, for the most part, had no place to go and therefore would not move, nor would they cooperate and pay rent.

At one point, there was so much malicious destruction to the property that astronomical water bills in excess of $3500 per month occurred because people broke pipes and let water run freely throughout the project. Unfortunately, it was difficult to get a plumber to go into the area since it was such a high crime area. Even the police were reluctant to enter the project!

The project abutted commercial and manufacturing areas. The location itself was quite marginal. Nearby housing in general was of a low income level. There were, however, some nice government-subsidized housing programs in the general area that were newer and well-kept.

The project was finally sold to a developer who actually paid $27,000 for the entire property.

In my own mind, I questioned the value of paying $27,000 for it. Based on the area and on the product itself, certainly a turnaround by improving the physical structures as they were would be a fruitless effort. To demolish and start over would be the logical program, but I would question developing any facility of this type in this particular location.

Hamilton Village is not alone as a turnaround opportunity that initally seems attractive because it is available at a low price but turns out to have no practical value for the turnaround investor. Important physical defects, a poor market without great potential for improvements, and a poor location can add up to no value at all.

Problem Analysis — What's Wrong and How Do You Find Out?

After a turnaround opportunity qualifies in the areas of market, physical condition, and location, you are ready to invest the time to find out why the project is not presently maximizing its potential. What in fact are the problems, and why do they exist? When you have those answers, you can go on to determine which factors can be changed in a profitable manner.

To find out what the problems are, it is necessary to examine both the income and expense sides of the ledger. Isolating problems is usually a matter of seeing the obvious. Determining the reasons for the problem may take a lot more digging. Following are guidelines to assist in problem identification:

Income Factors

- *Occupancy rate* — Breakeven will depend on area rent levels, but as a rule of thumb, look at occupancy under 92% as a danger sign. Compare to area competition as a further check. Plot occupancy rate by month for the past two years to establish trend and spot major changes which may indicate special problems.
- *Tenant Turnover Rate* — Normal rate in large projects runs about 33% to 50% turnover per year. Monthly move-outs will vary from 3% to 6% depending on seasonal influences and local practices.
- *Rent Schedule* — How do rents compare with competition? Is there a proper difference between one, two, and three-bedroom units based on market demand and availablity as well as square foot costs? Are extras such as view or additional space in particular units being reflected in rent rates?

Cost Factors

- *Management* — Cost is usually measured as a percentage of gross rent collected. Larger developments (over 150 units) are able to utilize professional management services including rental, maintenance supervision, accounting, cost control, collection, and tenant relations in a range of 4% to 7%, while smaller projects may cost 7% to 10% for adequate but somewhat less professional services.

- *Maintenance* — This cost area will show wide variance according to the type of construction, age, climate, and size of project. Acceptable ranges run from 7% of gross rents to 13%. Monthly figures may vary widely unless work has been well-planned and managed. Plot trends on a quarterly basis to spot artificial efforts to increase net income by deferring maintenance.

- *Deferred Maintenance* — In a well-run project, there should be no major costs for deferred or delayed maintenance. However, this can be a sizable one-time expense in a project which has been suffering economic problems. Carefully inspect "non-essentials" including landscaping, exterior paint, hallway paint and carpeting, exterior door locks, and unrentable units in which appliances have been cannibalized to repair those in occupied units. Estimate costs to bring all deferred work up to standard.

- *Advertising* — Normal cost for large projects is 1% to 4% of gross rent income. Check records to spot any measurable change which may indicate specific rental difficulty, or artificial cut-back to increase net income.

- *Taxes* — Are taxes levied fairly compared to other commercial properties? Are they set on the same basis as single-family residences? Does the government provide full services such as street lighting, snow removal, etc.? Most important, do the taxes reflect the current true value of the property based on present costs and income? Remember, taxes can be appealed and possibly lowered after you buy distressed property. That can immediately improve your cash flow. Taxes vary greatly around the country, from 8% to 25% of the collected gross income.

In considering income factors, they must be viewed relative to competition in the area. Obviously you should check out rental rates in competitive projects and estimate occupancy by personal inspection and conversation with managers.

I have discovered one of the best ways to find the underlying reasons for low income or high expenses is to go to the tenants and employees and ask for their opinions. Simply knock on some doors and ask some basic questions. You will be surprised at how frank and helpful people will be. If you merely ask someone to help, it is gratifying to see how many people are willing to spend the time to do you a favor.

In a situation where the records indicate a high tenant turnover and high vacancy rate, the residents are usually well aware of the underlying reasons. When they learn that you are considering purchase of the property, they will feel a new hope for relief from their problems and frustrations. They may overwhelm you with their desire to give you the facts.

Ask simple, direct questions; dig for facts instead of sweeping statements. Listen carefully and you'll find this kind of research very profitable.

Employees in a distressed operation are almost always frustrated because they want to take positive steps toward improvement, but usually are held down. They, too, have every reason to be straightforward with you if given the opportunity. Since they do have a job to worry about, it is helpful when possible to have the present owner instruct them to give you total cooperation and to hold back nothing in their conversation with you.

In-depth opinion surveys of tenants throughout the area can help provide a comparison with attitudes in the project you are considering.

Personally interviewing residents is the most accurate and expedient method you can use in assessing the quality of a complex. Face to face, you are able to interpret facial expressions, evaluate living habits, and establish a rapport that a mailed questionnaire cannot provide.

Interview occupants of different types of apartments on both the project in which you are interested and competitive complexes. Be sure you interview in both the daytime and evening so you don't omit the working segment. Your goal is to reach a cross-section of age, social, and economic factors within the resident profile. Based on the size of the complex, you can get a reliable feeling by interviewing about 5% to 10% of the tenants.

If the owner objects, it will be difficult to formally interview a lot of residents. But just talking on a casual basis, can get many of the questions answered. Something as innocent as stopping someone in a parking lot and engaging him in conversation can effectively accomplish most of the results of an otherwise more formal interview.

The following is a guide to basic questions from which to probe. Remember that each interview will flow differently. You are looking for specifics, so encourage the subjects to speak by listening carefully, expressing interest, and making plenty of notes.

"GUIDE TO PERSONAL INTERVIEW OF RESIDENTS"

Introduce yourself.
State your purpose honestly.
Ask for help.

1. How long have you lived here?
2. How is the service?
   a. Are your maintenance requests taken care of? How long does it usually take?
   b. Do you have many maintenance requests?
   c. Do you feel the halls and other public areas are clean?
   d. Are the management people courteous? Do they seem to know what they are doing?

3. Why did you choose this place to live?

   (possible responses to look for)

   — Close to employment
   — Good management reputation
   — Good price
   — Spacious
   — Better schools
   — Like amenities
   — Like neighbors

4. How do you feel these apartments compare in value and features to others you have seen in the area?

   — Superior
   — As good as
   — Inferior

   Why?

   What is your rental rate on this apartment?

5. Are you planning to stay here? Why? Why not?

6. Personal information to learn:

   — Size of family?
   — General age?
   — Work in the area?
   — Estimate their income level — *don't ask.*

Use Research with an Open Mind

As you consider the findings of resident surveys, keep in mind whatever people "think" is what creates their attitudes. You may see the facts quite differently, but their perceptions are what really count.

Let the market speak for itself. Review findings with an open, objective mind. I recall a situation where I had an opportunity to buy a downtown office building at an extremely low per-square-foot price. It appeared to be a deal that could be very lucrative. I tied the building up with an option and then proceeded to do some personal people research. I had all of the other aspects checked out including a complete physical inspection and a very professional look at the market in general. This building was located in the downtown area of a city of 100,000 population which was undergoing extensive urban renewal. The building had a great deal of character and class. It had been built in the 1890's, constantly maintained and upgraded, but still retained the charm of the turn of the century.

After meeting with the city fathers and the various groups and organizations who were promoting extensive development downtown, I was excited and impressed by the location. Personally, I was ready to close, but I decided to stick with my policy of checking with the real experts, the potential tenants. I went around to other office buildings in the area and talked to managers and secretaries alike. Almost universally, they indicated they were interested in moving out of the downtown area and into the growth areas on the edge of the city.

Their reasoning was not completely logical, but the point is they were the market. They believed that even though you made the building perfect in every respect, the downtown area still lacked proper security. The suburbs were seen as bright, clean, and providing a more secure feeling for secretaries and an improved atmosphere for managers to attract good help. In fact, many of the secretaries told me they would not park in the new parking structure which was being built, since they would have to ride up and down in an interior elevator and they were afraid of being attacked or robbed in it. Perhaps these fears were totally unwarranted, perhaps not. In any event, they were real enough in the mind of the marketplace to make me thankful I did not acquire the building. I understand now, some four years later, that building's occupancy has gone down.

Bonus Conditions — Does the Property Have STA?

Super Turnaround Ability, STA, consists of those bonus conditions that really help make a turnaround opportunity extremely profitable to the purchaser. In addition to making sure your turnaround opportunity meets the vital requirements discussed thus far, look for and try to obtain the property which has some or all of these bonus conditions. STA can stand for extra profit for the turnaround investor. The primary STA conditions include overbuilding, special use opportunities, and a seller under financial pressure.

Overbuilding

Look for properties in which the owner has included deluxe features which may be ahead of their time, or has built in more quality than the current residents are willing to pay for. For example, I have bought buildings which have marble windowsills and steel construction. Residents are not willing to pay extra rent for these items, but over a period of years, they keep the building in better shape and enhance its value. Further, things like washers and dryers in each rental unit, special bathtubs, deluxe carpeting, extra-large balconies, or other similar amenities are items which can be big value extras if not paid for in the purchase price.

If you are buying a project built by someone who was progressive in their thinking, they may have been a little ahead of the times. I have bought properties with amenities which have eventually become most valuable in renting at improved rates, but the first owner was too early for the market to have it pay for his investment.

Usually when you are buying something that is overbuilt, it is the result of a builder's ego. At one time or another, many builders try to build a monument to themselves and their career. Unfortunately, there is a very thin market for this highest quality construction and design, so it is quite common for such projects to not produce the appropriate return required to carry the extra cost of such building. When the turnaround investor buys such property at a reduced price, the quality turns into a bonanza.

Special Use Opportunities

Many times an existing owner will miss a complete concept or way of using the property. This can be a hidden opportunity for the new turnaround purchaser.

For example, I once bought a project that had a super-deluxe clubhouse. The clubhouse was actually a liability, because it was so deluxe that it had very high expenses. The increased apartment rental income and theoretical increased occupancy resulting from the nice facilities were not enough to offset the increased cost.

Then I discovered a special use opportunity. By improving the clubhouse a bit more, it was converted into a very desirable private health club. A stiff membership fee was charged to those not living in the project, creating a new meaningful source of income for the development. In addition, free memberships for apartment renters (at no cost to the owners) actually did add value to the apartments and increased occupancy.

Seller Under Financial Pressure

If your timing is good when buying a turnaround property, you may find you are dealing with a seller who is under tremendous financial pressure. This pressure can manifest itself in an emotional strain and a very real dislike for the property.

In many of the transactions in which I have been involved, the owners have been under so much pressure they are willing to sell their equity on very "soft" terms. The usual result is they receive very little cash, and most of my up-front dollars go into the project itself. This is fair and realistic when a project is suffering a continuous operating loss. The owners want to be relieved of those losses, so even though they may have significant cash equity in the property, they are willing to give flexible terms on the balance of the purchase price just to get out of the deal.

How STA Made Lilac Terrace a Good Turnaround

Lilac Terrace was an apartment project of 449 units located in a large suburban town. When I first looked at Lilac Terrace, I found a very interesting situation. It was a project that was basically in a good location for the market. Physically, it was reasonably well-built, and the potential of the market, while somewhat soft at the time appeared to be upward trending. Therefore, it fit my basic vital requirements.

I also found all of the bonus conditions which provide STA. The owners were under tremendous financial pressure. They had not been able to make their tax escrow. They had borrowed secondary debt on the development, and the project was getting further and further into financial difficulty. The occupancy was always stable at a fairly high level of 80%-90%. However, turnover was extremely high. Expenses were also quite high and out of line for a development of that type.

The project itself contained certain very deluxe amenities and was overbuilt for its time. There were four very well-done reflecting ponds in courtyards which had a view from most units. The community clubhouse was an outstanding facility, which I have already mentioned to illustrate the special use opportunity. It consisted of 10,000 square feet and included sauna and steam in the locker rooms for both the men and women, a complete exercise area, large whirlpool with a waterfall coming into it, and a large indoor-outdoor swimming pool.

By applying the turnaround techniques, we were able to really make good use of all three STA bonus conditions in this case. First, I was able to negotiate a purchase which involved virtually no money down on a 10-million dollar property. Next, I was able to take the overbuilt ego dream of the builder and turn it into added rentability for the project. Since I hadn't paid for some of these deluxe facilities in the price, I was able to make use of them without the overpriced cost which residents would not return in higher rental rates. Finally, as explained earlier, I took advantage of the special use opportunity in the clubhouse and created additional income from outside health club members.

A Decision Making Tool

The best way to select a good turnaround opportunity is to actively study at least two similar situations at the same time. This will force you to calculate which is the best opportunity and will help you avoid the problem of developing false enthusiasm for the "only game in town."

When you get right down to it, the acid question is, "Can I realistically expect to solve enough of the problems at a reasonable cost to effect a profitable turnaround?" There is a good technique available to develop a reliable answer. I call it a "test MAP."

In a later chapter, I present details of how to set up a detailed turn-around MAP, or Management Action Plan. Essentially, this is a written budget, schedule, and allocation of efforts designed to organize and control the work required for a turnaround. It is the blueprint for problem solving which will guide all the activity required for the turnaround.

You will rarely have the time, or can you afford the energy, to prepare a complete MAP prior to closing a purchase. But you can and should do a test which will encompass the basic problems you have identified as critical to the turnaround. These are usually few in number, but they may pose very difficult challenges.

Let's face it, if you can't detail a solution before buying, what reason is there to believe you can solve the problem later? By basing your decision to go or to pass on your success with a test MAP, you are simply forcing yourself to be realistic instead of emotional. If your test MAP strongly indicates that basic problems can be resolved at a prudent cost in time, dollars, and effort, you have a green light. If not, you have a very definite caution light.

Run the Real Numbers Game

The final key to deciding if a project makes good investment sense relates to two future factors:

1. What is the potential profit once the deal is turned around?
2. What is the risk and cost of turning the project around?

As to potential profit, there are various ways to look at it. The main thing is to decide what you believe the project will be worth to a conventional investor when you complete your planned turnaround. At this point, you must change your point of view, and estimate with conventional methods of evaluating smoothly operating properties. This, of course, requires a realistic view of the way in which values are actually established in your area.

In most cases, I have found that conventional evaluation is based on some degree of over-optimism. Purchases of productive properties are usually made at somewhat higher prices and somewhat lower yields than most buyers like to talk about.

More insight into the value of turned around property is provided in Chapter 16, entitled, *Selling Is the Time to Celebrate.*

Assuming you are considering a truly distressed property, at a price that reflects the distress, your estimate of potential profit will usually warrant enthusiastic interest.

The next question is what are the costs and the risks involved in getting to the projected profit. Costs come in the form of dollars, time, and transaction involvement. Since there is only a finite amount of time, ability, and effort, these are the costs you must guard most carefully. When you invest them in a project, you lose other opportunities. Obviously it is important that you use personal effort only in the most profitable turn-arounds rather than simply choosing what is available at the moment.

Quantifying financial risk is largely a matter of experience and your own confidence in your MAP. This is the major reason that it is intelligent to start an investment career with small properties and then move up. It is remarkable how fast you will be able to gain real experience and valu-able judgment that will reduce your risk to a very acceptable level.

There are a number of ways to limit your personal financial risks. These are explained in the next chapter. As important as this is, don't lose sight of the fact that risks of reputation are at least as important as dollar risks if you are to succeed in real estate. You can only grow as your credi-bility and your reputation as a winner grow. The final word on risk evalua-tion is to remember that real estate investment is a business. Realistic risk based on intelligent planning is acceptable. But "fliers" or "longshots" never make sense no matter what the potential rewards.

Summerhill — A Great Opportunity but not for Us

Summerhill seemed like a real dream opportunity. A hamburger millionaire (owner of a chain of fast-food operations) had decided to get into real estate. He had a beautiful project under construction, with a mil-lion dollars in cash already in and funds for completion committed by a lending institution. He had come to the realization that he was way over his head in terms of lack of knowledge and management skill. Because he liked my company and trusted me, he was willing to give us a package with no cash down, and a profit potential of at least $500,000 waiting when we completed the construction and rent-up. To put it mildly, I was enthused.

However, after a final review of the risks and costs, I terminated this negotiation. In the nick of time I realized I was about to step out of the field I knew — turnaround of existing projects — into the position of developer of a multi-million dollar project. With no experience in the in-tricacies of construction and development, I would have been committing a flagrant sin of excessive pride. I would have been operating in areas outside my specialty, and the transaction costs would surely have soared.

There was very little financial risk involved in Summerhill, and a large potential profit. The chance of major time costs and damage to my reputation simply outweighed the profit. I passed, and I've never been sorry.

After being involved in over $100,000,000 worth of real estate trans-actions, I'm convinced the way to profit is by treating it as a very logical and conservative business. As long as you take the time to get the right numbers and facts, create a detailed test MAP, then consider everything without emotion, you will be all right.

III
BUYING

Chapter 6

Special Methods of Buying
Turnaround Property

As we consider the subject of purchasing turnaround properties, perhaps the best starting point will be to forget everything you already know about buying real estate. You have probably had some experience in this area, but if it relates to buying or selling a personal residence, it simply does not apply.

Residential buying tends to be a technical matter, following well-organized procedures. Some negotiation over purchase price may be necessary, but in an active market, the range for that discussion tends to be very limited. In most situations, financing is routinely available to allow an average family to buy a home and make the payments from their earnings, so that is rarely a subject of negotiation.

Certainly there is considerable effort and expertise required in every real estate transaction, but the key word in the hundreds of thousands of residential purchases each year is "routine."

On the other hand, each turnaround investment purchase tends to be a unique transaction, developed and tailored to meet the specific needs of the property and the individuals involved. These needs multiply whenever real estate is being purchased for investment rather than personal use; they explode in number and complexity when the purchase is made for turnaround.

Frequently, in a turnaround purchase, the buyer, the seller, and the potential finance source may seem to be light years apart in terms of their needs. Here is a description of a common kind of situation.

- *The buyer* needs a high percentage of financing in order to handle the purchase and provide the cash necessary to handle immediate physical, cosmetic, and marketing improvements. He also has to recognize the limited ability of the property to generate income to handle debt, at least until the turnaround starts to take effect.

- *The seller* is intellectually anxious to sell but psychologically unable to admit to the reduced value of the property based on actual operating results. He wants a price that reflects pride rather than market value.
- *The Mortgage lender* looks at the economic difficulties of the proj ect and is something less than enthusiastic. The resulting financial support may be far less than required to meet the needs of the buyer or the desires of the seller.

At this point, the buying process must be approached more as art than science. What is required is a highly creative effort which will bring the diverse positions together.

Brokers Can Be Helpful

Most new real estate investors start by relying on their brokers for assistance in negotiating the financing and other buying details. This makes sense because brokers who specialize in investment properties do become very knowledgeable about the buying process. They can be very important while you are learning, and should always be a part of your buying team.

Still, you cannot ignore the fact that the broker is motivated by the desire to create a commission, while your motivation must be the strength of your investment. As you move into larger and more complex turn-arounds, you will recognize the importance of becoming more personally involved in the structuring of your deals. You will find that financing, purchase terms, and the trade-offs between price and terms will have as much bearing on success as the selection of the property itself, and you will be unwilling to merely delegate the responsibility.

Investors Need to Develop Skills

My experience has convinced me that the serious turnaround investor should actively develop his ability to be the catalyst in buying situations. Certainly negotiating skill is required, and extensive knowledge of all the alternatives available for financing and structuring a deal is imperative Even more, there is a need for innovative thinking and a willingness to consider new solutions with an open mind.

All of this will come with time and experience. As a start, the next four chapters will provide fundamental knowledge and share buying experiences I have had.

Eliminating Personal Risk

One of the most important things I hope you will learn from this book is how you can create your real estate fortune without exposing yourself to more than a small degree of personal financial risk. You have undoubtedly heard of millionaire real estate investors who lost everything as their real estate pyramid came tumbling down. This has created the impression that big risks are necessary to make big money in real estate. In fact, this is simply not true.

By far the largest risk in real estate is on promissory notes secured by mortgages on the properties you purchase. More than one large real estate company or individual has gone bankrupt after having a net worth of millions of dollars by having one liability after another come back to haunt them. Their total disaster developed because the promissory notes carried personal liability of the borrower in addition to being secured by the mortgaged property. This is normal on many loans, but it is not necessary.

The key is to negotiate each transaction so your personal liability is removed or "exculpated." Personal liability does not have to be spelled out in an agreement to be in force, it is assumed that you are responsible for everything to which you agree. Therefore, it is essential that specific language be included both in sales agreements and the corresponding loan documents to exculpate your personal liability.

When using a sales agreement to purchase a piece of property, one of the first things you should do is make sure you have no liability to close the property and that your earnest money deposit is your only "at risk" money. Insert a clause similar to the following to accomplish this:

> "In the event the purchaser for any reason does not close this transaction, seller's sole remedy shall be to keep the earnest money deposit as liquidated damages. In no event shall the seller be able to sue the purchaser for specific performance."

By inserting this clause you have stopped the seller from suing you to force purchase of the property if you change your mind after signing the sales agreement. You have further stopped the seller from suing you for damages in excess of your earnest money. I know of many cases in which investors have signed sales agreements without this type of language, changed their mind, and then been sued for specific performance. They ended up having to buy the property as originally committed for in the sales agreement, or paying significant damages in excess of the earnest money deposit. There is no reason this should occur since most sellers are very agreeable to the clause limiting liability.

Limiting Risk on Seller Finance

When purchasing a property with the seller taking back some of the financing, additional exculpatory language is required. Make sure the sales agreement includes a clause that will limit your liability on the financing the seller will be taking back on the property.

> "The seller will agree that the sole exclusive recourse on the seller's

portion of debt as herein described shall be limited to the property itself. The seller shall have no recourse against the purchaser personally for any payments or deficiency in the event of foreclosure."

Language such as this will specifically eliminate your liability from any financing being taken back by the seller. Make sure that the same type of language is inserted in the loan documents themselves. If you are buying on a land contract, this language should be included both in the sales agreement and the land contract itself. In the event you are buying the property with the seller taking a second mortgage, this language should be in the sales agreement and the promissory note on the second mortgage.

Now let's assume that you are buying the property and you are paying cash down to the seller's existing first mortgage. Normally, the sales agreement would be written to indicate you will be assuming the seller's present debt financing. Avoid the word "assume." An assumption is when you take over somebody else's liability. It may not excuse their liability, but it definitely does make you liable. You should point out to the seller that he is already liable on the financing, and there is nothing to be gained by both of you being liable to the first mortgage holder. To avoid liability when buying down to the seller's existing financing, always include language like the following in your sales agreement and all loan documentation:

"Purchaser agrees to take the property subject to, but does not assume, the existing financing."

When negotiating with a seller to arrange taking property subject to existing financing, or having the seller take back financing, there are several good arguments you can give the seller when he questions your "no personal liability position."

First of all, you should take an offensive rather than a defensive position. If the seller is saying to you, "I want you to be personally liable," you should turn it around and say, "Wait a minute, is the property worth what I have offered to pay for it, or isn't it?" Then point out that you are giving him the property as security for the debt, and if that is not good enough, you obviously must be getting a bad deal. This position will, of course, cast a serious question on your willingness to proceed with the purchase. It will usually gain quick agreement to the exculpatory language.

If you are forming a limited partnership to own the property, there is another good argument to have the debt non-recourse, or without personal liability. In the event you are personally liable as a general partner, the limited partners, of course, are not liable, and limited partners' ability to write off tax loss will be limited to the amount of cash they put into the transaction. Normally their write-off ability would be extended by their proportionate ownership interest in the property, including the percentage of non-recourse debt. If the debt is recourse to you it would by law eliminate a lot of the limited partners' tax basis or ability to write off tax losses. This would be an untenable position for a limited partnership. Unfortunately for many general partners, they are not well-advised of this fact and when the Internal Revenue Service audits and finds that they did not have adequate tax basis for the write-offs taken, these write-offs must immediately be reversed with penalties.

Eliminating New Mortgage Liability

The other type of major liability that you will, of course, want to avoid is on a new mortgage itself. Language such as the following will do the job:

> "The borrower hereunder shall have no personal liability. The sole and exclusive remedy of the lender being limited to recourse to the security of this note."

You might wonder what lender in his right mind would agree to a clause of this nature. Certainly many lenders will not agree to it. I suggest you avoid using these lenders, because there are a good number who will agree to the clause. Some will charge an extra ¼% or ⅜% to cover the additional potential risk. Others will include the desired language as a matter of course if they are asked. Many large life insurance companies automatically exculpate the personal liability of borrowers of large real estate loans.

Lenders who do not insist on personal liability realize it is simply not realistic to look to the borrower as a major source of comfort in securing large real estate loans. They are interested in the borrower's credit standing as background to assure intent to repay and ability to manage investments so they produce the necessary cash flow to make repayment possible. They make their loan decision on the value of the real estate, not the personal credit of the borrower.

In discussing this with the lender, I have always used the position that if I were to sign personally on a given loan for one lender, it would likely mean that I would sign personally with other lenders. Very quickly, my personal liability would far exceed my personal net worth. Failure of 5% to 10% of my property would virtually assure that all my properties would fail, and all my lenders would suffer. I have been involved in over 100 million dollars worth of real estate transactions, so if I were to have signed personally and been liable on those loans, it could be most detrimental to my stability, my personal financial position, and my ability to maintain the financial well-being of my investments.

Keep in mind that in the real estate business, even the smartest and brightest operators make mistakes and not all deals will be profitable. If you are personally liable on any number of loans, what good are you really doing a lender if two or three other lenders are suing you and you cannot make good on the property? I have told my lenders that the most important protection for them is that I have the financial strength, the ability, and the moral character to assure that I will make every possible effort to keep my investments operating and making the required loan payments.

Another important factor to keep in mind is that each time you sell a property, that doesn't automatically end your liability. If you are liable, the only way that ends is by paying off the loan, or by the lender giving you a written agreement to remove your personal liability. Of course, once a lender has your liability, there is very little reason to expect a release without something in exchange from you. Your best bargaining position is at the front end while you are making the transaction, not afterwards. In my case, I have been very tempted at times to sign personally on a loan in order to make a deal. Usually I can find alternative financing, but there have been a number of deals that I have been unable to make because I refused to accept personal liability. I don't regret this position in the least. I have still been able to make many successful transactions. Further, I realize that if I had accepted liability on just one of those deals and a significant loan had gone bad, I would be tied up in lawsuits for a long period of time and be subject to potential liability that could cause the loss of my good properties. That risk is simply more than any deal is worth.

I have built up some very high net worth corporations and am now in the position where if it is absolutely necessary to have personal liability, I will have one of these corporations sign personally so that all of the assets of the corporation are subject to liability on the loan. This still insulates me from personal liability but also gives me the flexibility to engage in some types of transactions that I wasn't able to finance previously.

I strongly urge you to make a firm personal policy to use the exculpatory language clauses that I suggest and promise yourself not to sign personally. It is better to go a little slower and not make quite as much money, but to do it on a safer basis, than to be rich one day and poor the next.

Beware of Finance Clauses That Bite

In mortgaging your property it is always advisable to obtain legal counsel to review the documentation. In addition to any undesirable elements they may call to your attention, there are a couple of frequently used clauses you should try to avoid: the closed note provision and non-transferability. It is not always possible to avoid these clauses since you may need the lender more than he needs you. However, it is worth trying, and there is no harm in attempting to negotiate even with a bank or savings and loan. Of course there is even a better opportunity to successfully change language to your benefit when dealing with a private finance source such as land contract lenders or you seller.

Closed Note

A closed note is a promissory note which cannot be prepaid during a certain period of time. This is done for the lender's protection so he can count on earning a minimum amount of interest on the loan. It seems harmless when you are taking out the loan, since you have no knowledge of when you may want to pay it back, and no intention of paying it back in a hurry. On the other hand, there are many possibilities that can make this clause a serious problem. At some point you may try to sell the property and the new purchaser may want to refinance with a new first mortgage.

Many times lenders will negotiate away their closed note provision and insert instead a penalty. Even if the penalty is of a fairly steep nature, such as 5% of the entire loan balance during certain years, this is better than having no right to prepay at all. Usually, the lender will go for a penalty which reduces on an annual basis, starting perhaps the first year at 5% and going down ½ % per year, or something similar.

Non-Transferability

Many lenders today are putting in a clause which requires their approval of any transfer to the property. This includes not only legal assumption of their mortgage, but in the event you sell the property on land contract or transfer the property subject to their loan, the lender has a right to approve the transaction. In the event you have gone ahead and sold the property without lender approval, they theoretically have the right to accelerate and call the entire balance of the loan as due and payable immediately. There is a great deal of question as to the legality of the non-transferability clause. To my knowledge, as both a lender and borrower, I am not aware of a clear-cut case where a lender has taken someone to court and won on the issue of accelerating the loan based on the fact that the owner sold without the lender's permission. However, it is unlikely that you would want to be the first case of this nature, and therefore normally you would seek the lender's approval of any sale. Assuming interest rates have gone up in the marketplace, the lender would only grant his approval with an additional fee being paid or a higher interest rate.

This situation will cost you the leverage of selling the property with an older, lower interest rate. This lower interest rate can help you get a higher price on the property. It is therefore very important to try to negotiate the elimination of any clause giving the lender the right to approve transferability.

Writing the Offer

Probably the key action in the buying process is writing the offering, usually in the form of a sales agreement. When you do this, what is specified and how it is worded is vital to making the deal and making it right.

The sales agreement becomes the underlying contract for the entire structure of the purchase. It is legally binding and it usually dictates the detail of all the documentation and closing actions which will follow. As a matter of fact, the offer frequently will control details of both the buyer's and the seller's performance for a long period beyond completion of the "sale" in the sense of control and possession of the property passing from one party to the other.

The reason I stress this is that if you have selected the right property, you are in a buyer's market even if the seller won't admit it. You can assume the seller desperately wants to sell. In fact he may have to sell rapidly to avoid foreclosure. With these facts in mind, it is frequently in your interest to consummate the purchase rapidly even though it may not be possible to get every detail tied down before closing. This sounds frightening to many people, but in fact it can be a very comfortable position if the seller's future action commitments are all made a legally binding part of the sales agreement, and if you have the leverage of owing money to the seller.

Possession Is Nine-Tenths of the Law

This cliché is both true and important. There is no question that a man in possession of the property is in the strong position no matter what disagreements or difficulties might develop.

If you draw up a detailed contract covering 30 things a seller is to remedy prior to closing, and he is unable to handle ten of them properly, what can you do? You can delay the closing, which will probably hurt you at least as much as him. Or, you can sue him, which will surely hurt you more than him since this will surely delay the closing for an undesirable period of time.

On the other hand, if you close and take possession with 30 things still to be done by the seller, where are you? Assuming you have legal agreement covering the things to be done, and assuming you owe the seller suitably substantial amounts of cash, preferably due at a fairly early date, you are in absolute control. If the seller does not perform to your satisfaction, you simply withhold portions of cash payments which will allow you to have the work done, or will allow you to pay the bills that weren't paid, or will reimburse you for tenants lost through the seller's stupidity, or compensate you for whatever problem is created. Now, the shoe is on the other foot. If the seller feels you are being unfair, he must bring legal action and prove you are in the wrong. Things usually fall into line quickly when you have the leverage of actual possession under the right circumstances.

One caution. Don't be tempted to abuse the power of possession by trying to renegotiate or being unreasonably tough. Not only will the seller resist, but you can do irreparable harm to your reputation. I like to be in a position of strength, but I find the biggest benefits are derived when I conduct myself honorably, with absolute fairness and always in keeping with my verbal assurances. My strategy has been to work as rapidly as possible toward possession, secure in the knowledge that my ability to achieve performance of promises by the seller will be strong when I am in the property, controlling its destiny and collecting its income. Of course, I must have the leverage of owing money to the seller, and his representations and warranties must be properly spelled out in the written sales agreement.

Because the offer is so critical, I would suggest you always have an experienced attorney work with you in its preparation. Real estate brokers often write offers on forms. These rarely include all of the necessary warranties and representations and contingencies that are generally appropriate for investment properties. In addition, the real estate broker is usually not an attorney and does not have the expertise to protect you. Once you establish yourself with an attorney, you should be able to get offers drawn in a very expedient manner and at a very reasonable cost. Perhaps you will end up doing most of the basic work yourself in preparing offers, merely having the attorney review them.

Warranties and Representations of Seller

It is extremely important that your sales agreement is properly worded to legally bind the seller to responsibility in various matters of fact which you cannot easily confirm prior to closing. In general, it is important that all warranties are worded so they remain in effect beyond the closing. Specific items are discussed briefly in the following sections. I am presenting these in legal wording, as the easiest way to illustrate important protection you need to consider. However, I am not suggesting you simply use these clauses (or any other legal language used in the book.) That is bad practice since proper wording will vary from state to state and situation to situation. Use your attorney to protect your interests.

Title

The seller must represent that he will convey fee simple interest in the property, subject only to specific mortgages, easements, or other restrictions as scheduled in the sales agreement. Language like the following is suitable, subject to obvious adjustment depending on the actual details:

> "The project being purchased hereunder is correctly described in the legal description attached hereto as Exhibit A.
>
> Seller has good and marketable title in fee simple to all the real estate described in Exhibit A, and all of the improvements situated thereon, subject to no liens, encumbrances, restrictions, or easements of any kind whatsoever except the following:
>
> (i) Existing permanent mortgage on the project in favor of _____ _____with a principal balance not exceeding the sum of _____Dollars as of the date of the seller's acceptance hereof. Said mortgage secures a note bearing interest at _____% (no income participation) with a remaining term of approximately _____years requiring monthly principal and interest installments of _____ _____Dollars. Said mortgage is presently not in default and shall not be in default at closing date. Seller shall make all principal, interest, and escrow (if any) payments up to and including the month of closing.
>
> (ii) The rights of tenants in the project, under leases, which shall not extend for more than one (1) year date hereof. All of said leases are presently current and existing and there are no defaults by lessor or lessee thereunder.
>
> (iii) Easements and restrictions of record which do not in Purchaser's sole discretion adversely affect the operation of the subject project."

This does not eliminate the need for title insurance[6] which should always be provided by the seller.

Always avoid weasel clauses with wording like "to the best of the seller's knowledge..." This offers practically no protection, and should only be accepted in those areas where the seller may, in fact, not be able to make a statement with complete certainty.

Physical Condition

Start out by trying to achieve the broadest possible protection with language like this:

> "The buildings located on the property described in Exhibit A, and all parts thereof (including, but not by way of limitation, the plumbing, electrical, heating, air-conditioning, and mechanical systems therein) are in conformity with all applicable, governmental, and other

legal requirements, including, but not by way of limitation, conformity with the health and fire code of the applicable municipality and the building and safety engineering department, or similar department of the applicable municipality. Said plumbing, electrical, heating, air-conditioning, and mechanical systems are, and at the closing date will be, in good operating condition, and the capacity of such systems are sufficient to adequately service the project. All of the buildings, structures, and improvements upon the subject properties are in good maintenance and repair and there are no repairs of any type or sort whatsoever which may be required presently or at closing date, and there are no latent structural or mechanical defects presently or existing at closing date which need to be repaired in order to render said buildings, structures, and improvements or parts thereof safe and reasonably maintained. All buildings, structures, and improvements upon the subject properties were constructed in accordance with the original plans and specifications. Further, all vacant space is in leaseable condition, without further preparation necessary."

The major purpose of physical condition warranties is to make the seller reveal information about the property. An astute seller's counsel may advise his client to negotiate away some of the protection you are asking for, and within reason you can afford to compromise as long as you remember your major purpose. For instance, the seller may not be willing to warrant that the capacity of the systems are sufficient to service the project. He many want to water down the matter of "no repairs of any type or sort whatsoever" to "no material repairs." They may also want to delete the last two sentences. Your agreement will depend on your strength in the negotiation.

There are some sellers who may insist on your accepting condition "as is." I would not recommend this unless the deal is so favorable that you feel you can afford the considerable risk involved.

Records

Have seller warrant as true and accurate all records to be provided to you, using language like this:

"The financial data contained in Exhibit C attached hereto is true, correct, complete, and accurately indicates all of the information referred to therein."

Employees

Have seller warrant as true and accurate the payroll and employment records. In addition, he should agree to protect you against any employee claims in a clause like this:

"The schedule of employees attached hereto as Exhibit E contains the name of all employees of the project, their salary, any concessions made to said employees, their fringe benefits, length of employment contract, vacation pay, all accrued benefits, and all other pertinent information concerning said employees, which Exhibit is true and accurate in all respects. Seller agrees to indemnify Purchaser from any claims by or on behalf of persons who are or have been employees of Seller on or prior to the closing date for actions arising and claims which may have accrued prior to such date."

Rental Occupancy

Have seller warrant as true and accurate the records of rents established, collected, and occupancy to be supplied, using a clause like this:

"The rent roll attached hereto as Exhibit D is true and accurate in all respects.

"None of the tenants in the premises were given any concession or consideration for the rental of any space except as otherwise indicated herein or on exhibits attached hereto, and no tenants are entitled hereafter to any concessions, rebates, allowances, or free rent for any period after the closing.

"The collected monthly gross rental income from the project is and shall be at the time of closing not less than the sum of _____ Dollars."

The seller may have to water this down if the actual management has been handled by a management company.

Contingencies

Generally, you will not want to take the time and effort or spend any extensive amount of money to get all of your research done prior to making an offer. The way to handle this is to make an offer with one or more contingencies. The contingency is merely a condition that must be met precedent to your being liable to close on the terms of the offer. I would suggest the following types of contingencies which are very simply written, but very effective:

"This offer is contingent upon satisfactory new financing by purchaser. If said financing is not obtained within 30 days from the date of acceptance by seller, this offer shall be null and void, and the purchaser's deposit shall be returned to purchaser without any further liability on either party."

In the case of physical inspection of the property, you might have a clause like the following:

"This offer is subject to and contingent upon purchaser's satisfactory physical inspection of the premises including all mechanical, structural, plumbing, and heating as well as roof, grounds, etc. If said physical inspection is not to purchaser's satisfaction, then he shall inform seller of same and this agreement shall become null and void. All money hereunder shall be returned immediately to purchaser. The purchaser shall have 30 days from date of execution of this agreement to make his inspection. In event that the seller has not received a contingency removal at the end of 30 days, the offer shall be null and void."

In essence, both of the above contingencies are simply providing the purchaser with a no-money option. The earnest money is merely "show money" which is being used to exhibit good faith. It may seem to you that a seller would be foolish to agree to something along these lines. On the other hand, if the seller really believes that the deal is likely to go through, that you are a credible, honest buyer, he may be very willing to go along with it. It has been my experience that contingencies for 20-30 day time periods which actually make the transaction into an option are almost always agreed to by the seller. He sees it as a necessity to make the deal he wants and needs.

Title Protection

Wherever possible, specify title insurance "without exceptions." In some localities title insurance is not widely used, and instead lawyers give title opinions. I strongly urge you, if at all possible, to avoid an opinion. In the event a title defect does occur, you do not want to be in a position of having to sue an attorney. Even if the attorney is properly insured, if he makes a mistake, it will be much more difficult to collect than to turn a claim into one of the large title insurance companies. Of course, there is usually no problem. However, it only takes one time to be severely hurt if you do not have the proper coverage.

Total Price Versus Terms — The Trade-Offs

In planning the purchase of a specific property, you will certainly establish some initial idea of the price you are willing to pay. As I indicated in the previous chapter, concern with the profit potential and the profit versus risk analysis should be your key considerations. Certainly, you want to make as favorable a buy as possible, but if you get hung up on conventional methods of appraising real estate and try to apply them to turnaround opportunities, you will rarely make any deals at all.

Even though the property you want is in great economic distress, you will rarely be able to buy it based on conventional appraisal of its cash value at the time of your acquisition. The seller will probably have psychological hang-ups that may make such a price absolutely unacceptable. He may also have economic pressures such as liability on existing financing that make a true value cash offer almost valueless to him.

As a general rule it is wise to anticipate that you have to "over-pay" based on conventional appraisal methods. I accept this and forget all the old ways of establishing value in favor of balancing my offer against the bottom line value I know I can create by employing turnaround techniques. I know I am getting a bargain as long as the property will later be worth far more, and result in a large profit for my effort.

While I accept the fact that I may have to give on total price, I do expect something of even greater value in return. That is favorable purchase terms from the seller, and possibly from his existing finance sources as well. A lower down payment, a favorable interest rate, or a stretched-out term of repayment may be much more profitable in the long run than a lower purchase price.

New mortgage financing on a turnaround property is likely to involve a high interest rate and a relatively low loan amount since you are dealing with a property that has a very unattractive track record. This means that deep participation of the seller in financing your purchase may be an absolute necessity. The way to achieve this under most favorable conditions is to plan a trade-off between total price and purchase terms.

The chapters which follow will examine the details of finance and negotiation which will be your tools to turn the basic trade-off strategy into reality.

Chapter 7

The Art of Finance

Selecting the Best Finance Method

There are numerous methods of borrowing money to finance a real estate investment. The right choice for any given situation depends on balancing a number of key considerations.

- *Cash purchase advantage* — It is normal for the seller of investment property to ask for cash but to expect to assist in financing the purchase with favorable terms and interest. On the other hand, the seller may be willing to accept a much lower total price if the buyer can arrange other financing and make the purchase for cash.

- *Term and amortization of loan* — The term of a real estate loan is the number of years agreed to by the lender for total repayment. Amortization is the period of repayment time used to calculate the size of the regular payments of principal and interest to be made. It is becoming increasingly common for commercial real estate loans to carry a shorter term than amortization schedule. This creates payments which can be handled by the income produced by the property, but it also creates a "balloon" to be paid off in a lump sum at the end of the loan term.

- *Cost of loan* — This factor obviously includes the interest rate, but should also include service fees and "points" which are essentially prepaid interest. One point equals 1% of the amount of the loan. For comparison, you can figure that one point is the equivalent of 1% interest over a term of eight years.

- *Cash required* — Within economic limits, the less cash an investor must put into a real estate purchase, the more favorable the profit potential.

Suppose you are able to control a $100,000 property with only $5000 of your own cash. You have a highly leveraged position with each of your dollars doing the work of $20! Now let's assume that you are able to improve the property and sell it at the end of a year

93

for a net profit of 5%. You sell the $100,000 property for $105,000, plus commission and costs. That's not too impressive until you consider the return on your $5000 investment — a cool 100%, thanks to leverage.

The critical limitations on leverage are the size of loan available, and the ability of the property to produce income necessary to repay a high leverage loan. In general, leverage of at least four to one is a minimum prudent level. Considerably higher leverage is possible under favorable conditions. However, high leverage structures should be carefully examined to be sure enough cash will be available from operations and your initial capitalization to cover all reasonably anticipated exigencies.

- *Ability of property to service debt* — As a general rule, any income-producing real estate investment must be structured as a self-supporting business, with all operating expenses and debt service to be paid from current income. In the case of turnaround purchases, initial expenses required for physical improvements or extraordinary marketing efforts should be capitalized and financed as part of the purchase price. Complex turnarounds may have to be structured to produce little or no cash flow during the period of improvement — possibly even for a period of years. But in no event is a planned negative cash flow economically justified except for short periods of time such as the turnaround start-up immediately after a purchase.

  This finance philosophy may limit leverage and require more cash up front, but it is your best protection against turning a financial failure into an even bigger failure the second time around.

  As a key element in planning your purchase, it is essential that a careful and conservative analysis be made to accurately estimate income and expense. The resulting "Income Before Debt" figure will indicate the absolute maximum which can be committed to principal and interest payments.

- *Freedom from personal liability* — In Chapter 6, I detailed the reasons I believe investors should refuse to accept personal liability on the financing of real estate purchases, and the techniques which must be followed.

  In considering various finance options, it is important to recognize that certain sources will tend to insist on personal liability. I will point these out in the following review of finance sources and vehicles.

Checklist of Finance Methods

Conventional mortgage loans are the most common method of financing purchases in which the seller is to receive the full cash price. A conventional loan refers to one made from a source other than the seller, and not under a government guarantee program. For properties under $1,000,000, the best source is usually a local savings and loan institution. Local banks should also be checked, but they will usually offer less attractive term and amortization because they are not primarily in the long-term mortgage loan business. The same institution will usually charge higher interest and offer to loan a smaller percentage of the property value for a commercial or investment property than for an owner-occupied residential property.

Be sure to get figures for the specific property you want to buy, as conventional lenders tend to be very selective. For example, it may be very difficult to find any source of conventional mortgage money for many older apartment buildings, and if it is available it will be extremely expensive. The poor economic showing of most turnaround properties will probably result in a high interest rate and low percentage loan amount from conventional lenders.

In general, conventional mortgage loans will probably not be as favorable in one or more respects as some of the alternates reviewed below. However, a higher interest rate or shorter term may be more than offset by a deep discount in the selling price for cash.

As a matter of tradition, most local lending institutions will insist on personal liability. Interestingly, the life insurance companies and extremely large savings and loan institutions who are the best conventional lending sources for properties valued over $1,000,000 are frequently agreeable to exculpatory personal liability on their loans!

Purchase subject to the seller's mortgage (assumption) can be an excellent method of finance in that a mortgage made some years ago is likely to carry a substantially lower interest rate than a new mortgage. There are additional savings in that no fees, points, or closing costs are involved.

In terms of personal liability, your takeover of the seller's mortgage does not relieve him of his liability. However, if your agreement is properly worded, you need not share liability. The proper procedure to protect yourself was detailed in Chapter 6.

The major potential disadvantage to assumption is that the mortgage may be paid down to the point that you will have to put up too much cash to achieve reasonable leverage. In general, if you have to pay down more than 25% of the total price, you will not be receiving enough leverage.

Seller taking back financing is a method which can frequently solve the leverage problem in assumption. Let's say the favorable existing mortgage will cover 60% of the purchase price and you do not want to come up with the 40% balance in cash. The seller may be willing to accept 15% or 20% in cash and take back a second mortgage for the balance.

The same vehicle can be used to give you better leverage with a new conventional mortgage. Let's assume the conventional lender offers a loan of 75% of the value. If the seller will take back a second mortgage for 15%, you will have excellent leverage in the purchase and the seller will still receive most of the purchase price in cash.

Another method for the seller to take back financing is the use of an instrument in which the seller retains legal title to the property and in essence grants you a right to title. You have all the beneficial ownership rights to use of the property, cash flow, and tax benefits from the time the transaction is made. You have the right to receive the deed for the property when you have complied with your contract with the seller. The form of this type of financing instrument varies from state to state. In Michigan, for instance, it is called a land contract. In other states, it is a deed of trust, contract for deed, or something similar.

In operation, this approach is the same as an assumption plus a second mortgage. You agree to put a certain amount of money down and make specified monthly payments to the seller to cover principal and an agreed interest rate. The seller maintains the payments on the existing mortgage underneath.

Some form of seller participation in financing is probably the most effective way to buy most smaller, and even many larger, apartment developments today. More than 70% of my purchases have been accomplished with the seller taking back portions of the financing.

Down payment over time — In the case of a conventional mortgage, cash purchase, or even a land contract type of purchase, you may also want to negotiate an agreement for the seller to take the down payment over a period of time.

It can be advantageous to both the seller and purchaser to pay a portion of the price over a period of years. To the seller, this can amount to spreading his tax liability on the sale by making the sale an installment transaction. To the purchaser, there is the obvious benefit of postponing the need to lay out cash. Also, as you will note in the section on equity financing later in this chapter, extending the down payment over a period of several years can be very advantageous in raising funds from limited partners.

Private land contract source — This is a finance method which is not in wide use, probably because it requires special initiative on the part of the purchaser. Nevertheless, it can be more than worth the effort.

You simply line up a private source who will pay the cash price for the property you want, then immediately resell it to you on a land contract or contract for deed basis. In essence, you get the best of both worlds. You can usually make the purchase for a better price than if you had bought it on a land contract direct from the seller. At the same time, you will probably have far better leverage than if you had structured a typical cash purchase with a new conventional mortgage.

You find a property, negotiate to buy it on a cash basis, then, prior to closing, you assign your rights to the sales agreement to a third party.

This third party is a friend, or someone you have previously located and established as your finance source. This associate has cash dollars to invest and is looking for a low risk investment with relatively high return. In essence, he is becoming the lender on the project, but is in a secure position because he is acquiring title to the property. He may or may not put a mortgage on the property, depending on how much of his own cash is available. Let's assume that there is to be a mortgage and he is putting the difference down in cash between his mortgage and the price of the property.

To be specific, let's say you find a property and are willing to pay up to $50,000 with $5000 down. It turns out, however, that the seller wants cash and is asking a price of $52,000. You offer him $37,000 cash and he counters with a price of $43,000 cash. You end up agreeing on a price of $40,000 cash.

You then go to your private land contract source and assign him the agreement to purchase the property for $40,000, agreeing to buy it from him for $45,000 with $4000 down. He goes ahead and buys the property for $40,000, puts down $10,000, and borrows $30,000. He then immediately sells the property to you for $45,000 with you only putting down $4000.

The private source now has $41,000 owed to him on the property, with a debt of only $30,000. Since he has gotten back $4000 of his original $10,000 for, in essence, financing your $6000, he has received a $5000 paper profit which he will receive with interest over the period of years that he holds your land contract.

You, on the other hand, were willing to pay $50,000 for the property and instead have bought it for $45,000. Further you have received it for $1000 less cash than you actually would have been willing to put down.

The seller came out with what he wanted which was a cash deal. You have come out with what you wanted, and the private finance source has come out with a tidy profit. This is a good deal for all three parties involved. This is often a good method of acquiring smaller properties in particular. This area is discussed in somewhat more depth in Chapter 17, "The Magic of Paper."

Wrap-Around Mortgage

This is an excellent vehicle to allow you to take advantage of a large existing first mortgage with a favorable rate, in a situation where the seller cannot take back financing to help you pay down to the existing mortgage.

In essence, this situation is financed by a lender who wraps a new mortgage around the existing one so you get the advantage of a combined rate which will probably be considerably better than the rate on a new conventional mortgage. The lender also gets a better return than he would on a new conventional mortgage and he has excellent security. In short, you and the lender split the benefit of the low rate on the existing mortgage.

To illustrate, let's assume that you are purchasing a property for $800,000 which has an existing mortgage with a balance of $400,000 and a term of 13 years remaining. The annual payment is $44,000, including interest at 6%. The net before debt on the project is $76,000.

You plan to raise $150,000 of equity money for a cash down payment, so you need an additional $250,000 to pay down to the mortgage.

One alternative is a new conventional mortgage for the total $650,000. At present, this is available at 9¾% for a 25-year term and amortization which will require an annual payment of $69,508.72. The property can support this, but it leaves a cash flow of only $6492 which is a rather skimpy 4.3% return on your $150,000 of equity capital.

The wrap-around mortgage should be available at about 8¼% on the total of $650,000. The lender will take over the $400,000 mortgage and therefore retain the difference between the 6% interest being paid and the 8¼% being charged, and this will not be offset by any cash advance from the lender. On the $250,000 additional cash, the lender will make 8¼% Collectively, this will give him an 11.85% return on the $250,000 the first year, and it will get better year by year as the loan is paid down. Obviously this is a good deal for the lender.

From the borrower's point of view, the 8¼% overall rate is much better than the new conventional loan. It will increase the cash flow to $14,500, or a respectable 9.6% on the $150,000 of equity.

An Example of Seller Participation

My introduction to the "seller taking back" method came with the second building I ever bought. With my first purchase under control, I was anxious to move on to bigger and better things.

The property was a rambling old mansion, converted into apartments. After some negotiation, the price came down to $69,000, but the owner absolutely insisted on cash even though I tried to get him to help with financing.

My next step was the local S & L. I was amazed to get a good first mortgage of $55,000 — about 80%.

Now all I needed was $14,000 worth of equity money to wrap up the deal. Personally, I had only $1000, so I planned to bring in one or two outside investors to supply the equity money. It was a good idea, but a bit over-ambitious for me at that moment. My prospects ran out when I got to $6000. That gave me a grand total of $7000 for equity, including my own cash reserve.

I went back to the seller with the bad news, and one last effort to get him to take back some of the finance. His response was not enthusiastic, but rather quickly we did arrive at his agreement to take back a $7000 second mortgage. Since there wasn't much net before debt left in the deal, he even agreed to interest payments only for ten years, with a balloon payment of the $7000 principal.

Thinking through the whole experience, it became obvious that this seller had no desire to become a financier even though it was a fair investment for him. His motivation was to salvage the sale. Once he was psychologically committed to the sale and was virtually counting the cash, it was much easier for him to bend a bit. The lesson I learned was to be very careful about the timing of requests for sellers to participate in financing. The same plan might turn a seller off completely in the early stages of a negotiation but wrap up the deal at the right time.

Equity Financing

Up to now, we have concentrated on the debt side of finance, but if you want to be an aggressive real estate investor, equity finance can be just as important. The cash down required for your earliest purchases may come out of savings, but after that you will almost certainly have to find a source of additional equity cash if you are going to broaden your investment base. In some cases, this equity may in fact be short term borrowing or debt secured by assets other than the purchase.

How Home Improvement Loans Can Help the Small Investor

In my own early experience, I found home improvement loans to be most useful in expanding my real estate program. The home improvement loan is usually made by your local savings and loan or possibly a bank. Many of these loans have government support which helps keep the interest rate down. Usually the loan is a five to seven-year term and amortization. The monthly payments are fairly high, but you usually can justify the payment through the cash flow of your real estate.

Since these loans are made available to help owners improve their property, you cannot use this kind of finance until after you have purchased at least your first investment and are in a position to fix it up.

You make a list of all the improvements you intend to make to the property. Use the full cost of these improvements through a contractor as the basis for the loan. Borrow the maximum amount the bank is willing to loan you on those improvements. By doing much of the work yourself, the amount of money that you can keep out of the loan after paying for the materials and necessary outside labor can be very substantial. You can then use this money to help as down payment on your next investment.

For example, one of my earlier properties was a two-family purchased in very poor condition. The price was $16,000. I then borrowed a home improvement loan of $7000 and did an extensive amount of repair and rehabilitation work to the property. Even though the property was greatly improved, I spent only $4000 of the $7000 I had borrowed. Of course this did not count my own labor. So I had $3000 to be used towards the purchase of my next building. In addition, the improvements helped me raise my gross rent income by more than $250 per month. Since I was paying off the loan at $120 per month, the home improvement loan proved to be a most lucrative way of leveraging that particular transaction.

In general, you will find that home improvement loans are readily attainable and excellent sources of financing improvements. By doing the work yourself, you can quickly earn equity dollars to help finance future purchases. This can be a key to building the base of your real estate fortune from a very small start.

How Angels Help Make Deals Fly

One of the greatest ways I have found to finance the equity portion of turnaround acquisitions is by bringing in limited partners. A limited partnership is an interesting and effective vehicle for real estate acquisitions of this nature. As the active partner, you become the general partner and have all the management decisions and control-making power of the partnership. Your investors become limited partners and are in a passive position, somewhat similar to stockholders in a corporation. A written limited partnership agreement specifies, among other things, the nature of the splitting of benefits between the limited and general partners.

As a general partner, you should expect to receive substantial benefits from the property even though you have little or no cash invested. However, the most effective way to attract investors is to allow them the first priority in the profits of the transaction. Let them have their money out first, and then if the deal is extremely profitable have them receive a portion of the profits for putting up the dollars at risk, while you participate in a portion of the profit for putting up the hard work and expertise.

I have syndicated many millions of dollars worth of real estate in limited partnerships, and I have found that by treating limited partners in a fair and equitable manner, it can be a mutually satisfying relationship. Because my syndications have been very beneficial to the limited partners as well as to my company, our investors have helped me grow by introducing me to friends and associates, and by demonstrating a continuing interest in new projects.

I have various formulas which I have used in splitting benefits in syndications, but in all cases, I do everything possible to watch out for the security of the limited partner's money. In fact, if I ever have a deal that does get into trouble, I will do anything possible to make sure we never have a limited partner lose a penny. The general partner's reputation is extremely important to limited partners, so their satisfaction is a key to success.

A solid relationship starts with selectivity in the type of limited partner with whom you get involved. I always want to make sure that I have investors who understand real estate programs and can afford the lack of immediate liquidity, and have the degree of patience required in this type of investment. I believe that the more an investor knows about the type of business I am in and how I work, the better the relationship will be for both of us.

During initial periods of real estate activity, while you are dealing with smaller properties, most of the investors will come from your circle of friends. As you expand you will begin to get investors from many sources. Your reputation grows very fast in the real estate business. It can quickly become a most valuable asset or a most damaging liability. Nothing breeds success like success. I have found that honest, careful treatment comes back tenfold in the syndication business. I stress this, because in some areas limited partnership investments have been abused and have developed a bad image. This should not deter your interest.

When developing your "angels," the limited partners, make sure you check with your local State Securities Bureau as to how you register or exempt limited partnerships in your state. It is really essential to hire an experienced securities attorney to investigate and guide you in these matters.

The securities law is a very complex area, but you should not be frightened off by the mystique. Once you have determined the rules under which you have to do business, it is generally not too difficult. The key requirement which should guide all syndication activity is complete and absolute disclosure of risk and facts. It is time-consuming and creates a certain amount of expense, but remember that operation within the regulations is for your protection as a general partner, as well as to protect investors.

Almost all limited partnership interests you would be selling would fall within the securities act of your state as well as under the jurisdiction of the U.S. Securities and Exchange Commission. Many of them will be automatically exempt from registration from the Securities and Exchange Commission. Depending on your state law, you may or may not be required to file forms with the state. The penalties for violation of the securities law vary, but generally include the right of limited partners to sue and easily obtain a recision which would cause the general partner to refund the investment, usually plus interest! This can be extremely detrimental if the deal does get into trouble. Further, there may be criminal violations for not having properly complied with the securities laws. However, if you make a sincere effort to work within regulations, and you demonstrate a desire to be open and honest with investors, you will rarely have any problems with Securities Administrators.

How a Limited Partnership Pays Off for All

Morgan Pointe is a 68-unit apartment project located in Ann Arbor, Michigan. At the time of purchase, I had a fellow general partner whom I later bought out. He and I managed to borrow, on a very short term basis, the entire down payment of $80,000. The total purchase price was $820,000 with a $740,000 land contract balance. Immediately after purchasing the property, we turned around and syndicated it to a limited partnership.

In this particular case, the limited partners put up 100% of the money, paying back all the loans that my fellow general partner and I had borrowed to get the original down payment of $80,000. The limited partners put up additional cash which was required to operate and improve the facility as part of the turnaround plan.

In total, the limited partners provided $145,000. Each unit of partnership required an investment of $14,500. The total of ten units was subscribed by seven investors.

In the case of the Morgan Pointe partnership, the general partners received a 30% interest without any cash investment except the costs incurred in buying the property. This was a 14-year-old complex that appeared to have stalled economically. The actual cash flow on the property had been going down somewhat in the years just previous to our purchase. The owners were suffering, but did not feel they could raise rents.

We made certain physical improvements and operational changes to the property, similar to many of the things discussed in later chapters of this book on specific turnaround techniques. The turnaround program steadily increased the net before debt and cash flow of the property. Within a year of the purchase, it was obvious the project had become far more valuable than when we took over.

Two years and two months after the property was purchased, I sold the project for $1,050,000. This represented a good value to the new owner, based on the improved operation. For the partnership, it produced a profit of $230,000 on an $820,000 investment. The limited partners received 70% or $161,000 in profit. This, of course, was in addition to the tax benefits and cash flow they received during the ownership of the property. As the general partner, I received $69,000 with no investment for part-time work during a little over two years. It is another example of a transaction where the turnaround techniques and sound financing proved profitable, for all parties.

The exact structure of any given limited partnership in terms of the split of benefits to the limited partner investors and the general partner organizers should be tailored to the specific circumstances. In my experience, it is reasonable for the general partners to receive a 10% to 30% interest without cash investment in return for their work in finding and negotiating the investment for which the partnership is formed, and as payment for the work to be done in operating the venture. The specific share depends on the amount of work, on whether the general partners are to receive any other fee such as a property management percentage, and on whether the general partners' direct expenses incurred in buying the property are to be reimbursed.

In order to assure limited partners that this dilution will in fact only be reflected in times of successful operation, I frequently agree in advance to subordinate the general partners' interest in cash distribution in any year in which the limited partners do not receive a 10% return on their investment. At the time of the sale of the partnership assets, the general partners' interest is subordinated until the limited partners' total return equals their original investment plus a 10% per year cash flow.

Another basic approach is for the general partners to receive a moderate ownership interest, between 1% and 5%, plus a major participation in operating and sale profits based on a sliding scale formula. This might call for all profits to go to the limited partners until 10% return is achieved in any year. Then profit is split ⅔ to limited, and ⅓ to general until the limited partners receive 15% return. Beyond that, everything is split 50-50.

The point of this detail is to illustrate how much flexibility there is in structuring the limited partnership arrangement. I believe the best thing a general partner can do is to lean over to be fair to investors, by taking healthy profits for himself only after the investors have received an outstanding return. This giving attitude will quickly bring back amazing profits for everyone concerned.

How to Increase Leverage for Limited Partners

In structuring the purchase of large properties with equity financing supplied by a limited partnership, I have found an excellent advantage in negotiating arrangements to pay the cash down on the property over a period of time.

As an example, let's say I am buying a five-million-dollar apartment complex by paying $800,000 cash down to an existing mortgage. In addition, I need $200,000 cash for immediate physical improvements and an initial turnaround marketing program. Total requirement is $1,000,000.

This might be syndicated in 50 limited partnership units of $20,000 each. Investors who can handle units of this size and larger are available.

However, like any other investors, they are anxious to maximize their return, and the larger the cash outlay, the harder it will be to make the sale.

The answer is the installment investment. By negotiating a down payment over time with the seller, I am able in turn to offer the limited partners an "investment over time" with numerous advantages.

Our example requiring $1,000,000 cash might end up requiring $200,000 immediate cash for turnaround expenses plus a $200,000 cash down payment on closing, then additional annual payments to the seller of $200,000 each year for the next three years.

The effect on the limited partnership is dramatic. Each investor puts up $8000 cash and signs a note for an additional $4000 payment in each of the following three years. The total is the same, but psychologically the investors find it much easier to make their decision, and the partnership will be sold out much more quickly.

Furthermore, since the investor immediately starts to receive his full share of the profit and loss of the project, he is receiving a highly leveraged return during the installment years. In a typical situation, a turnaround investment of this size might project a tax loss of $15,000 per unit during the first several years. For the investor in the 50% tax bracket, this has an economic benefit of $7500 in deferred taxes. Think how much more dramatic this is when his cash investment the first year is $8000 rather than the full $20,000.

A project of this type might also project a tax-sheltered cash flow of $1500 per year starting in the second year. Based on the full $20,000 investment, that would be a satisfactory return of 7½%. However, with the installment arrangement, the investor gets an extra advantage because the same cash flow is generated by far fewer dollars invested during the first years. A $1500 cash flow in year two would amount to a 12½% tax-sheltered return, and in year three would be 9⅓%

Tax Considerations

While your primary motivation for buying and turning around financially distressed real estate should be cash profit, you must also be cognizant of the tax advantages allowed by the government to encourage real estate ownership. They can add to your personal wealth, and they will frequently be a major incentive for people in high income brackets to become your limited partners.

Because our tax laws are subject to revision, I will not go beyond a basic presentation here. I suggest that you research this area with a qualified tax attorney or accountant so you will have completely current knowledge of the subject. Be sure to get information specifically applicable to real estate. The Tax Reform Act of 1976 severely limited many types of tax shelter, but it maintained attractive tax treatments in connection with real estate investments.

These tax incentives basically work by creating tax losses through writing off non-cash loss items. These are items such as interest and depreciation on the property. The tax loss which is created can be used by investors to defer the payment of taxes on other income, as well as to shelter the cash flow from the real estate itself. The greater the write-off, the more inclination limited partners in high tax brackets will have to invest with you in a particular apartment transaction.

To prepare for effective tax structuring of an investment, it is advisable in your sales agreement to allocate the purchase price between real and personal property. At the same time, you should take an inventory of the personal property involved to establish exactly what is being obtained. The more of the purchase price that is legitimately allocated to personal property, the better off you are. Personal property can be deducted over a shorter term than the building itself and therefore gives you a greater depreciation tax loss.

In addition, in your sales agreement or any other documentation at the time of purchase and during operation of the project, make sure you carefully establish each item of expense to the partnership. Expenses, of course, can be written off. Certain of your organizational or syndication costs may either have to be amortized over an organization period, usually five years, or may not be allowed to be written off at all. Land cost, for instance, as well as the payment of syndication fees to someone to raise money, are items that you cannot write off. Therefore, you will want these costs to be as small as possible.

Try to establish the value of your land in the sales agreement. Again, however, this must be a reasonable established value. During an audit by the IRS, you may be called on to support your value. If this situation occurs, it may be necessary for you to hire an appraiser or engineer to allocate purchase price between the various components of land, building, and personal property. To the extent that you have previously had an agreed upon amount for these items in your sales agreement, this can be very helpful in supporting your position.

Chapter 8

The Art of
Successful Real Estate
Negotiation

What Is Negotiation?

Most people don't realize that each of us is involved in negotiation throughout our lives, virtually on a day-to-day basis. Anytime you have a meeting to discuss an opportunity, a problem, or a need, either business or personal, you are involved to some extent in negotiation. Because we do negotiate so frequently, there is a tendency to take the activity for granted as just another routine event.

Actually, negotiation is an art — the art of achieving things we want through diplomatic or verbal means. As an art, there are definite skills and strategies which can contribute to success. As a matter of fact, the first step in becoming a consistent winner is to realize that a large body of knowledge and experience is available to guide the individual who wants to be a competent negotiator.

Pre-Negotiation Preparation

Too often the participants in a negotiation think only about the nose-to-nose meeting. In fact, many negotiations are won or lost before the people ever meet. The negotiator who goes to a meeting without any strategy, or even without a clear idea of his direct objectives, is almost sure to be sliced into little pieces if his competitor has properly prepared.

The use of the word "competitor" is really not out of place. You can realistically think of negotiation as a highly competitive game.

To win, you have to sharpen your skills, learn all you can about your opponent's methods and current situation, create a game plan, and finally get yourself "up" psychologically.

Considered in this light, pre-negotiation preparation must include four elements:

1. Establishing your objectives.
2. Gathering facts about the property.
3. Gaining knowledge about your opponent — the seller or the lender with whom you will negotiate.
4. Establishing basic strategy.

Knowledge — A Needed Asset

All of this adds up to the fact that the real key to success in negotiation is knowledge. Know what you want to achieve and what cards you hold, and you are well on your way. This will require a great deal of homework: tough digging for information and careful consideration of what you learn. The results will inevitably pay for the effort. There is no substitute for effective preparation.

As an example, let's suppose in doing your homework you learn that the seller has significant cash obligations coming up soon on the property. You proceed to negotiate, and he is not divulging the full extent of his situation but you already know his needs. He is trying to negotiate from a position of apparent strength but you know differently. You play along with his game, right down to the wire. You stall a bit compared to what you might normally do in making a specific price and terms offer. When you realize the timing is right, you come in with an offer that is very favorable from your standpoint, but that meets his immediate desperate cash needs. Perhaps to add a touch of drama, you bring in a certified check for an amount of money that you know will take care of his needs and problems.

Even though it may mean selling the property for far less than he would normally accept, the seller in a desperate situation will frequently jump at the chance. Make sure that during this course of action you do not rub the seller's ego the wrong way. I have seen people refuse to do business with someone who has ridiculed them, choosing to lose a property through foreclosure rather than see someone they dislike gain by their misfortune. Hard bargaining strategies have to be tempered with careful personality considerations.

Establishing Your Objectives

If you are the would-be buyer, obviously your overall objective is to arrange the purchase of the property. But, at what price? With what terms? With what special rights? With what financial support from the seller?

In my own case, I go beyond establishing overall objectives, and before each meeting concerning a purchase I establish my specific objectives for that meeting. In this way I am constantly reviewing my progress toward the big objectives, and establishing step-by-step goals to keep moving forward. This ties in closely with setting up effective strategies.

As a general guide, objectives should be specific but not inflexible. Going back to the "trade-off" philosophy expressed in Chapter 6, you may find it helpful to establish your objectives in a range instead of in absolute terms.

Facts About the Property

Naturally you will have reasonable familiarity with a property as a result of your consideration leading to the decision to buy. However, to be effective as ammunition for negotiation, your knowledge of the property will have to be well-organized, and even more detailed than during your initial consideration.

Let's say you are interested in buying a mobile home park or apartment building for turnaround. The more you know about what is wrong with the property, the better off you are. As you point out highly specific, detailed facts to the seller, you are proving you are well aware of the negatives of his situation, and you will be moving him toward your price and terms position.

Then, if you can add to your presentation knowledge of the detrimental aspects of the location, or the economic condition of the area, or some other important aspect outside of the property itself, you may really take charge. Your preparation will pay extra dividends if these factual negatives come as a complete surprise to your opponent. It can happen, but only if you really do your homework exceedingly well.

Sizing Up the Seller

It is important to know with whom you are dealing and have as much information as possible before entering the first meeting. Some of the areas you should look into when negotiating with a seller include the following:

1. *Associates* — Who does the seller associate with? Do you know any of these people? What type of people are they? Can any mutual friends be of assistance to you in any way?
2. *Reputation* — Is the seller's reputation one of honesty and fair play, or is he known as someone who has to be watched carefully? Does he have good or bad credibility in the business community?
3. *Financial condition* — What can you find out through local banks and "street talk" about the financial condition of the seller? Check

suppliers and outside services. Get a local credit report and **Dun
and Bradstreet** report on his company if it is an important meeting.
Learn as much as you can about the seller's current financial position as well as that of the property. This may materially affect how
and what you do in your negotiation.

4. *Personality traits* — The factors of what a person's ego is like and
   how he reacts to various types of business negotiations are extremely important. Some people, for instance, have a father image. If
   they befriend someone and help him out, they are willing to do anything for him. Other people have a need to be loved and an ego
   problem which you can use to your advantage. Some people are
   abrupt and businesslike and appreciate people with the same type
   of attitude. The idea is to get as much information as you can and
   adjust your approach accordingly.

Sizing Up the Lender

Negotiations with lenders are just as critical as those with sellers.
They too, require as much advance knowledge and personal understanding as possible. The relationship with a lender is frequently somewhat
more complex than with a seller. Most sellers are strong individuals, entrepreneurs rather than corporate representatives. Most lender negotiations
will be with an individual who is to some extent bound by institutional
policy and committee review. Therefore, when preparing for lender negotiation, it is best to learn as much as possible about the individual and
separately learn as much as possible about the normal posture of the
lending institution itself.

Seek the help of other lenders who may be willing to casually talk
about their competition. Talk to other investors and to all the knowledgeable brokers you know. People who have previously been in the same
lender negotiation position you are entering are your best source of pre-
knowledge. Because real estate is a small and friendly fraternity, they
will usually help, if asked.

Establishing Strategy

Your early consideration in this area should be very preliminary, and
subject to development as the negotiation progresses. The knowledge you
gather about the people and situation involved may dictate a highly specific strategy or only a general approach. Think it through, but don't be
concerned if you are not able to come up with a full-blown master plan.
Important negotiations are not fulfilled in one session. You will have ample
time to develop your plans more fully as personal contacts take place.

The Power of Doing Your Homework

I personally have developed a system of doing my homework on any important negotiation on a continuous basis. Prior to the first meeting, I do everything possible to gather and organize facts about the property, the people, and the situation; this is only the beginning.

Subsequent to each meeting I spend as much time as necessary, sometimes hours, making notes on my current perception of the facts, the personalities, my objectives, and my strategies. This may lead to additional research. It certainly leads to new ideas and major changes in thinking which affect future negotiation strategy.

I keep a file — sometimes massive — of all my written notes on any significant negotiation. This allows me to review the step-by-step thought process that takes place. I find that even though it is time-consuming, writing down the data helps me capture the full meaning of all the facts, and it has a definite bearing on the total results.

The Non-Zero Sum Negotiation

In a "zero sum" situation, one party wins and the other party loses. In a numerical sense, if there is a $+3$ gain for one player, there is a -3 loss for another player. Therefore, a zero conclusion or sum exists. Some people believe that in negotiating, all transactions are zero sums. One guy loses and one guy wins.

I personally have a strong theory and philosophy that negotiation generally can be a "non-zero sum." I pride myself on a sincere effort to make both myself and my opponents winners when doing my negotiating homework. I am generally trying to understand the need and motivation and psychology of my opponent relative to the facts and to my personal objectives. The more I can meet the needs and motivations of my opponent, the easier it will be to sell him on a program that is favorable from my standpoint. I personally look at all negotiations as a challenge where the desired result isn't to win by having the other guy lose, but to win by creating a plan or program that makes everyone a winner.

In real estate, negotiation isn't simply a matter of the seller wanting $50,000 and the purchaser wanting to pay $45,000, and therefore they both lose by giving up $2500 and compromising on a $47,500 price. In fact, if the parties consider the situation carefully enough, perhaps they are better off if the seller accepts a lower price and gets something else he didn't even think he wanted, or perhaps it is better for the purchaser to pay the higher price but to get better terms than expected. The point is, oftentimes there are alternatives to what we think we want that will actually improve our position.

If you accept the challenge that more than one person can be a winner, one of the key requirements is to get to the guts of the issue and establish what is really in the best interest of each. Keep in mind that frequently your competitor won't have clear-cut objectives. Further, he may not recognize what is best for his interests when it is put in front of him. It is your job to understand and "get inside the head" of your competitor to help him figure out what is in his best interest. Once you have established that, then you can indeed end up with a non-zero sum negotiation.

Don't Forget the Other Point of View

In your honest desire to help the other party see the "facts," it is easy to lose touch with reality as seen by your competitor. Remind yourself frequently that obvious facts to you may not be recognized as facts at all by the other side. Taking the leadership position in a negotiation may be good strategy, but it is well to temper it from time to time by looking at your own position through the eyes of your opponent. After all, he is the one you have to convince.

Keeping an open mind and being flexible as to your method of handling the situation can be the key to keeping control. At all costs, avoid becoming emotional or subjective. Try to keep an objective perspective on all negotiations and discussions. While always keeping in mind your primary objective, be flexible as to how you will get there and what you can give away in the process.

More than once, I have seen an individual come into negotiation with a very rigid personality and end up on the short end when there was no real reason for this result. This kind of person tends to lose his temper or disagree so violently with others that they end up taking a hard stand. A hard stand is one that often pushes an opponent into a corner. Once you have lost the flexibility of allowing your opponent to gracefully agree with you in the end, you have lost a great deal, probably the entire negotiation. Despite your personal feelings at any point in time, be as careful as possible to contain yourself. Remember, negotiation is a dynamic and challenging game of wits.

Developing Your Own Style

Many people will tell you how to negotiate in terms of the style you should use. I personally believe that styles can vary tremendously and still be effective. The key is that your style works for you and is comfortable for you. Beyond that, the style you choose should be one that gets the job done. If you know where you are going, whatever works for you and gets the job done is the right style.

For example, I have seen some people who are effective with a style of haggling and constantly needling the opponent until he is tired. I have seen some people who are excellent negotiators speaking in a constant monotone, displaying a very calm, detached attitude that puts opponents off-guard. Other people are very effective with a screaming style, commanding authority and intimidating their opponent into a position of vulnerability. However, all of these effective styles will be more effective with some people than with others. I believe good negotiators have the ability to use more than one style. They learn quickly to adjust their primary style to a secondary style as needed with a particular type of personaltiy.

My Personal Style — Constant Credibility and the Big Picture

The style that I have come to use as my natural approach to negotiation involves maintaining a high degree of credibility throughout. I am careful not to pull any punches or mislead my competitor. I avoid major changes in basic positions and hold true to my word on any and all verbal agreements or obligations.

I am not the type of negotiator who likes to offer substantially less than he is willing to pay. In fact, although I pride myself on being able to change my negotiating style when necessary, I find some types of discussion very difficult. For instance, negotiating with someone who wants to haggle over nickels and dimes on a big transaction is very difficult for me. I am generally interested only in the big picture.

An example of the type of negotiating I have a difficult time handling is that of the typical single-family buyer or seller. In the typical owner-occupied single-family negotiation, both the buyer and seller want to get the best deal they can in terms of price. Even more, they seem to place great value in getting in the last word. Buyers of houses I have personally sold always seem to psychologically get the last nickel out of me, and the cost in irritation has been very high. Because I see that this is a weak area of mine, I have one of the people who work with me take over when I sense a haggling match developing. They generally are better at it than I am.

My style is really very effective only when dealing with a negotiation of a complex nature. I look at the big picture, decide what my objectives are, go in with a very sincere, honest tone, and really "don't sweat the small stuff." I generally am very easy to get along with and let my opponent win all the small points so that I can get my major objectives. In addition, I am a sincere believer in the real challenge, which is getting a good deal for my opponent as well as for myself.

Should You Negotiate Alone or with a Team?

This is a tough question without a precise answer. Nevertheless, it is a question you should carefully consider. There are definite advantages and disadvantages to either personal or team negotiation, and both strategies will probably be useful to you under different circumstances.

Here are some of the potential advantages of team negotiation which you should weigh:

1. As you learn to be realistic about your own negotiating weaknesses, you can find complementary strength in other individuals and let them do parts of the negotiation. For example, when it comes to a detailed negotiation over a price on certain types of things, I always farm it out to one of my employees. I know that they take a much stronger stand than I would and end up getting a better deal for me and the company.

2. By having the team present at all sessions, you can compare impressions after meetings and come up with strategic plans and programs that may be better than you can do on your own.

3. By using the team, you can do the old "Mutt and Jeff" routine, where if all members of the team are not present during negotiation, you can use an absent member as an excuse to avoid an immediate decision.

4. In a team negotiation, you can always have one individual act as the nice, compromising, good guy and another act as the tough, hardnosed, bad buy who must be convinced. If this is used sparingly by experienced negotiators, it can create a highly effective whipsaw that will keep your opponent off-balance to your benefit.

Certainly one important consideration is who will be the members of your team if you do decide to work with other people? In most negotiations, your real estate broker or attorney can play a role. Additionally, as your operation expands, you may have employees who will be qualified to do parts of the negotiations for you.

Be careful when using a team to make sure you maintain control of the negotiation. Particularly in the case of attorneys, you will find that many of them enjoy negotiating on behalf of their clients. Unfortunately, many attorneys are not the expert negotiators they like to think they are. In fact, some attorneys are frustrated businessmen, and at your expense may attempt to take over the businessman's role and end up blowing your deal. This, of course, must be controlled quickly.

A good reason to use outside assistants is objectivity. Many times you may become emotional on a subject. By using an attorney, in particular, or another third party, you may have a teammate who will remain more objective and take a better look at all the facts. I have found this particularly effective when re-negotiating the finance of some of my older properties which have emotional involvement for me.

There also are advantages to negotiating alone. First of all, you do not get whipsawed yourself by making mistakes that can be made in a group negotiation. Secondly, it is easier. You know exactly what is happening and can make your own decisions without consultation and argument. You don't have one of the individuals on your team giving away your position or saying things that are inconsistent. Finally, it is wise to remember that you can depend on yourself better than on anyone else.

Hopefully you know yourself well enough that you can make proper evaluation of using other people in any given negotiation. Based on your knowledge of your own strengths and weaknesses, and based on the knowledge of your opponent, and finally the considerations of what talent you have available, you should make your decision as to whether or not in a particular negotiation, you are better off alone or with a team.

Use of Brokers

I have seen brokers make and break deals during negotiations. As a principle, I feel they should be used as a member of the team, but only under your control and to play very specific roles. Many brokers feel it is part of their job to handle the total negotiation for you. Therefore, it is essential that you clearly advise the broker exactly what you want him to do and what you will do for yourself.

In making your decision in this area, you will have to weigh the broker's experience and personality against the fact that he is motivated by one thing and one thing only — that is a commission. I am not saying that a broker, which I happen to be, is a crass or ruthless person, but he does work on a commission basis, and you cannot afford to forget it. Used effectively and with control, your broker can be an excellent tool and he can earn the money he makes in the transaction.

Always try to have the broker communicate all the negative things possible about the property. Oftentimes, the broker can more sincerely indicate to the seller that the property is only worth "X" and the seller would be lucky to get out. The broker can act as a third party talking as a middleman; if you use him properly, he can be a middleman who is really doing the work you want done.

On the other hand, I have seen brokers who have been privy to inside information as to a purchaser's ideas and strategies, and rarely do they keep them for the purchaser's advantage. They are simply too anxious to make the deal. So, you must sell the broker just like you are selling the seller, and use him to reinforce your position.

In addition, learn to use a broker as a fact gatherer. Let him do all the running and errands necessary to get the data on the property. The good broker realizes that this is part of his function and will be very diligent in helping you obtain the necessary information. Check the accuracy of the broker's information. He can be most helpful, but his interpretation of the meaning of the information will tend to be slanted to encourage the sale. Depend on your own interpretation to plan your strategies.

The Ego-Ego Theory

It is important to realize that negotiation is not a situation where you necessarily win if you have the best arguments. Having the best arguments can help you win, but how you present them is probably even more significant. In fact, you must put together a combination of knowing what you want, having the right ammunition, and then putting across your points in the right manner. That is the winning combination.

Part of putting your points across in the right manner involves knowing the other person and knowing how to use their ego rather than abuse it. In my own situation, I have had a problem of my youth creating an atuomatic ego problem for many of my opponents. For instance, I have negotiated with lenders where I have put myself, by virtue of manner and means of acquiring property, in a position of leverage over the lender. This, combined with my success at a young age, tends to upset some ego-insecure lender types. They are then subconsciously saying to themselves, "I'll show that little upstart that he can't make a deal with our bank." I have started off with an abused ego problem even before negotiation started.

In this situation, I do everything possible to attempt to sincerely and honestly change the opponent's image of me. Image in negotiations is most important. Oftentimes, we have a preconceived image of our opponent or our opponent has a preconceived image of us. The more we can do to effect a favorable image, the better. We certainly don't want to do anything to abuse the other person's ego and have him feel personal affronted. To consider a negotiation as a business competition is healthy, but if it deteriorates into a personal confrontation everyone loses.

It is never sensible to go in and brag about how smart you are when you are negotiating to buy a property from a man who is in trouble. It is generally better to be sympathetic to his problems and appreciative of some of the good things he has done. Very few people respond to obnoxious or arrogant opponents. On the other hand, getting to know your opponents on a personal basis and understanding them is a way of using their ego rather than abusing it. It doesn't hurt to take a real interest in their personal life and think about why they may or may not have done certain things. It also doesn't hurt to know when to keep your opinions to yourself.

The Art of Asking Questions

One of the best techniques for appealing to the ego is to ask questions from time to time in order to involve your opponent and create a climate of confidence.

Questions can invite friendly sharing of thoughts, or they can put the opponent into a corner. It is not enough that you make a statement with a question mark at the end. If you are to use questions effectively, you have to develop a special skill in framing them properly.

For example, if you want to encourage participation, don't ask a question which can be answered with a simple "yes" or "no." Don't ask closed questions like, "Do you think this problem can be solved?" Ask open questions like, "Joe, what do you think we can do about this problem?"

Another important technique is to encourage an expanded response by using hitchhike questions after you receive an answer. Ask things like:

"Why is that?"

"How do you happen to feel that way about it?"

Both of these questions are intended to encourage more discussion by expressing friendly interest. But they could also come across as argumentative challenges, depending on the tone of voice. Try it. You can give these questions exactly opposite meanings depending on how you say them. This is an important clue to effectiveness in negotiation: be sure your voice and your face reflect the feeling you want to project.

If you become conscious of the value of questions in negotiation and deliberately plan their use from time to time, you will quickly develop an effective style and skill in this area.

The Art of Listening

Obviously, if we are to use questions effectively we have to listen to the replies. Really listening is another skill which has to be developed. All too often, in a desire to maintain leadership of the conversation, we half-listen while we are really concentrating on our next thrust. This is the sure way to miss the nuances and details which can help understand the opponent and his ego.

When dealing with a particularly talkative opponent, there can be a tendency to break in and take over because he seems to be talking in circles. My experience dictates patience. More than once, I have had talkative opponents end up supplying valuable information I had not even thought to ask for.

When to Be Tough

In any style, there is a time and place to be tough. In my own case, probably because I am very straightforward, whenever I feel my opponent is being unfair or dishonest I can become very difficult to deal with. Another time to become tough is in a situation where you feel that particular style will have a good effect on the competitor. Some people are intimidated and react to a tough, strong posture. Again, the flexibility of accommodating the necessary tone and style to get your objective from a particular opponent is the key.

When to Be Cooperative

Oftentimes in negotiation, the best possible strategy is to cooperate and do what your opponent asks. The more you can give your opponent, the more indebted he becomes to you. Keep looking for things that are important to the opponent but which will not seriously hurt you. You may be able to give up ten things and end up just getting one major point which is your entire objective. This can be the perfect path to non-zero-sum results. Remember, the more positive and cooperative the tone you establish, the more willing your opponent will be to cooperate in return. Just don't lose sight of your objective and don't give up on the major points you require.

The Power of Silence (Or When to Shut Up)

One of the most effective tools in negotiating can be keeping your mouth shut at the right time. When you are at a critical stage in the negotiations, review the facts, make your point, and then shut up. The next guy who talks, loses.

Think about this the next time you are in a negotiation. At a certain point, if you say what you have to say and then shut up, the silence can create fantastic pressure. If you immediately follow your point with another comment or reason, it simply dilutes your position. If you make the point well and then wait for the opponent to respond, you are going to win.

I have been involved in negotiations where there has been a pause as long as three to four minutes when no one says a word. It may seem like an hour, but inevitably the next person to speak gives in and loses the point. It is a fascinating thing to watch the power of silence. Make sure this pressure is used to your advantage and not used against you. Make your point, back off, and shut up. If your opponent has done the same, wait him out, let him make the next move. Even if you are there for 20 minutes without anyone saying a word, make sure you are not the first one to speak in the "silence challenge."

Everything in Good Time

One of the worst things you can do in any negotiation is push at the wrong time. Try to pick your own time and place for important negotiating breakthroughs so you put the leverage on your side. If you really believe there is always another good deal available, you will be able to put patience on your side.

The person who doesn't need to make the deal usually makes the best deal. This is because he has the confidence and power to wait it out. The man who is aggressively in need of a deal blows it. I have seen this with real estate brokers who are on their last nickel and show it. Nobody will do business with them. On the other hand, I have seen some people in tremendous positions of weakness negotiate as though they had all the strength in the negotiation, and because of their guts and fortitude they came out of the negotiation as winners.

How Patience Made an "Impossible" Deal

One of my early transactions offers an interesting example of the value of patience in negotiation. It also points up the fact that negotiation is not limited to specific sit-down meetings. In this case, the negotiation also involved a series of very brief, informal contacts over a two-year period.

Rolling Hills is a beautiful 400-unit townhouse development built in the heart of Ann Arbor, Michigan by one of the big three automobile companies that had gone into the real estate business. They did not spare anything in terms of quality. The site was beautifully landscaped and made for a really exciting rental project.

I was interested in the complex since its completion. During the early rent-up, I felt that they had set the rents too low, and they would ultimately find they were not going to make money on the project. I tried to make an offer on the property at that time. However, it wasn't easy for a very small real estate entrepreneur, 23 years of age, to make an effective offer on an eight million dollar property. Since at that time I had very little money, my interest wasn't taken too seriously and the corporation continued to own the property.

Over a two-year period, I kept in contact with their attorney and with other people involved in the operation. I had a firm conviction that this property was losing a great deal of its profit potential through inefficient operation. It has been my experience that large corporate organizations frequently do not operate with the flexibility and fast decision-making capability that marks most entrepreneurial real estate operators.

My beliefs held true with this particular development, but the company continued to hold the property and was not too concerned about profitability. Then, toward the end of a calendar year, policy changed, and it was suddenly decided to liquidate two or three of the company's larger real estate holdings in an effort to boost year-end profit.

Since I had constantly expressed my interest, an attorney who had worked on the property with an associate of the auto company owner contacted me with news of the property's availability. We decided that he and I, and eventually a third individual, would acquire the property together. We would then syndicate it to raise limited partner equity money as I had done with other developments.

As a result of the attorney's previous work with the auto company, our team had credibility and we were immediately able to enter into effective negotiation. The closing and purchase of the property took place less than 60 days later. We initially raised a 10% down payment or $800,000 and bought the $8,000,000 property.

This negotiation was only possible because of my perseverance that led to being in the right place at the right time and, most particularly, to being involved with the right people. This was a transaction that was simply out of my league at the time, but with the right partner and a lot of patience, I was able to become a part of a very successful turnaround.

Chapter 9

Advanced Turnaround
Negotiation Techniques

Essentially the basics of negotiation apply to all real estate invest-ment purchases. Of course, some will be more complex than others. Turn-around purchases tend to be more complicated and more dependent on creative solutions. As a result, success may require a highly developed ability to ferret out the real needs, rather than merely the stated require-ments, of the opponent in negotiation.

An Example of a Creative Negotiation

The owners of Lilac Terrace let it be known that they wanted to sell their very attractive 449-unit apartment development. We, as well as a number of other potential purchasers, expressed interest and entered into discussions. As we got into the numbers, it became obvious there was no way the property could support the price on the basis they were asking. Interest in the property diminished, but the owners held fast to their ex-pressed need for $2,600,000 cash down to an existing $6,980,000 mortgage.

The project was not doing well and there was pressure on the gen-eral partners to sell. The problem, however, of getting their price and still having the deal make sense to the potential purchaser seemed insur-mountable. We negotiated for an extensive period of time, and after sev-eral months of discussion it became apparent, piece by piece, what the real needs of the sellers were.

On the one hand they did have certain rather immediate cash needs: about $75,000 for outstanding bills, and $250,000 to cover second and third mortgages which were scheduled to balloon in a short time. The general partners had personal liability on the quarter of a million dollar debt, so they virtually could not afford to sell without those debts being covered. We segregated these items as being "real" cash needs from the seller's point of view.

The balance of the cash requirement, we finally found out, represented the $2,000,000 which had been invested by 44 limited partners. To their credit, the general partners did not want to sell the property unless it would cover the complete return of the limited partners' money. Of course, if the project could not be sold for a sufficient amount, this investment might well be lost through bankruptcy. Therefore, we labeled this portion of the price as a "psychological" need.

Extensive negotiation followed, and we were finally able to arrange a purchase plan that completely satisfied all parties. We paid $75,000 cash, and took over the responsibility for the second and third mortgage balloons. We created a unique kind of wraparound land contract that combined the existing first mortgage and the limited partners' investment. A low interest rate was established on this wraparound so in essence there was no finance cost to us for the limited partner portion of the debt.

Our payment schedule on the combined debt was geared to the proven ability of the project to generate cash flow. This was sufficient to cover the first mortgage, but the limited partner portion was deferred until a balloon payment matured in 12 years.

While we essentially paid a higher price than the property was worth at the moment, $2,000,000 of the price would have no bearing on our operation for 12 years. During this period, turnaround improvement plus a very moderate inflation rate would provide more than enough growth in value to assure payment of the $2,000,000 balloon.

This was an excellent example of non-zero-sum negotiation that was only possible after a real definition of the needs of the various parties. Technically, the deal was structured to maximize everyone's tax position, and through mutual concern, everyone won.

Since the purchase, the project was turned around and became a money-maker. It has recently been sold at a good profit.

Recognizing the Seller's Needs

In any transaction you are dealing with human beings, and therefore all your considerations must be subject to the frailties of logic which all of us possess as people. I personally feel that the question of a seller making a big profit or taking a substantial loss should have no bearing on the value of a property. However, from the "people" point of view, I simply cannot ignore the seller's profit or loss. It is important to know what the seller is doing in terms of gain or loss for the psychological effects it may be having on his ability and willingness to make a deal. You may easily lose a deal because you don't know what the real needs of the seller are. If you do know them, you may be able to structure a transaction that will be in your mutual best interest.

Unfortunately, many people feel they have to play a game of "hide the facts" when they get into a real estate negotiation. They have a feeling they will weaken their position if they explain their situation in plain language. In these cases, it may take several meetings before you can get down to the real needs. I can only suggest that you keep asking, keep hammering for the facts, and don't forget the importance of this strategy.

Another important need to try to establish at the beginning is what the seller's tax position is. I have been through a number of lengthy negotiations right down to the wire where a deal was about to be made, only to have the seller take it to his accountant and find he will have tremendous tax liabilities from the sale and can't make the deal. When this happens, the seller has wasted a great deal of your time and done so in a manner that seemed to be in good faith. Tax considerations to a seller are extremely important. Therefore, it is essential for you to understand what his position is so you can determine whether or not a deal can be made on the terms you are considering.

A final important need to consider is how much the seller really needs cash and how much of his demands are psychological. A seller who is in desperate need for cash is obviously much easier to deal with than a seller who is dealing from a position of strength and wants cash but doesn't need it. On the other hand, a seller who doesn't need cash and is willing to admit it can be the most lucrative to work with from a standpoint of profitable terms.

Techniques for Satisfying the Seller's Needs

There are many techniques to consider when satisfying the seller's needs. Obviously, these vary considerably depending on what you have established his needs to be. Some of the techniques you can use are as follows:

1. *Compromise* — If the seller is a personality who needs to win points, compromise with him in all of the small things, but make sure that you get tough when necessary on more important issues. Frequently, when a guy is busy winning many issues, he is willing to give in on a few, and he doesn't differentiate well between the small and large issues.

2. *Let Him Beat You Slowly* — Sellers like to win and many look at everything as a game. Unfortunately for them, a smart buyer knows the real objective of the game. While he is letting the seller slowly beat him into submission, he is truly giving up none of the important objectives. The seller thinks he has come out with the ultimate victory, but ends up with just his fair share, despite all of his effort.

3. *Finance Suggestion* — Whenever possible develop alternative methods which will satisfy the seller's real needs and be advanta-

geous to you. Particularly, study all tax consequences as these frequently offer opportunities that are not realized by the seller.

4. *Cosmetics* — In order to meet the psychological needs of the seller who may have too much money in a property, you may have to come up with a plan to buy the property for a higher price than you would normally pay, with some agreement that if you pay it off at a certain point you will receive a large enough discount so that you will end up paying what you wished to pay in the beginning.

The First Meeting — Setting the Tone

The first meeting should be extremely important. The effect of your homework and clear-cut objectives is critical. I would suggest that you prepare an agenda and give consideration as to the tone and approach you want to use that best combines your own style and what you have heard about the opponent.

During your opening remarks, make sure that you establish your position clearly but without polarizing the situation or backing the opponent into an untenable corner. Present your agenda for consideration as a suggested approach. If the opponent has not prepared an agenda, yours will probably be accepted and start things as you desire.

I primarily use the first meeting as a fact-gathering session. Even if I know the answers to questions, this is an opportunity to re-assess and get facts about the property from the "horse's mouth," so to speak. In addition, as you are asking the questions, you will be able to get a firsthand reading on the seller. I have found first meetings to generally be an opportunity to establish the personalities and get a feeling that will help establish strategy for later meetings.

By digging in with questions and establishing what the seller's needs are, you can usually take control of the situation. From the beginning, you can establish that your basic approach is attempting to understand the entire situation and to best meet everyone's needs. If the seller takes over and starts asking you questions, answer them in as short and concise a manner as possible, avoiding detailed substance. Then turn around and continue to question the seller as to his motivation, needs, etc. This will help you keep control of the meeting and build the rapport you will need later on.

The First Offer

Your first offer should always be made from a position of strength, and should of course reflect a very favorable price for you as the purchaser. On larger properties which usually require seller participation in finance, the best way to indicate strength is to make a cash offer.

In fact, you may not have the cash to support your offer, but it has been my experience that if your offer includes a reasonable time period to arrange finance, you will usually be able to make the deal if it is accepted. Of course, your offer should carry adequate contingencies to protect you if you are unable to close.

A cash offer will be a very strong consideration to the seller. It should, however, be a price significantly lower than the seller is originally asking for. In many cases the seller is not necessarily going to get a cash sale and he may be very impressed that you at least made a cash offer. This will make him believe that you have a great deal of financial strength and capacity. Certainly do nothing to discourage him from feeling this way. This will work to your advantage in the balance of the negotiations.

If your cash offer is accepted, you then have the problem of raising the money. Generally, your offer will have been low enough that you can get conventional financing on the property and have very little actually involved in completing the transaction.

In the event your first offer is not accepted, you then seek a counterproposal from the seller. He may automatically state this, or you may have to ask him what he would take for the property. In any event, at this point, you are in a position to say, "O.K., if I have to come up with a higher price, it will have to be with you as the seller taking back a purchase money mortgage on a portion of the price."

At this point, you have established credibility and substance. You have registered your position as to cash value and established the necessity of the seller to participate in the finance.

How to Present the Offer

Presentation of the first written offer is frequently the climax of the negotiation. It is always a very critical stage and should be planned for maximum effect.

If there is a broker involved, he will usually want to present the offer. As a general rule, I think it should be presented by you as the principal. You may or may not want to have the broker or other people present. This will depend on the nature of the relationships that have been developed. In addition to presenting the offer, present your deposit check. If the check is going into escrow, which I would always advise, make a copy of the check and give that to the seller with the offer. Presenting a copy of a certified check or showing him the check itself can have a major psychological effect. In addition, it is often helpful to write a cover letter. This should be brief, but make the key points as to why your offer has been framed as it is and why it deserves favorable consideration.

When you present the offer, do not expect an immediate response. If you push for an immediate response, it may be negative. Suggest the seller review the matter. Demonstrate the seriousness of your offer in your verbal presentation. Answer any questions he has and explain to him why you believe this is in his best interest. Build up a positive atmosphere without any hint of defensiveness or apology. Keep the presentation short and leave with the anticipation that the deal will soon be accepted.

Time Is on the Buyer's Side

The more time you spend and the more meetings you have with the seller, the more likely you are to make a deal. As long as there is a reasonable end to it, it is generally helpful to spend a lot of time in negotiations and meetings before you get into a meaningful offer position. While this is not always practical, at least in the initial stages of your real estate career, it is well worth the time. During your many meetings with the seller, you should constantly, subtly, but strongly jab at the seller with all the negative points you can think of regarding the property. In essence, you are making a concerted effort to condition the seller's mind so that when your offer is finally made, he will be expecting even less than you offer.

Let's suppose you are interested in a property being offered for $150,000. You have decided it is worth only about $100,000 because it has serious cash flow problems and requires a great deal of turnaround work. If you were to go in and make the offer of $100,000 during the first, second, or third meeting, you might get thrown out of the office. Instead, you spend a great deal of time inspecting the property. Have seven or eight meetings during which you develop a friendship with the seller while constantly pointing out deficiencies of the property in the nicest possible way. Then make your offer, and the response will be entirely different. If you have done your job, the seller should not be surprised and may even be receptive.

Do not become discouraged by a seller who may constantly say, "If you offer less than my figure, you may as well forget it; you are wasting your time." You must differentiate between the seller who is saying this as part of his ego and the seller who is dead serious. Some sellers are very serious when they make a statement of that nature. Many, however, are really saying, "Hey, I know my property isn't worth what I want; keep coming, I'm interested." You must learn to read these signs and eventually they will become second nature to you.

The Seller Who Is Wasting Your Time

Some people who own real estate are frustrated professional sellers. I say this half in jest and half seriously. The problem is that these people who consider themselves professional sellers are really not sellers at all. They will negotiate, negotiate, negotiate — but they don't really want to sell at all. It is difficult to tell if an individual is a serious seller or just someone who is wasting your time.

I remember one project in which I was interested which included 800 units. I was really excited about the property and felt after weeks of negotiating that I had gotten to know the seller's needs. He was in a situation where his building partner of many years had passed away within the last two years. This left the gentleman I was dealing with and the widow of his partner as 50-50 partners in a number of apartment buildings. He was doing all the work in management and she was getting half the profit. He was tired of that position. He had enough money to sell and enter other ventures, and that seemed to make good sense for him.

The particular property had a great deal of financial trouble, and at the time they had not been keeping up with the maintenance so the project had run down. The run-down condition caused them to get a lower-class resident profile, and accordingly they were having rent collection problems even though the rents were not as high as they should have been.

When it became apparent that he was half interested in selling, and half not, I worked out a very interesting program for him. In my transaction, he would have ended up selling the property, while still maintaining an involvement in the new entity that bought the property. His involvement would be passive in nature, but would still give him ownership benefits. Most importantly, it was a situation where he could make money and still satisfy his ego desire to own property. It sounded like a perfect solution.

Unfortunately, at the last minute, I came to realize that this man was not a seller at all. We were not able to get together on the deal. As far as I know, some three or four years later, he still hadn't sold the project, although he was actively negotiating and talking to many, many people.

This problem is not unique. Many owners will simply use your time and are not serious sellers. You must keep this in mind when you are talking to a seller as it can obviously be a most time-wasting experience. This is not a conscious thing, and perhaps is something similar to the emotional problem of cutting the cord as your children get older and go off to school or get married.

The way to spot a non-serious seller is by flushing him out in the early stages with real questions. Establish firm areas that he would agree to if he really wants to sell. Frame your questions in such a manner that you are not indicating that you can necessarily live with whatever you are suggesting, but are merely asking for a point of beginning. Ask direct questions on timing, dollar amounts, etc. and then make your own judgment as to the sincerity of the responses.

Lender Involvement in Turnaround Negotiation

As you get involved in larger turnaround opportunities, you will find that an existing lender will sometime become an important part of the total negotiation. This relationship may become extremely important to you, and it is important to realize that in many ways it will be quite different than negotiating with sellers.

A lending institution may become involved for several reasons. They may have foreclosed, and in fact occupy the position of seller as well as lender. Or, the property may be in serious default on its mortgage subject to foreclosure, and it is necessary to create some relationship with the lender either as a part of the total purchase package or to be finalized immediately after purchase. As the purchaser of a property in financial default, you may feel the only way to structure a viable purchase will be with the assistance of the existing lender through renegotiation of the terms of the underlying loan.

The Lender's Needs

While you will negotiate with an individual lender who must be treated as an individual personality, the over-riding fact is that this person is the representative of the lending institution. Of necessity his needs will be dictated by established policies, by state laws, by committee approvals, by outside auditors, by accounting practices, and by the protocol of his institution.

As a result, there is far less personal psychology involved than when negotiating with entrepreneurs. In some respects, it is even more difficult to pin down the needs of your opponent, and when you do there may be less opportunity for creative maneuvers.

Nevertheless, there are many opportunities to negotiate successfully with lenders, for they too have their problems that you can help solve. Indeed, lenders really need help with distressed properties, and if you can convince them of your ability and credibility, they will work with you, but only within the requirements they must meet to satisfy legal, auditing, and sound business practices.

Building Credibility

Credibility with lenders comes with time, with professionalism, with paper, and with personal relationships.

Because of the importance of the individual member of the lending institution meeting its performance standards, he cannot and will not make snap judgments. He must accumulate demonstrated proof of your ability and accomplishments. The banker will intuitively react well to a steady stream of reports and documentation of actions and results.

Suppose you are managing a foreclosed property for a lender and hope to buy it from them. A paper blizzard will be in order to first establish the inherent problems of the property, and second your command of the situation and its future.

Even though you are dealing with an institution, in the final analysis, an institution is made up of individuals. Ultimately, if you are to be accepted, you must have a sponsor. Someone within the institution must accept you on a personal basis and believe in you. Thus, the building of friendship and close rapport with selected individuals is important.

Tenacity Pays Off

Probably because of the great number of decisions constantly before lenders, they will sometimes tend to procrastinate on complex situations that are not clear-cut. If you feel this is happening, establish a campaign to provide as much information and substantiation of your position as possible — always in writing. Don't let the deal die. Don't press too hard, but keep the matter viable and alive until you get action. Too often, buyers or borrowers are intimated because they don't understand the operation or personality of the institution. Make it your business to dig beneath the surface. Get to know the people, and help them get to know you.

Learn All You Can About Lender's Accounting

The more you know about the accounting practices of the lending institution with which you are working, the better your position. Lenders are, of necessity, motivated by their accounting practices. For example, what is the write-off policy on foreclosed properties being held by the institution? If it is a five-year write-off, that means the institution's asset is being dissipated on their books at the rate of 20% a year or 1⅔% each and every month! They should be highly motivated to turn this loss into a sale, even with excellent terms.

Various lenders have differing policies about the cash down required when selling a foreclosed property to an investor. In the past, many would make no-cash deals with purchasers who had the necessary ability and experience to make the property pay. Today, however, many lenders feel they must have a financial as well as a mental commitment. It may only be 3% or 4% down, but some cash must be involved. In the case of insurance company lenders, state law may require them to get 10% minimum cash. The point is there are needs, and the sooner you check them out the better.

Foreclosure Is a Last Resort

A major premise in working with lenders is that while they can legally foreclose on properties that are in default, they would much prefer to find another way to protect their loan and the interest income it should be producing. Foreclosure is a long, expensive, and troublesome procedure. It ends up with the lending institution owning and operating real estate, and they know this is not a profitable or desirable business for them.

I am a firm believer that a bank or lending institution wants to deal with someone who is in possession. Rather than foreclose and operate or sell, they will make a workout with an existing owner if possible. If, for committee reasons, psychological reasons, or other reasons they cannot work with the existing owner, they are desirous of working with whoever is closest, most local to the area, and who can provide the services they need.

The "On-the-Spot" Maneuver

This belief regarding lending institutions has led to the development of an approach which has some risk of time and effort, but a good chance of creating a favorable purchase. I have gone in as a management agent on properties when I have known that the prospective seller is very close to being foreclosed. I let the seller know in advance that I intend to deal with the lender as well as himself to try to do my job as management agent during this difficult time.

I will not go behind a seller's back and try to cut a deal for my own benefit, as long as he owns the property. If, however, the property does go into foreclosure or is taken over, I hopefully will have established a rapport with the lending institution so I may have a chance to continue in management and eventually buy the property. In some cases, this is advantageous to a seller. The seller is interested in doing anything he can to save the property, and, if he realizes what your position is, he is usually willing to go along.

In the particular case of the Colonial Circle property, we took over management of a 310-unit apartment development with the property behind on its mortgage and in a physical state of disrepair. There was extensive deferred maintenance and many latent defects from original construction. The property was over two years old at the time, but had never really taken off. We were made aware by the owner of the possible foreclosure on the property. The owner was concerned since he had limited partners involved who would suffer severe tax consequences from such an action.

As a first step in our management, we did a complete analysis of the property. We came up with facts that indicated the property needed extensive funding in order to be turned around. The property needed a new image, physical improvements, and significant dollars to keep the mortgage current until there was satisfactory occupancy so that the project could generate money to pay its way.

The lender was in a position that was becoming increasingly more serious. Realizing this, they decided to take whatever actions were necessary to get the property. The seller was in a position where he realized that his time was almost up. We were in a position where we were technically agents of the seller, but with his permission had some relationship with the lender. We were, however, in a position where we might end up losing our management contract.

What happened was most successful for all parties involved. We ended up negotiating a deal with the lender and the seller. The seller agreed to a very low down payment and long-term land contract sale, subject to our satisfactorily renegotiating the loan underneath the land contract.

We then, on our mutual behalf, negotiated with the lender. The lender agreed to defer the back interest and grant reasonable temporary relief of current mortgage payments while we put money into the project as well as time and effort in order to turn it around.

This was most profitable for everyone involved. The seller had established an installment sale for tax purposes which greatly minimized the disadvantageous position of a foreclosure to his investors. In fact, there were certain other advantages to the sale over foreclosure from a tax standpoint, and the investors came out much better than if the property had been foreclosed. The lender came out quite well because he avoided all the time and effort involved in litigating a foreclosure. In addition, the lender got an immediate new buyer who was willing and able to make the necessary commitment to the property to turn it around. Our investment in the turnaround process considerably improved the lender's position.

We were, of course, happy because we were able to favorably purchase a turnaround opportunity. In addition, this was a turnaround opportunity concerning which we had complete knowledge. By knowing what the problems of the project were we were in a better position to negotiate, bringing up all the negative aspects possible. Even more important, we were in an excellent position to evaluate the property.

Never Go Against the Grain

Negotiation is a fascinating subject, and one I believe can profitably be studied for a lifetime. Obviously, it is complex and difficult to recap in a few words. However, I believe the old cliché introducing this paragraph may be the best of all guidelines for effective negotiation.

Too often, I have observed people taking adversary positions apparently just to try to do the other fellow out of something. That to me is "going against the grain."

If you simply take a position based on logic and sound reasoning, and that meets the needs of all parties involved, you are on the way to winning. And that's what negotiation is all about.

IV

MAKING YOUR
TURNAROUND WORK

Chapter 10

Tips on Taking Over
Turnaround Properties

The moment of truth has arrived. After searching, analyzing, negotiating, and financing, you have closed the deal. The turnaround property is yours, complete with its problems and its great promise for the future. Now your real work begins.

Whether your purchase puts you in possession of a faltering four-family or a 1000-unit economic disaster, you can quickly become the "white knight" I described in Chapter 1. The moment you take over, you are in the spotlight. Residents, suppliers, employees, and your lender are all waiting and watching for action. They don't expect miracles, but they do expect you to get your arms around the project; display an understanding of the problems and begin a program for improvement.

The Importance of Having a MAP

The old saying that the shortest distance between two points is a straight line certainly applies to turnarounds. That is the reason we prepare a MAP, or Management Action Plan, for each turnaround I undertake. This is our detailed planning and control mechanism that establishes the specific "who, what, when, why, and how much" of a particular turnaround. It puts us on that straight line and helps keep us there.

Certainly it is possible to run a business by the seat of your pants, but in my experience consistent success in turnarounds requires carefully conceived plans that coordinate all of the activities necessary to solve all of the property's potential problems. Furthermore, I am convinced the plan should be in writing. The mere act of putting your thinking on paper will force you to be more precise, both in your planning and your reviews of progress.

133

Developing Your MAP

The MAP approach applies equally to large and small properties. Obviously, a large development will probably require a much more complex plan because it will have more complex problems. Nevertheless, the basic principles are the same:

— Identify the problems, their root cause, and relative seriousness.
— Establish improvement objectives.
— Determine how much time and money you can afford to achieve each objective.
— Develop specific action plans in line with the time and cost allowances to eliminate the problem or at least reduce the negative effect.
— Establish personnel responsibilities for each area of action.
— Communicate the plan to all those involved, gaining absolute understanding and agreement.
— Monitor activities to control and coordinate while you evaluate and adjust to assure maximum effectiveness.

For planning purposes, we examine the turnaround in terms of its needs in each of four areas that usually require some degree of effort: finance, operations, physical, marketing. A large turnaround property may require numerous actions in each of these categories. Each of the next four chapters examines one of the turnaround areas in detail, with actual examples from successful projects.

To organize this material, we use a simple form laid out horizontally on 8½" x 14" paper, like this:

Property _____ Date _____		
Activity _____ Date Revised _____		
Problem	*Remedy*	*Result*
A highly specific and detailed description of each major problem.	The essence of the planned action, or at least the general type and direction of the effort planned to develop an ultimate solution. May include cost allocations.	Clear communication of the end result objective. Includes time goals.

This form is used in planning. When it is finalized, it is duplicated and used for communication to people who will carry out the remedies, to investors, to lenders, and to the operating staff managers in larger projects. Chapter 15 presents a complete set of these charts just as they were filled in to plan the turnaround of a $16,000,000 property.

When to Start Developing Your MAP

As I indicated in Chapter 5, a test MAP limited to ultra-critical problems is one method of analyzing whether or not a potential investment is feasible for a turnaround. This activity during the selection phase will give you a running head start on the development of your MAP. Actually, you will be gathering action plan facts and ideas constantly as you go through the buying process.

As soon as the sales agreement has been accepted, you should move ahead to expand and finalize your MAP. Ideally, your complete management action plan will be ready for use when you close the purchase. If this is not possible, it should have top priority after you close.

Tips on Planning

As a part of the buying process, you will certainly have become aware of all the major problems of your purchase. Nevertheless, it is smart to take another, more detailed look as you start to finalize your plans.

If you did not carry out an in-depth opinion survey among tenants, be sure to do it now. Their thoughts and reactions are vital to planning your marketing, and very helpful in identifying some of the priorities in operations and physical upgrading. Also be sure to have the project shopped by a few friends playing the role of prospective renter. Find out how they are treated and how effectively the selling job is handled.

Another worthwhile activity at this point is a "walk-through." With notepad and pencil in hand, cover every bit of the building or complex. Look at it closely and critically. Don't merely accept what you see, but aggressively look for opportunities to create improvement. Concentrate on appearance, amenities, housekeeping, and maintenance. Note specific work to be done, as well as overall impressions.

As you start to write down problems, remedies, and results, be sure to note your thoughts about the urgency of the work and the estimated cost. As you put it all together, you will have to recognize that everything can't be done immediately. You should work on several objectives at the same time, but there is rarely the time or money to do everything at once.

If you establish the relative importance of each activity, and cost estimates, you will be able to consider the trade-offs and establish intelligent priorities.

High Value-High Priority Opportunities

In setting priorities, it just makes good sense to tackle those areas which will be most meaningful either to you or your tenants. Anything which will quickly improve cash flow or build up tenants' image of the project, should get top-priority attention. Here are some good possibilities to consider:

— *Rent Collection Program:* If there has been a growing trend to delinquency or slow payment, nip it in the bud. Remind delinquents promptly in writing. Follow up when necessary. Take legal action to evict and do it without delay. You may lose some tenants, but you will be able to replace them with a higher resident profile as other aspects of your turnaround become obvious.

— *Security:* Nothing is more negative to residents than fear. Tackle this problem fast with armed guards patroling the property if it is necessary. Get a police department expert to talk to a meeting of residents to advise them of what they can do to improve their own security.

— *Deferred Maintenance Activity:* This will create a quick impact on residents if the condition of the project has deteriorated enough to become annoying. Deferred maintenance will have to be caught up sooner or later. "Sooner" will prove to be a much better investment.

— *Reinstate Curtailed Services:* This might include such things as window washing, hallway cleaning, etc. Such improvements will gain quick appreciation.

As a matter of strategy, I have found it is very effective to put on an extra show of strength in areas like these during the first 90 days in a turnaround investment. For example, if security has been a serious problem, I will bring in twice as many security patrols as we plan on a permanent basis. The sight of a patrol car every few minutes is dramatic proof of improvement to the residents, and it will also go a long way toward solving the problem.

Setting Up a Consolidated MAP

A series of "Problem — Remedy — Result" sheets reflects your planning in detail, but it is not a convenient tool for reviewing and controlling progress. For this purpose, we consolidate the action decisions made in all the turnaround areas. I suggest you use a form like the following:

MANAGEMENT ACTION PLAN				
Project _____		Date		
Action Required	Responsible	Budget	Progress Check Dates	Final Completion Dates

With a MAP as simple as this, you will not lose touch with even the most complicated turnaround. However, remember that this is just a tool of management. It won't do anything by itself, but it will help you stay on top of your job effectively.

While the finalization of your MAP is a top priority immediately after closing, there are a number of other activities that will demand immediate attention. We'll look into these now.

Take-Over Assistance from the Seller

Certain legal documents will be required from the seller at the closing and these will be specified by your attorney. However, unless the attorney is very knowledgeable about property management, he may not be aware of the many other items you will need to plan your turnaround and carry on day-to-day management. These too should be covered in the sales agreement, and to the extent available, the seller should be willing to give you these documents. Important information and materials include:

— *Accounting Data,* which should include statements of operation for three years prior, and an interim statement for the current year. These should be audited statements, if available. In addition, the seller should agree to retain all books and records for at least two years, and make them available to the purchaser for inspection during that period.

— *Leases and rent roll* should identify each unit which is rented at the time of closing, the name of the tenant, expiration date of lease, rent rate established, security and other deposits made by tenant, any special concessions made to the tenant such as rebates, allowances, or a free rent period. All leases should be legally assigned to the purchaser as part of the closing.

— *Keys,* including master keys, keys to maintenance storage and other non-rental areas, resident keys for every unit. Be sure keys are securely tagged, properly identified, and stored in an organized fashion.

— *Maintenance records* should be transferred if they exist. If not, be sure to have the seller list in as much detail as possible all maintenance carried out in the past year. Invoices from outside contractors may be helpful.

— *Tenant files,* including any complaints, rent collection problems, or other special situations.

— *Employee information,* should include names, addresses, social security numbers, salary or hourly pay, working schedule, job description, date of employment, and evaluations and previous employment history, if they exist.

— *Announcement of change in ownership* should be made by the seller in a letter to all residents and vendors. This should be followed immediately by a letter from you as discussed later in this chapter. Sometimes this can be done in a joint letter by both of you.

Recognize the People Factor in Turnaround Success

If your turnaround property is large enough to require an on-site management or maintenance staff, it is vital that you evaluate the people you inherit and orient them to your program immediately.

Arrange to meet the staff as a group so you can briefly introduce yourself and your plans for the property. This should be immediately followed by a private meeting with each employee of the project. If standard personnel data covering education, experience, and so on is not available from the seller, have employees fill out an employment application form in advance. These are available from office supply stores. They will provide you with a quick overview of each individual. Further, they subtly indicate that each person is being re-considered or re-hired, and that is a good position to take.

A good way to start each interview is to have each person describe his job in detail. Ask questions to help evaluate qualifications, personal goals and ambitions, economic needs, enthusiasm for the project, flexibility, ability, and willingness to learn new ways. This interview should be the beginning of your decisions as to who to keep and what changes to make in the staff and their procedures.

During the early weeks following a take-over, it is essential to have your presence constantly felt by the inherited staff. You may have to arrange to work with them personally for part of each day. Or, if you have other employees who know your style and methods, you may find it valuable to bring several in as a temporary "task force" to install systems, train the staff, establish proper attitudes, and further evaluate each individual.

Do not hesitate to release inherited employees if you feel they are not qualified, or if you do not feel they are needed to properly run the project. The only caution is to keep key people, those who know what has been going on, so your task force can become properly oriented.

Gaining Credibility with Employees

All employees make a better contribution if they believe in their company, and feel they are part of a "winning team." However, this is particularly important with project employees who are usually detached from the business headquarters and who frequently operate with a minimum of direct supervision. There are many things you can do to create a favorable atmosphere, both when you take over, and from time to time as you go along.

Acquaint new employees with your company history, your plans for growth in the future, your successes and problems. Keep them aware of your plans for their project; not only the work which they will do, but the total picture. A real estate turnaround is a very exciting and satisfying experience. Given an opportunity, employees at all levels will identify with the challenge and many will make unexpected contributions.

I strongly suggest that you have a policy of promoting from within, and that you point out the opportunities to all employees. In my own case, this has had excellent results both for the company and staff members. Here are a few examples of individuals who have been promoted several times to the level of their present positions: a project secretary has risen to corporate level property manager; an inherited project manager and assistant project manager have each become presidents of key subsidiary companies; a project marketing director has become assistant vice-president of our securities corporation.

It is essential to pay competitive wages and benefits. Check out the prevailing rates with the owners of similar projects in the area of your purchase. If you find serious discrepancies, don't hesitate to make adjustments, either up or down. Employees will respect the owner who says he will do the right thing and then proves it.

The early days of a take-over are likely to be tough on employees. You can help most by providing effective supervision and moral support. A meeting is a good start, but it is equally important to be available regularly for guidance and leadership. Encourage questions and suggestions. Keep two-way communication alive.

Establishing Credibility with Residents

The tenants in place when you purchase a property can become a very important asset. Their feelings about the desirability of living in the property will radiate into the community and play a major role in creating your image.

Generally, you will find the residents of a distressed property will not be too happy. The property's distress is certain to have had its effect on them. You owe it to the residents and to yourself to keep them advised of your plans and your progress. You should also make a point of encouraging them to let you know their needs.

Start by informing all residents of the change of ownership. Introduce yourself in an appropriate way, with enough background to give some assurance of results to come. Do not make specific promises at this point; simply express a general intent to meet the needs of the residents through development of a program of improvements. Too many early promises can create undue pressure for action before you are ready to perform.

Then, as quickly as you start to accomplish real improvement, communicate further with residents. Point out what has been done, and discuss your next action plans in advance. Invite suggestions for further improvements. This step-by-step communication will create an atmosphere of constant improvement that will build resident enthusiasm and loyalty.

In larger developments, it is possible and profitable to create a "community feeling" through regular scheduling of social events geared to the interests of the residents. We have had events ranging from ladies' physical fitness classes, group trips to major football games and skiing weekends, Halloween costume parties, bingo, dances, and even a 4th of July parade! Different events attract different residents, but they're all well-attended and fun.

Organizing a steady social program requires real interest and effort, but it pays off. In addition to building goodwill, we have found an interesting long-term effect. Through the social events, residents meet each other, discover mutual interests, and become good friends. When people are surrounded by friends, they have a desire to stay put rather than move frequently as so many apartment dwellers do. I have found that "community feeling" has a very positive effect on the stability of a project.

To further build mutual interest in large complexes, we also publish professional quality monthly news magazines that run about 24 pages and cost us nothing! All costs are more than covered by paid advertisements eagerly placed by area merchants.

In properties of any size, follow-through with residents is essential. You have to regularly demonstrate that the management "cares." That's really all most people want. For example, don't just put through an order for repairs, follow through with a phone call to the resident to be sure of satisfaction. Don't just survey residents' opinions when you take over, repeat the process once or twice a year to let them know you are still interested.

Establishing Credibility with the Public

If you are going to be active in real estate, you should also play an active role in the community. Get to know a variety of leaders in business, government, and civic groups. The best way is to be active. Take part in local elections, the Chamber of Commerce, and charity activities.

Establish fair arrangements with local vendors, and always pay promptly for goods and services. Whenever possible, patronize local business.

In the case of large developments, the community at large also has an interest in the economic well-being of the property. No one wants to see a run-down eyesore in their midst. They welcome the news of improvements and increased popularity. Most local newspapers have a real estate section. They will be interested in publicizing your activities once action is underway and specific turnaround activities can be cited.

Throughout your communication efforts with residents and the public, make it a basic rule to hold back making promises until you have already shown some results. It is very easy to create the impression that you are bragging, and this will lose confidence fast. Unfortunately, most communities have had the experience of a flamboyant real estate developer promising perfection but delivering a mess. To accomplish a successful turnaround, you need all the cooperation and support possible. The way to get it is to provide what the people want, and then talk it up so they appreciate what you have accomplished.

Maintain Flexibility

I have stressed planning as a vital activity during the takeover period. Well-defined plans are critical, but do not fall into the trap of considering a written action plan an absolute, unchangeable decision. Successful management requires a fine balance between dedication to making a plan work, and flexibility that allows reconsideration and adjustment when conditions warrant a change of direction.

If your planning is properly handled, it will reflect complete consideration of all the information available at the time. Alternate courses of action will have been considered in detail and carefully compared until the desirable decision became obvious. On the basis of sound logic, your established plans are the best available, and they should work.

That is theory. The real world may throw you a few curves. Conditions may change from the time of planning, or you may have used some incorrect assumptions in establishing your plans. This will usually not be disastrous if you are constantly monitoring results, and constantly testing your plans with a willingness to adjust as necessary.

As an example, we made some interesting errors when we took over Deer Park, a 180-unit apartment development in a rural community with a population under 2500. Since it is only 20 miles away from a metropolis of about 200,000 population, we made the assumption that our marketing should largely be aimed at the nearby city. This resulted in an advertising allocation of $7000, largely in the big city radio and newspapers, plus billboards designed to catch commuters.

Fortunately, my management personnel are trained to check every prospect to determine where they live at present, and what interested them in our project. Very quickly, the weekly demographic reports pointed out our error. Most prospects, and especially those who became residents, were not commuters from the big city. They were local area people: young married children of nearby farm families, teachers, police, local business people who no longer wanted to care for a residence, and so on. This resulted in a major marketing shift and a sizeable saving in the advertising budget!

Follow-up, Follow-up, Follow-up

Starting action is easy, keeping it headed right at the objective is an art. Properly organized, your MAP will become the nerve center of your follow-up effort. Each major activity will have key follow-up dates established, and your detailed planning sheets will establish specific results to be achieved by each activity.

That's all you need for effective follow-up. That and time to really probe for the facts. It's really much easier to follow up when you have staff people or outsiders involved in the work. You can ask pointed questions to determine specifically what has been done and what results have been experienced. A tough review session will quickly indicate whether progress is satisfactory and will lead you to necessary decisions to guide the next period of activity.

On the other hand, follow-up is somewhat more difficult when you are personally acting both as supervisor and worker on a smaller project. It's very easy to be carried away with enthusiasm, and confuse activity and effort for results and achievements. In this situation, remember you are "wearing two hats." From time to time, put on your manager's hat and hold a hardnosed review situation with yourself. Ask the tough questions. Answer them honestly, then make the decisions to guide your next round of work.

In the next four chapters, a number of monitoring systems are introduced. If you are in a "no staff" position, you may be tempted to skip over these forms and reports lightly. Don't. There is just as much need for the individual operator to know where he is as the big organization.

One of the great things about real estate, and especially turnaround investing, is that a small investor can very quickly become a large operator. Just start out thinking and managing like a large investor, and you'll soon be one!

Chapter 11

Financial
Turnaround Techniques

Financial considerations are, of course, the backbone of every turnaround. Since the ultimate goal is to make a profit by increasing the value of the property, one part of your mind must constantly be on the financial side of the picture. Operations, physical improvement, and marketing are your turnaround action areas, but all of these are ultimately related to financial results.

As a basic rule, always evaluate any planned activity on the basis of its ultimate financial contribution. Turnarounds are a business. Therefore, all of your time, energy, and effort must be considered as part of your investment assets. They are limited. You can't afford to squander them, anymore than you would invest cash in a physical improvement without some assurance that it will create a specific financial return.

Set Specific Financial Goals Early

Obviously, you expect to be able to make money when you buy a turnaround opportunity. But how much? All too often this question may be answered with a shrug of the shoulders and some mumbled words about how difficult it is to forecast the future.

The truth is, a reasonable forecast of the future is vital to intelligent planning of your turnaround budgets, both dollars and effort. There is one aspect we can't forecast, and that is inflation. In general, we know the inflationary pressure tends to increase, but I would not want to invest my money solely in the hope that inflation will make the property worth more. There simply is not enough potential in that approach. Since inflation cuts the buying power of money, the profit I make from inflationary forces may not really be worth much.

The real profit forecast must be based on the value of the property in terms of established investment formulas. You will generally realize your turnaround profit when you sell. Therefore, your consideration should be the point of view of the investor who may buy the property from you once it has been turned around.

Methods of valuing income property vary slightly from one area to another, and from time to time. Obviously, you should be constantly aware of the prevailing thinking in your market. In general, however, there are two rules of thumb you can use for forecasting future value to a conventional investor. These are multipliers of current results from the property that are used to indicate an approximate realistic buying price:

1. 5 to 7 times the annual gross rent collected, and
2. 10 to 12 times the net before debt.

Certainly there is no absolute, guaranteed selling formula that will apply in the future. However, these are good enough indicators to guide your planning. The important point of these two guides is that the future value of your project will be based on:

— Increased rental rates
— Increased occupancy
— Reduced operating expense

A Dollar Earned Is Much More than a Dollar

The fact that income real estate is valued on the basis of a multiplier gives tremendous velocity to even small improvements in a turnaround. It doesn't take huge monthly rent increases to create a major selling profit. They are multiplied by 12 for an annual rate and the effect on the selling price can be five to seven times the annual increase! Net before debt increases have an even more dramatic impact on the selling price since they are usually multiplied by 10 to 12 times. This places major importance on operating efficiency. The saving of just $100 of wasted expense in a year can result in an extra $1000 when the property is sold!

A word of caution. Your real goal should be to increase the net by a combination of effective spending, coupled with control that will minimize waste. Simply "saving" your way into increased net doesn't work. It quickly leads to false economies that reduce the desirability of the property and ultimately reduce income. There is no profit in that direction.

The Power of the Multipliers

Let's look at a typical situation to see how the conventional buying formulas can allow you to forecast turnaround financial goals. Suppose you are purchasing a 72-unit apartment development which has been underproductive because management has not provided competitive appearance, maintenance, and other services. As a result, the vacancy rate has been running 15% to 20%, and the rent scale has had to be held 10% below area norms.

You are convinced that you can upgrade the project to be fully competitive, and then with aggressive marketing you will be able to increase rents and still achieve a higher occupancy rate. You have organized your basic finance to provide enough reserves to get your programs instituted. Now, there are two important questions. How much additional ongoing operating expense can you intelligently build into your turnaround plan? How much profit at sale can you expect from your efforts and anticipated results?

Look at the numbers. Let's say the average rent in the complex at the present time is $280. Your objective is to increase them by 10%, which will simply put them in line with similar-sized units in the area. This will raise the average monthly rent per unit by $28. Multiply by 12 for an annual increase of $336. Multiply by 72 units for a total annual improvement of $24,192.

Of course, there will be some vacancies, so we have to adjust for that. The rate has been 15% to 20% in this property, but your study of the area indicates the better-run developments are maintaining at least 90% occupancy. Since high vacancy is apparently not a market problem, you feel your program will improve this element, so you deduct only 10% from your indicated rent increase improvement. Total is now $21,772.

In addition, you will benefit by having some apartments rented which were vacant under the previous ownership. This is the difference between a 10% vacancy and the previous 15% to 20%. Let's say an average of five more units rented at all times. Multiply this by the present $280 average rent, since the planned increase has already been included in the earlier calculation. $280 x 5 units x 12 months adds $16,800 to your rent income improvement forecast, for a total of $38,572 per year.

Let's be sure we understand this is the analysis of the results anticipated from a turnaround plan. It will happen over some period of time, based on the speed of improvements. Certainly the rents cannot be increased until the value to the residents has been increased. Based on this forecast of increased income, you can take a look at one of the rule-of-thumb value indicators. Assuming a gross rent multiplier around 6X, you have an indication that your $38,572 rent income improvement can result in an increased property value at sale in the area of $230,000.

Of course, the gross rent multiplier approach doesn't take into consideration the expenses of operating the property. That's why conventional buyers also use the net before debt multiplier approach. You can now use this formula to estimate how much additional ongoing operating expense you can safely incur as you make your turnaround. Obviously, you aren't going to be able to increase your rents and your occupancy without some extra cost. How much can you afford?

Another rule of thumb applies here. Expenses will usually run in a range from 33% to 50% of gross income. The exact percentage will depend on the area, the economy, and your management skill. You can control some expenses, but not all.

For test consideration, suppose your rent income increase of $38,572 increases your expenses by about half that amount. This might include extra labor for cleaning and maintaining improved landscaping, more advertising, a better rental hostess, and so on. Okay, that leaves an improvement in net before debt of only $19,286. Using an 11X multiplier indicates an increased value of $212,000. That's considerably less than the $230,000 indicated by the gross rent formula. The indication is that to maximize your profit potential, the rent improvement should be brought about with a cost allocation closer to 45%. Plans and budgets should be adjusted accordingly.

Of course, when you are projecting future value based on net before debt, you have to consider the existing expense ratio, as well as the expense you can afford for the improved income. The future buyer will look at the total picture. Any improvements you can make in basic expense will certainly pay off.

The Net Rent Increase Concept

The above walk-through of financial goal-setting and forecasting is essential to planning turnaround success. My experience gives it so much importance I have formalized a programming procedure referred to as the "Net Rent Increase Concept," which is a major element in planning what will and will not be done in each turnaround.

Net rent increase is defined as that portion of the total increase which does not reflect increased operating costs. It is the "profit" we earn by providing improved value to the public, and therefore, the amount that will be reflected in the net before debt multiplier formula.

To use our net rent increase concept for planning and forecasting, we follow four simple steps:

1. Ignore inflationary value increase on the assumption that inflationary rent increases will merely be passing through inflationary cost increases. The result will be no net rent increase.
2. Estimate the increased rental value of proposed physical and operational improvements, based on realistic analysis of the market and competition.
3. Work backward to establish the additional costs the project will be able to absorb and still produce an increase in net before debt, which will produce an acceptable profit when the turnaround is sold.
4. Based on the indications in steps 2 and 3, finalize the turnaround plan by selecting those potential improvements which will contrib-

ute the most profit relative to their required investment of time, energy, and money. This will guide your MAP decisions, and will also provide an ultimate net rent increase goal and a profit-on-sale objective.

The Effect of Rent Increases on Occupancy

Residents like improvements, but they aren't always willing to pay for them. We find it is important to be conservative in the timing of rent increases — conservative, but certainly not reticent.

It is important to recognize that each increase will force a certain amount of turnover. Some residents will simply not be able to afford the additional amount, regardless of the value you are providing. Others will be able to afford the increase, but will resent it, and will at least consider moving. The right strategy is to move as fast as possible, but slowly enough to hold on to these "borderline" cases. Another important factor in timing of rent increases will be how rapidly you can fill up the vacancies you will inevitably create.

In our experience, it is necessary to stretch out planned rent increases to meet the situation after you test it with a moderate increase. In a typical situation, you may receive notice of intent to move from as many as 50% of your residents even though you greatly improved your product before announcing the increase. Don't panic. Before they move, these residents have to find new quarters. Many of them will have been out of the market for a while, and they don't know the reality of rental rates. In our experience, if your increase is justified, half of those who give notice will rescind after they do a little shopping for another apartment.

You will still have to fill an important number of vacancies each time you adjust the rent. It must be faced as part of the turnaround job. In addition to the economic benefit, the turnover will also help you upgrade your renter profile, which will add stability to your operation.

In general, it is well to plan any sizeable rent increase in a number of steps over a considerable period of time. For example, a 20% to 40% total increase may require a period of three to six years for implementation without creating a serious occupancy problem. Remember, in addition to our rent increases to get to our total "net rent increase" goal, we must be raising the rent to pass along to the residents increased expenses due to inflation. For example, assume you believe you should have a net rent increase, over three years, on a given apartment of $15. In fact, you might initiate a raise in the first year of $10, of which $7 may go to cover increased inflationary expenses and only $3 will go toward our net rent increase goal. In the second year let's assume we increase rents by $15, with $8 going toward inflationary expense increases and $7 toward our net rent increase. The third year we might require a raise of $10 in order to obtain a net economic raise of $5 which will get us our total $15 net rent increase over normal increases needed to cover expense increases.

Opportunities to Effect Savings

Some owners get so tied up in bringing more money into their properties, they never notice the dollars leaking away through waste and inefficiency. Controlling these sums can be important to the achievement of your profit goals.

The first step is to build your awareness of the need to control expenses. Regularly analyze your expenditures and consider alternatives. Stay away from any idea of saving by cutting down. Concentrate on how to maintain or improve all necessary activities, but at a lower cost.

A good example is maintenance work in a small complex. Add up the bills from various outside services. The lawn people, the painters, the janitor service that cleans halls, etc. You may be surprised to find the total is more than enough to hire a general handyman, either full or part time.

In larger complexes, this same principle may extend to more sophisticated maintenance. Of course, you don't want to have a high-priced plumber on staff, but only working occasionally. The trick is to keep careful track of all maintenance work, analyze the costs, and then take steps to reduce them where possible. My company now sends some of our general maintenance staff to schools to learn how to repair our refrigerators, ranges, washing machines, and dryers. The result is a sizable net savings in dollars, plus the ability to provide same-day appliance repair service to our residents.

Property Taxes Can Become Profit

There is a tendency to accept "death and taxes" as inevitable. In the case of a turnaround investment, there may well be something you can do about the size of your property taxes. In view of the fact that a turnaround property has presumably had an underproductive history, and may have been in serious financial difficulty, you probably have good grounds for a tax appeal.

This doesn't mean you will necessarily win a reduction, but it's certainly worth trying. Keep in mind that property taxes are almost always the largest single expense of income property. Even a modest reduction can be a big improvement.

In most states, the assessment is based on true cash value as determined by the assessor or an appeals board. At best, this is an inexact science, especially when it involves a distressed property. Therefore, I have found it is best to meet with the assessor for a background discussion before the time for the appeal to the board.

Assuming you bought the property for considerably less than its assessed value, this will be your opening reason to expect a reduction. However, the assessor will probably say, "We're talking about value, not price. After all, the market isn't established by any one price." Now it's up to you to prove the price you paid was indeed a reflection of real value. It will help if you can show the property was exposed to other qualified buyers, but you were the highest bidder. A letter from the seller or broker can be very helpful in this regard.

Be prepared to show records of the earnings of the property over a period of years. The assessor should be aware of the reasonable return expected from properties of various values. However, if it is advantageous to your position, be prepared to demonstrate the value indication of the property's figures when they are plugged in to various buying formulas.

If you purchased the property on favorable terms, you may well have paid more than your estimate of the true cash value. In this case, it is essential that you convert this misleading figure to a true cash price. One way is to retain a respected local appraiser to supply this information to the assessor and appeals board.

Additional professional evidence can be supplied by an accountant's evaluation of the value of your term purchase to the seller when discounted for cash. Obviously, if you buy a property with a very low down payment and favorable interest rate, you will likely pay a much higher price than if you had bought the property for cash.

As I previously have indicated, you should consult on a personal and logical basis with your assessor before filing a formal appeal. The formal appeal usually puts the assessor in a position where he is an adversary backed into a corner defending his assessment. I heartily recommend meeting with assessors even before the assessments are out for any given year, merely to discuss facts about the property and approach to its value. In my experience, open, honest communication is well-received and very successful in establishing fair and reasonable tax assessments.

If the assessor is not willing to change his position, do not hesitate to make a formal appeal. By and large, local boards try to be fair and reasonable, and it is in the interest of the community to cooperate with your effort to salvage property which might otherwise go into bankruptcy and disrepair.

Renegotiating Debt Finance

In Chapter 9, I discussed various aspects of lender negotiation, and pointed out that when buying a property in default on its mortgage, you may find the only way to structure the debt will be with the assistance of the existing lender in renegotiating the terms of the existing loan. This may or may not be possible to achieve before you consummate the purchase.

If circumstances indicate you should close before completing negotiations with the lender, be especially conscious of the need to exculpate personal liability. Even with that protection, realize you are risking any cash paid to the seller, as well as cash put into operations.

Immediately after the closing, advise the lender of your new position and provide a complete review of the facts concerning your purchase and your plans to turn the property around. Attempt to negotiate "breathing room" from the lender so you can put a portion of payments back into the property for a period of time. Point out to the lender that this kind of cooperation will result in a strong property which will be able to support full payments. On the other hand, an effort to continue the full payments now will surely result in operating deficits and eventual repossession of a losing property.

As negotiations progress, request a specific mortgage modification or forebearance agreement. Once the lending institution really believes it is in their interest to cooperate, they may well create a whole new situation that will virtually guarantee the success of your turnaround. A typical renegotiation of a 9% mortgage with 25 years to run might result in the following:

— All principal payments waived for a period of perhaps three years,
— Interest reduced to 4% for one year, 6% for the second year, and 8% during the third year, with 9% resumed in the fourth year.
— All deferred payments, plus the previously delinquent amounts to be incurred and due with interest, along with the balance remaining on the mortgage in a balloon payment in perhaps 15 years.

As you work with the lender to achieve this kind of modification, keep working on the turnaround, and keep advising the lender of your plans and activity in writing. Credibility is your big need, and the best way to get it is by demonstrating results.

Refinancing Existing Debt

Even though you buy a property with a debt structure you can handle from cash generated by operations, there may be future opportunities to profitably refinance.

Keep in mind, the cost of money goes up and down with supply and other economic factors. When the mortgage market is favorable to borrowers, it may be possible to obtain a mortgage larger than your existing debt, and at a more favorable rate. This may allow you to actually take cash out of the new loan, and still be able to handle payments from the cash flow of the project. This is an excellent way to provide money for another investment while you continue to work on your current turnaround.

The possibility of refinancing makes it especially important to try to avoid "close note" provisions which do not allow payoff ahead of maturity. A pre-payment penalty clause is far more desirable, as this at least gives you the flexibility to refinance if it is worth the penalty cost.

Make it a point of checking the mortgage market a few times a year, even if you are not in need of finance. When it is attractive, review your existing debt and consider refinancing.

Chapter 12

Physical
Turnaround Techniques

It's a safe bet that every turnaround will involve some physical improvement of the property itself. Inevitably, the "downward cycle," which created your opportunity will have given the product a shabby look that must immediately be erased if you are to present a desirable image. The physical problems may be just skin deep, or they may be much more serious and more expensive. Your first step in this area is a detailed analysis to come to grips with all of the needs so you can budget and schedule the work in coordination with your other plans.

Physical needs don't go away, they just get worse if they are ignored. Furthermore, most product defects cost you everyday by holding down occupancy or deflating the rent you are able to charge. If you have planned your financing properly, you should be in a position to face up to the total challenge, and move ahead rapidly to bring the project up to par.

If economics force you to upgrade the property over a period of time, you should set your priorities with an eye to immediate return in terms of improved rentability. For example, if there are maintenance needs that have made some units unrentable, these should get first attention. This might include inoperative door locks, broken windows, inoperative appliances, roof leaks, and so on.

The next priority should go to cosmetic improvements; those visual areas that instantly create an image of the product in the minds of prospects. Cosmetic improvements usually pay the highest return per dollar, and they can make a dramatic contribution to a turnaround. It's amazing what a little paint, grass seed, and fertilizer can do to the "feeling" of a property; and this applies just as much to a 200-unit complex as a two-family investment.

Of all the areas of turnaround activity, physical improvement is the one which is most immediately obvious to both residents and prospective tenants. Certainly your planning and activity should cover all aspects at the same time, but I suggest physical work should get the most attention in the early days following the take-over. This is particularly important relative to undertaking an aggressive marketing program. There isn't much sense in spending a lot of money to attract prospects if you don't have an appealing product to show them. Don't kid yourself. It is almost impossible to rent units on the basis of promises of improvements to come. Residents simply see what they see. They can't seem to visualize your plans, and even if they can, they won't believe your promises.

Perhaps the best way to illustrate the power of product improvement is to consider some actual cases. Here are two at the opposite ends of the investment scale, one involved a $16,000 property and the other purchased for $3,700,000. Both became profitable because of effective physical improvement. 805 South Tenth Street was the kind of property that is perfect for someone just starting to build their real estate fortune. The only problem with these kinds of properties is they look so bad they scare off most potential buyers. Fortunately, I had been through a few investments and I was able to see below the surface.

The house was old, maybe 60 or 80 years old, but it was structurally sound. It was within walking distance of lots of jobs. At some point in the past it had been converted to a two-family, and while it wasn't chic or modern, it did have big, spacious rooms that would be worth a lot to residents with children.

The house was owned by an estate, and rented by rather militant tenants who were systematically kicking it into a shambles because they felt they had been mistreated by the elderly lady who owned the property before her death. In fact, they probably had had some legitimate small complaints at one point, but at the time of sale, they had carried things to an extreme, and were not even paying their very modest $90 a month rent!

Unfortunately, the people handling the estate were not stupid. They knew the property was in a good location, so they insisted on getting the maximum value, with no allowance for the operational problems or the physical condition. I finally agreed to a $16,000 price with $3000 down and a very favorable land contract requiring a $100 a month payment. In addition, the sales agreement specified that the seller would have to evict the tenants prior to closing. From a conventional appraisal point of view, it was certainly overpriced, but based on my plans, I felt it would turn out to be a bargain. It did.

Earlier in this book, I mentioned this property in connection with home improvement loans. As soon as the purchase was closed, I submitted a list of proposed improvements, with contractor costs attached, to my bank. They loaned me $7000 for seven years, with monthly payments of approximately $120 a month. As the story unfolds, you'll see this extra expense created no strain.

Because cash is always in short supply for young real estate investors, I chose to do the improvements with as little cash and as much personal sweat as possible. The net result was an outlay of less than $4000, which left $3000 cash to be used as the down payment on my next investment. Here's how it worked.

When the tenants were evicted, they left the property literally knee deep in garbage, and with crayoned poems about the landlord on many of the walls. Both of these unexpected setbacks led to good ideas. First, I found two ambitious high school boys to help clean out the junk and refuse. They were so good, I kept them on as "apprentices" every Saturday and some afternoons throughout the three months of labor involved in the project. They cost me about $350 total, which was more than worthwhile because it gave me at least a three-week speed-up in getting to the point where I could start to collect the new, higher rents.

Second, since I discovered it is very tough to paint over heavy crayoned poetry, I decided to panel the walls where necessary. This cost more than paint, but it added so much "class" to the apartments, I was able to get much more than the additional rent necessary to compensate.

I had decided to devote practically full time to the work, but as I looked over the list of what had to be done, I realized I would be short of both time and talent. This put me into a hunt for a retired man with home improvement work experience. It took a lot of asking around, plus ads in the newspaper, but I finally lucked out. I found a really experienced man who was anxious to do some work instead of just watching TV. He would work about half-time, on his schedule, but he had good tools and was willing to work at a low hourly rate.

With about 250 hours of my expert's labor, over 500 hours of my own, plus the help of the two students, this is what we accomplished:

- Panelled some walls.
- Painted the balance of interior.
- Installed drop ceiling in kitchen with improved lighting.
- Reinforced flooring where necessary.
- Rebuilt two porches which were falling down.
- Replaced kitchen ranges and refrigerators (new, but not deluxe).
- Replaced kitchen linoleum.
- Rewired most of the electric service to meet code.
- Replaced worn carpeting with a sharp-looking red-and-black shag bought on sale.
- Repainted the entire exterior, replacing a peeling paint with an attractive light green and a contrasting darker green shade on the shutters.
- Painted the claws on the old-fashioned bathtubs.

That last item deserves some explanation. I wanted to replace the old fashioned high-legged tubs, but that was where I had to draw the line on major cash expenditures. In desperation, I decided to accentuate the "unique" nature of the antique tubs. I painted the claws flesh tone and added nail polish on each toe! It must have been pretty corny, but the new tenants thought it had real class because no one else in town had anything like it!

All in all, I spent about $1200 for labor, and $2000 for materials. Of course, my own labor was "free," but I certainly got paid for it in the long run. We should also add another $750 to the cost, as I had to make payments for the land contract, the home improvement loan, and utilities while the building was vacant.

When the turnaround was complete, the four-bedroom upstairs apartment was rented for $360 per month, and the three-bedroom lower went for $340. My gross rent was increased by $520 per month or $6240 a year. Even if you subtract a 10% vacancy factor, that increased the estimated property value by $28,080 when applying a 5 times gross rent multiplier. In fact, I enjoyed a very good cash flow from the property for two years, and then sold it for $36,000. The sale was actually at lower than 5 times gross multiplier due to the age of the property, but the venture was still super-profitable for me.

A 90-Day Wonder Physical Turnaround

In Chapter 9, I described the way we developed our opportunity to purchase the 310-unit Colonial Circle complex by taking on the management contract when the property was less than 65% occupied, and on the verge of bankruptcy. Now let's take a more detailed look at the turnaround which was largely a physical improvement challenge.

The key was that while the project was over two years old when we took over, the construction had never really been completed! This isn't as unusual as you might think. The original builder-developer had gotten into serious financial difficulties and felt his best way out was to quickly wrap up the construction and sell. In the process he cut a lot of corners. Essentially, the rule seemed to be, "if you can't see it, don't do it." Nevertheless, an occupancy certificate was received and rent-up was undertaken.

The second owner took over with excellent intentions of polishing up the poor product areas of which he was aware. Unfortunately, he had so much trouble with unanticipated problems he never got around to fixing much of anything.

As the management agent, we had ample opportunity to become thoroughly acquainted with the turnaround requirements. We budgeted the cost of immediate improvements at $150,000, and arranged our financing accordingly. The list of construction-related improvements was extensive:

— Complete drain tile had to be laid around several buildings to eliminate leaks that made lower level apartments completely uninhabitable.

— Carpeting, tile, painting, and other repairs were necessary in all of the previously flooded apartments.
— Extensive landscaping had to be added to the token plantings made by the builder.
— Large areas of cracked asphalt had to be replaced in parking areas and roadways, and sub-surface work had to be done to avoid a repeat of the deterioration.

In addition to these absolute requirements, we decided on one additional major expenditure that was an optional investment. The apartments had small interior kitchens. For no good reason, some had pass-through bars into the living-dining room, and others did not. The pass-throughs were so desirable, those apartments were always full, and at a higher rent. Therefore, we spent a considerable sum per unit to cut-in and finish off pass-throughs.

On the Verge of Disaster

The plan looked fine. We had the money for the turnaround, and we were absolutely sure the physical improvements would produce a product of greatly increased value.

How we goofed I still don't know, but we did in a big way. Suddenly after the work was moving at top speed in all directions, it became obvious that we had miscalculated the budget. This wasn't just a small error. It was a 100% error. The $150,000 anticipated costs suddenly became a $300,000 nightmare!

Since it was too late to cut back on the work, we covered our obligation with short term loans, and spent a lot of nights worrying about how to handle the long term situation. Then the "90-day wonder turnaround" came into being. Our work on the project attracted the interest of another investment group. They liked what they saw and entered into negotiation. Of course, we had not planned to sell quite so rapidly, but with the short term loans hanging overhead, we found the idea very appealing.

The end result was that within three months of closing our purchase of Colonial Circle, we had made the physical turnaround, started the improved rent-up, sold the property, and walked away with a $400,000 plus profit! Truly, it was a 90-day wonder.

That sounds great, but it was as close to serious trouble as I care to get. There is a lesson to be learned. The real estate turnaround business is a big business that turns on tiny details for success or failure. While it is fine to grow, it is not a business where you can get big faster than you are able to develop absolutely reliable people and systems to handle the multitude of details with absolute assurance of accuracy.

Budgeting turnaround plans is a critical activity that can never be shortcut. While turnaround real estate is a business where you can make millions, it is a business that depends on nickel-and-dime precision in planning and control for success.

Physical Turnaround Planning Guide

The following pages provide a collection of approaches we have found are most important to consider in analyzing critical areas of physical turnaround opportunity.

PHYSICAL TURNAROUND PLANNING GUIDE

Problem	Analysis/Planning Tips
ARCHITECTURAL STYLE AND DESIGN:	
1. Appeal to Market	Can cosmetic changes be made in the design and/or exteriors of the buildings and/or common areas that will add appeal? The addition of bright colors may change the entire flavor of an apartment complex. We find that yellow and green panels with dark trim are very effective. Inside rental units, consider whether the size and layouts appeal to your market target. Unit design should reflect the life-style of potential residents. Major layout changes are usually very expensive, but a pass-through, a mirrored wall, or some other minor modification may be profitable. Ask prospective renters what they would like.
2. Amenity Package in Larger Developments	Is the amenity package adequate and appealing to your market target? Should you consider addition of a pool, tennis courts, golf course, marina, exercise room, playground? Will these additions make your product more competitive? These facilities must be large enough to accommodate your resident population or negative feelings will result.
3. Inadequate Storage Space	Are there unused areas in the basement or under stairways which could be converted into locked private storage areas for each apartment?
4. Inadequate Laundry Facilities	Are laundry facilities convenient for residents? Are there enough washers and dryers? Should this service be operated and maintained by the complex or sub-contracted? Is there unused space in the basement which could be converted into additional laundry rooms? Are these laundry rooms attractively and functionally appointed? Many smaller apartment buildings have no laundry facilities. Consider the "edge" this would give you over competitors.

Problem	Analysis/Planning Tips
GENERAL CONSTRUCTION:	
1. Mechanical Systems	The mechanical systems must be operative and giving good service. What repairs or improvements should be made? Will a new, more efficient system be a better investment than maintaining existing systems?
2. Heat Loss	Does the owner provide heat or do residents absorb this cost. Should you caulk all windows and weather-strip doors? Is the insulation between floors and walls adequate?
3 Noise	Excessive noise may be the result of inadequate sound proofing; i.e., insulation or simply loud residents. Should you make improvements in the quality of the soundproofing or enforce tighter controls on loud stereos?
4. Roof Leaks	Many times a costly problem to solve. The amount of capital invested to rectify this problem should be in line with your plans for projected sale of the project. Can patching the existing roof adequately solve the problem for the time being or should you invest in a new roof?
5. Sewer Backups	Could there be a blockage causing backup? Have the sewers been properly graded? Be sure the system is adequate to accommodate your project at full occupancy before any heavy investment is made in alteration. It may be more economical to expand the system if it will have to be done eventually.
6. Obsolescence	If the project is old, consider if there are elements such as door locks, cabinets, or fixtures that are obsolete? Can suitable replacement sources be located to supply items which will fit? If so, should they be replaced instead of repaired?
7. Poor Condition of Roads	Can roads be patched or should they be resurfaced? Get expert advice as to the reason for the poor condition. What can be done to avoid quick reappearance of cracks and holes?

Problem	Analysis/Planning Tips
DEFERRED MAINTENANCE:	
1. Carpet Replacement	Should the carpeting be replaced or simply shampooed? Should replacement carpeting be of a higher quality to reduce the need for frequent replacement? In living areas, shag will last longer and look more luxurious than sculptured.
2. Appliance Replacement	Can appliances be repaired or should they be replaced? Would higher quality appliances reduce the frequency of replacement and maintenance?
3. Shabby Hallways	Consider commercial grade carpeting for longer life. Light-colored carpeting should be replaced by a neutral shade which shows dirt less. Paint the hallways with high-quality washable paint to eliminate the need for frequent repainting.
4. Nondescript Landscaping	Lawns should be lush and green. This may be achieved by proper fertilizing or new sod. Replenish trees and shrubs. Flower beds carved into lawn areas will add attractive accents. Landscaping is an important investment in "curb appeal," which will help keep units rented.
5. Exterior Wood Weathered	Do any of the panels need replacing? Would fresh stain of a darker color on trim enhance the building?
6. Dull, Chipped Paint	Should painted areas be repainted with brighter colors? Is a weather-resistant paint being used? Check for rust stains, and if any exist, paint the metal source with rustproof paint before repainting wood.
PARKING:	
1. Inadequate Parking	Are there unused areas that would be convenient for parking lot expansion? General recommendation is 1.5 spaces minimum per apartment. A high resident economic profile may require 2 spaces per apartment. If your market target is accustomed to covered parking and they will pay for it in higher rent, consider the feasibility of building carports. It can be an appealing and profitable investment.
2. Lack of Covered Parking	

Problem	Analysis/Planning Tips
3. Inefficient Utilization of Parking Lots	Parking lots must be properly striped with cement paint to insure maximum utilization of space. Take the time to work out an efficient arrangement.
4. Unsightly Recreational Vehicles	A specific area should be provided for the parking of recreational vehicles, including boats being stored out-of-season. Since this is a special service for some residents, it should carry an extra charge sufficient to cover all cost involved.
LOCATION:	
1. Difficult to Find	In large complexes, directional signs at strategic points are necessary to guide potential customers to the site. Analyze the project's proximity to major arteries and install directional signs along the least confusing route. Properly identify the entrance with bold signage. Proper on-site signs should easily direct traffic to the rental office and to various address areas.
2. Unsightly Surroundings	Is the residential or commercial property bordering the site shabby or run-down? The erection of an attractive fence around the complex will impede unattractive views.

Chapter 13

Operational
Turnaround Techniques

Operations are where everything comes together in any rental property. This is the day-to-day firing line of turnaround action. It is the center of business management and the source of tenant satisfaction.

In a small property, all operational responsibilities will probably be lumped into one part-time activity, and frequently handled by the owner. In a large apartment complex there may be a resident manager and numerous supervisors and staff people assigned to specific responsibilities in maintenance, security, accounting, collections, rentals, social activities, customer relations, and so on. At our largest present complex which consists of 1145 rental units, we employ an on-site staff of up to 50 people to handle all elements of operations. It is a big job.

Naturally there are some techniques available to the large property which are not practical for smaller operations. However, the similarity in basic approaches and requirements is remarkable. This is why earlier in this book I suggested property management experience as a highly desirable background for turnaround investing. Operational knowledge is highly transferable from one kind of property to another

The Essence of Operation Is Control

Any rental operation is a business. As such, it must be managed, or it will surely manage you. One key to successful management control is establishment of reliable information systems. These will regularly point out a project's progress, problems, and opportunities in sufficient detail to assure effective activity.

When a new project is taken over, be it a turnaround or a healthy property, the first operational move is to examine the information systems. If you are comfortable with their suitability and reliability, keep them going at least for a transition period. If not, move rapidly to install

163

your own systems. There is no way that you can really take charge until you have a steady flow of accurate facts.

My property management group has developed a complete information system that is used with all of our properties. The forms themselves are very simple, and not special at all. The thing that is worthy of note is that the systems exist and are applied consistently.

As a checklist for your consideration, here are the regular operational systems as used in the largest projects managed by my company. Smaller operations use simplified versions to fit their needs.

- *Rental Report (weekly)* — New rentals, cancellation of rentals, move-ins, move-outs, number of units occupied, number vacant, move notices received (with analysis of reasons for leaving), income, delinquents, skips, prospect phone calls received daily, prospect visits daily, rental applications daily. This report is organized to allow cumulative totals by month and comparisons with the previous month.

- *Demographic Analysis (monthly)* — A tally of various indicators concerning each rental prospect who visits the project. Breakdown factors cover present home location, type of occupation, age group, and advertising media involved in generating interest.

- *Service Call Analysis (daily/monthly)* — Tallies the total number of maintenance service calls handled, detailing each as to plumbing, heating, appliances, structural, and other. Special reports are submitted on any service request which cannot be handled within three days.

- *Security Call Analysis (weekly/monthly)* — All security calls are logged, and tallied according to the type of problem or complaint involved.

- *Delinquency List (updated daily)* — This report lists all tenants who have not paid monthly rent after a three-day grace period. A firmly established collection procedure is then followed with each step and response noted. Delinquency is controlled by early and consistent action.

- *Resident Complaint Follow-Up File* — Each complaint is handled on a separate report sheet for convenience in follow-up. The problem is written out in detail. After necessary investigation or consideration, action is taken and a follow-up statement is added to the report. All complaints are reviewed by the resident manager and corporate vice president.

- *Budget Report (weekly/monthly)* — This is the key financial control, although it is backed up by other daily bookkeeping procedures. Funds are budgeted annually in 22 separate categories, and are allocated monthly with seasonal adjustments. The report indicates actual expense compared to budget, and requires a written explanation of any variance above a specified percentage in any month.

All reports are reviewed regularly by on-site management to determine out-of-line conditions and special needs. Trends are carefully monitored to gain early awareness of changes in the market, in costs, or in any indicator of effectiveness.

Resident Satisfaction

Much of the work of operations is aimed at one gigantic objective: keeping residents. We recognize that even after we have turned a property around and gained high occupancy, we will have a continuing marketing requirement. Apartment dwellers, particularly those in large developments, tend to be highly mobile. Their jobs and other changes encourage fairly frequent moves.

However, turnover is expensive to the investors. We can afford a lot of effort and attention and a fair amount of money to keep residents more than satisfied if it will keep them with us for a longer tenure.

To earn this satisfaction and loyalty, we concentrate on superior response to all expressed requests from residents. Management pursues a never-ending routine of scheduled cosmetic and functional maintenance in large and small properties. In large apartment complexes, we maintain a 24-hour security force operated as an integral part of the project operation. We do not use outside services because they have been less responsive to the needs of tenants.

Above all, my property management operation tries to maintain a community feeling which people will not want to give up. This can best be illustrated by a description of the content of one of the project newsletters we publish on a monthly basis. The issue at hand happens to be for the month of February. It includes the following activity announcements and articles:

- Happy hour party with live music for dancing.
- Wine tasting party.
- Bingo party reminder (weekly).
- Feminine fitness class reminder (twice weekly).
- Weeknight and weekend ski trip announcements.
- Girl Scout troop formation.
- Snowman contest for resident children.
- Tips on growing house plants.
- Rental referral gift program reminder.
- Clubhouse rental availability for private parties.
- Overnight guest suite rental availability.
- Free classified ads for residents.

New Resident Communication

I am convinced that long term satisfaction starts with a smooth transition when a new rental is made. Therefore, when the marketing effort is successful, operations immediately take over.

When the rental application is taken, a printed information letter is supplied covering details of deposits, pet policy (extra deposit, additional monthly rent) arrangements for telephone installation, utility billing procedures, rent payment policy ($2 per day late charge after three-day grace period), move-in arrangements, etc. Our premise is that people get frustrated when they suddenly realize they don't know what to do about something. We try to anticipate their knowledge needs.

Immediately after move-in, a nicely designed personalized information package is delivered along with a tasteful "house-warming" gift. The packet contains the signed lease, a check-in inventory form on which the new resident is asked to report any damaged or worn elements of the apartment. These are immediately inspected and brought up to par or noted in the resident's file to assure no charge against damage deposit. In addition, specific information and suggestions are provided in the following areas:

- Personal property insurance
- Rules and regulations covering use of balconies, appliances, etc.
- Recreation
- Maintenance
- Energy conservation tips
- Security tips
- Community services
- Social program
- Babysitting and child care

A few days after move-in, the new resident receives a welcome letter from the vice president of the management corporation, and a questionnaire checking satisfaction with all aspects of the move-in. A second questionnaire asking for a much broader evaluation is sent after the resident has lived in the project for six months.

These surveys are not used just for "show." They are seriously analyzed and followed up when operational weaknesses are indicated. As a result, weaknesses in procedures or attitudes are discovered before they become serious. Steps can be taken to help employees correct potential problems. We rarely find major deficiencies because we are quickly reminded of any inadequacies.

Make Sure Your People Make the Difference

Despite the fact we are dealing in bricks and mortar, rental operations are still essentially a people business. Tenants want a good standard of living, not just shelter. The people who handle the operation make the difference.

The individual who is handling the whole show in a small property has a big advantage. He or she can be absolutely "sure" of motivation, effort, knowledge, and all the other factors that are required for operational success. The owner of larger properties which require an on-site staff has a more demanding problem.

Working through others requires the use of every available technique for effective supervision and training. We have found personnel evaluation a very helpful procedure. It is a difficult and demanding exercise but it is worth it. Each individual in the organization is evaluated by himself and his supervisor annually. We evaluate past performance, take an inventory of strengths and weaknesses, and mutually plan a program for improvement. The evaluation process helps us prepare individuals for promotion and better serve the needs of our investors and renters.

Small-Property Operational Opportunities

Small properties frequently offer really exciting turnarounds through concentration on operational changes that affect utilization. In modern, relatively new properties, an apartment is an apartment and utilization is pretty well dictated before the purchase. In older properties a great deal more flexibility exists if you have the vision and the willingness to create change.

My very first investment was an excellent example of an essentially operational turnaround. 427 Glendaloch Place was a nice old rooming house that was producing an out-of-pocket loss for its owner each and every month. He hadn't planned it that way, but that's how it had worked out. As a result, I was able to buy it for $27,500 with $4000 down. This purchase price was only 4.1 x the annual gross, far below the 6.5 x average which prevailed in that market at that time.

At purchase, the three-story converted building consisted of seven bedrooms on the second and third floors which rented for an average of $60 per month. This was a low price in the market at the time as management was poor, premises dirty and shoddy. The previous owner had established a common kitchen in the hope it would allow him to raise rents Instead, it resulted in fights about food being stolen from the refrigerator, and eventually in complaints to the City Board of Health.

The first floor was given over entirely to a very spacious apartment rented to a large family for $140 per month plus management services which were of dubious value. The basement was attached to this apartment. It was high and dry, but was only used for storage.

The most important part of my operational turnaround plan was to handle the management personally and make the apartment available for further conversion and better utilization. The seller had represented in writing that he had no lease or agreement beyond 30 days with the manager-occupant of the apartment.

Unfortunately, after the closing, when I went to discuss termination with the "manager," I got my first lesson in why seller representations should be verified. It turned out the manager had a completely valid verbal lease with almost one year to run! My dreams of golden profit were shattered.

I had no choice but to sue the seller. I won a judgement which ultimately netted me $1400; far less than I would have made from the planned changes in the first floor utilization. I charged the difference to experience, and proceeded with my plans for the second and third floors. The first floor had to wait a year.

The first step was to clean out the "kitchen" and convert it to an additional bedroom rental. This eliminated a great deal of trouble. To improve the desirability of the property, the entire second and third floors were painted with my own labor, and inexpensively carpeted. Due to the improvement and more aggressive renting, the eight rooms now rented for $75 each.

Eventually the first floor apartment was partitioned into a small apartment with a lounge room in the basement, plus three independant bedroom rentals and a common bathroom. The total rent for the first floor jumped from $140 plus services to $375 without the un-needed services.

The total improvement in income amounted to $415 a month, a 74% increase due primarily to operational changes which improved utilization. Some physical improvements were involved, but these were minor. My total cost for the change was approximately $1000 plus my own labor.

The addition of $415 per month to the income stream was sufficient to raise the value from $27,500 to $49,000 by the end of my second year of ownership! That's another story, and it is told in full in Chapter 17, *The Magic of Paper.*

Operational Turnaround Planning Guide

The following pages present a collection of the most important operational problem areas, with tips for analysis and planning.

OPERATIONAL TURNAROUND PLANNING GUIDE

Problem	Analysis/Planning Tips
SYSTEMS:	
1. Time-consuming and bulky weekly report	Analyze which information is pertinent to management on a weekly or monthly basis. Consolidate the report to reflect only the pertinent information.
2. Delinquency high	Analyze nature of delinquents, length of residency, income level and social factors. Develop a socio-economic guideline to follow in screening applicants for occupancy.
	Enforce stringent late charge policy as incentive for prompt payment.
	Enforce a strict eviction policy with action to be instituted when delinquency is evident.
3. Uncontrolled purchasing	Develop purchase order system whereby all purchases must be authorized by a purchase order signed by the proper management level.
	Instruct vendors that we will not be responsible for any purchase made without a purchase order.
PERSONNEL:	
1. Personnel cannot identify with residents	Are the personnel of similar background to the resident profile?
	Are the personnel too sophisticated for the resident profile?
2. Personnel not productive	Are they properly trained?
	Are their job descriptions well-defined?
	Are they well-supervised?
	Is the office conducive to working?
	Do they have the proper tools?
	Is the staffing adequate?

Problem — *Analysis/Planning Tips*

SECURITY:

1. High incident report

Analyze nature of incidents.
Do you have an undesirable resident profile?
Can you develop a rapport with local police?
According to nature of incidents, what preventative steps can be taken? (Example — daytime incidents — alert maintenance and hall cleaners to be on look-out).

2. Security agency too expensive

Can you hire and train your own security staff?
Can you offer rent-free apartments to regular police officers in return for their off-duty coverage?

3. Undesirable automobile traffic through project

Can parking stickers help eliminate the problem?
Would a gatehouse help eliminate the problem?
Can road "bumps" be installed to slow traffic?

MAINTENANCE:

1. Sub-contractors too costly

Can the quality of maintenance personnel be improved? Experienced, specialized maintenance men can be less costly than outside contractors.

2. Resident service requests not performed

Do the maintenance personnel have the necessary supplies and equipment? Are the communications between office and maintenance efficient? Are the maintenance men properly skilled?

3. Residents not satisfied with work performed

Is the nature of the problem clearly understood? When the work is complete, do you ask if resident is satisfied? Is the maintenance staff capable?

4. Resident unaware that work has been performed

Leave a card in the apartment explaining work performed.

5. Residents irate over delay in work

Do you keep residents informed when parts need to be ordered, etc.?

Problem	Analysis/Planning Tips
OFFICE LOCATION:	
1. Difficult to find	Can office be moved to more visible and accessible location? Should directional signs be erected? Is there a well-located structure that could be converted to an office?
2. Inadequate parking for office	Is there available space to increase parking? Can office be moved to a spot where parking is adequate?
OFFICE FUNCTION:	
1. Poor efficiency	Can desks be re-arranged or added for increased efficiency? Can walls be re-arranged to improve efficiency? Can office be moved to more efficient location?
2. Congested office	Is the office being used by persons who could have offices elsewhere? Is the office overstaffed? Is the office overfurnished? Can the office be moved to larger quarters?
3. Office is drab and unattractive	Can walls be repainted? Would wallpaper add accent? Would new drapes enhance the appearance? Is new carpeting needed?
4. Rental visitors are exposed to complaining residents	Can the rental office be separated from the administrative office? Can services be improved to decrease resident complaints?
OFFICE EQUIPMENT:	
1. Equipment not functioning	Can equipment be repaired? Does equipment need to be replaced? Can equipment be traded in for new?
2. Poor mix of equipment	Can adjustment be made by selling or exchanging excess items to get those which are needed?

Chapter 14

Marketing
Turnaround Techniques

We have now examined three of the four major elements of turn-around activity: financial, physical, and operational. You may be wondering why we left marketing until last. In fact, marketing as a major thrust is usually the last area of concentration. It isn't that the new owner is not anxious to create higher occupancy in a hurry. The fact is, most marketing expenditures simply won't pay off until the physical and operational turnaround is well underway.

Don't Push Marketing Until the Product Is Ready

The toughest thing to accomplish is to rent something that does not exist. Rental prospects are usually shopping for immediate action. They want to move soon, so they are ready to make their decision virtually without delay. If you are forced to describe physical improvements that will be done at a later date, you are creating a big psychological block. Prospects are not used to using their imagination. They are used to making a rental decision based on what they can see, touch, hear, and smell.

When you take over a turnaround property, you can assume there will be excessive vacancies. Obviously you must be prepared to rent as many units as possible from day one. That, however, is not "marketing." In our sense of the word, marketing is a deliberate, aggressive program to attract and rent to a specific type of desirable prospect. It means specific expenditures for advertising and promotion, and high quality contacts with prospects on-site. This level of activity is properly deferred until the basic physical and operational turnarounds are accomplished to a reasonable degree.

Decide on Your Resident Profile Early

The most basic marketing question that must be answered by a new owner is "What kind of tenants do I want?" The answer to this will direct many decisions in the physical and operational areas as well as in marketing. If you want a higher resident income, educational background, economic stability, etc., you must be prepared to offer a higher standard of space, physical condition, amenities, cosmetic appeal, security and day-to-day maintenance.

What you want and what you can attract may be two different things. Your decision must be realistic, based on the facts of the market and the current status of your project. If you are willing and able to change your project sufficiently, you can indeed change your resident profile, but it must be the result of a conscious decision and a total plan. The ultimate level of residents will be the result of the product you have to offer, the price you establish, where you advertise and what you say, how you show your product, and how you select the people to whom you will rent.

Owners Can Select Tenants

Many owners of rental property have a serious misconception about their legal position in terms of selecting the people to whom they want to rent. They think the law requires them to rent to anyone. This is simply not true.

In general, the intent of both state and federal anti-discrimination laws is to stop discrimination for reasons of race, religion, sex, or national origin. This does not mean that a property owner cannot establish and maintain tenant requirements in terms of income, employment stability, and credit record. The key to selectivity is that there must be a valid and fair basis for acceptance or rejection, applied equally to all. Since this is a matter of satisfying state law, it is an area which must be checked with a knowledgeable local attorney. The important thing to realize is that you do have the right to establish and maintain a desired class of residents if you can get the people you want to desire your rentals.

Selectivity Is Important for Small Properties

Owners of smaller rental properties frequently make a major error in thinking that things like "resident profile" and "selectivity" are just for the big boys, and they will have to rent their few units to whomever comes along. If anything, the smaller owner needs the stability and reliability of selected residents more than the large property owner. Every time one tenant in an eight-unit building moves out, the project has a 12½ % vacancy!

For a smaller property, size up the advantages you have to offer, match these with the most desirable tenant, advertise for specific types, and hold out until you find what you need.

Selectivity Is a Marketing Tool

If you establish a plan to upgrade your resident profile by being very selective in terms of income and stability, you will need to require considerable credit and employment information prior to offering a lease to prospective tenants. In many properties, we use an application form that requires information about present and past employment, about income, about charge accounts, car finance, previous landlords, etc. It does scare a lot of prospects away. However, it does not drive away the kind of reliable residents we want. They have nothing to hide, and, in fact, they are attracted to an apartment complex that obviously sets standards for the residents who will be their neighbors.

If your property is good enough to warrant resident selection, never apologize for the process. Your selectivity will be appreciated by good prospects; they will, in fact, consider your attitude an extra benefit.

Applicant Verification

If you have ever worked in any business involving credit, you are aware that the application is only valuable if it is verified. Unfortunately, everyone does not provide completely straightforward background information.

There are a variety of verification methods, and experience is usually the best way to establish a reasonable balance between cost, effort, and results. In our own case, we have decided that a formal credit check through the local credit bureau is too expensive for its value to us. We have found that verification of employment and income, plus a careful check with the present landlord, is sufficient.

The most convenient way to verify employment is to inspect a W-2 tax form or a current payroll check stub. If there is any question of employment stability, a phone call to the employer can resolve the matter. Self-employed individuals are usually willing to prove their status by showing a portion of their last federal tax return.

Marketing Starts with Employees and Residents

Too often we think of marketing as reaching out through advertising. That is just one small part of the total package. Much more basic is the role of employees and residents. Whether the owner encourages it or not, they will have an important effect on many prospective tenants.

If you trace the job responsibilities of various specialized employees in a large apartment complex, it's easy to see how each individual does in fact have a bearing on marketing. As an example, consider hall cleaners. The quality of their work certainly influences the feeling of residents about the quality of management and maintenance. This will have a major bearing on referrals. Further, the cleanliness of hallways is one of the "little" things that make a big direct impression on prospects. The same pattern of importance to marketing applies to all maintenance and management activities.

Recognizing the importance of all employees to marketing, we have made a specific effort to create positive attitudes. When maintenance or

Rental Application

PROPERTY NAME_____   APARTMENT NO._____

TODAY'S DATE_____ , 19__ MOVE-IN DATE_____ , 19__ DATE RENT TO START_____ , 19__

PROPERTY ADDRESS_____ _____ , MICHIGAN

CARPETED_____ DRAPES_____ FURNISHED_____ NO. BEDROOMS_____ RENTAL RATE_____

Full Amount
Security Deposit_____ Deposit Paid with Application_____ Deposit Bal. due_____

NAME		AGE	DATE BIRTH	☐ Single ☐ Married ☐ Widow
SPOUSE'S NAME		AGE	DATE BIRTH	☐ Divorced ☐ Separated
RES. PHONE	NO. CHILDREN	AGES		EXPECTING?

PRESENT ADDRESS:	STREET	CITY	STATE	ZIP	☐ RENT ☐ OWN
FORMER ADDRESS:	STREET	CITY	STATE	ZIP	☐ RENT ☐ OWN
PRESENT LANDLORD'S NAME		ADDRESS	CITY	STATE	PHONE

MILITARY SERVICE — Branch and type of discharge (or present classification):

DRIVER'S LICENSE NO.   STATE   SOCIAL SECURITY NO.

OCCUPATION		SALARY	PER	OTHER INCOME (explain):
EMPLOYER:	ADDRESS	HOW LONG	POSITION	BUS. PHONE
SPOUSE'S EMPLOYER:	ADDRESS	HOW LONG	POSITION	BUS. PHONE

	Name	Address	City	State	Phone
BUSINESS REFERENCE (2)	Name	Address	City	State	Phone
	Name	Address	City	State	Phone
PERSONAL REFERENCE (2)	Name	Address	City	State	Phone
BANK	BRANCH	CITY	STATE	☐ Reg. Checking ☐ Savings ☐ Spec. Checking ☐ Loan

PERSONS OTHER THAN APPLICANT TO OCCUPY PREMISES

NOTIFY IN CASE OF SICKNESS OR ACCIDENT

Name   Address   Relationship   Phone

AGREEMENTS:
1. The Landlord will either accept or decline this application upon receipt of credit report on above applicant. If accepted, any deposit received will be credited on account of the security deposit; if declined, the deposit will be returned to the applicant, thereby waiving any claim for damages by reason of non-acceptance of this application, which the Landlord may decline without stating any reason whatsoever for so doing.
2. Application is subject to standard form lease to be executed on or before_____
3. Applicant agrees to give thirty (30) days prior notice in writing before vacating premises.
4. In the event of cancellation by applicant, the security deposit will be subject to a service charge.
5. SECURITY DEPOSIT CANNOT BE USED AS THE LAST MONTH'S RENT.

_____ APARTMENTS   _____ Applicant

_____ Management Agent   _____ Applicant

other non-rental employees are hired, their involvement with marketing is carefully explained. On a regular basis, we share marketing plans and objectives with all employees. We keep them up to date on the occupancy situation, and we all celebrate together when we achieve a new high plateau. It's amazing how much everyone helps when they are aware of the need and opportunity.

Resident Referrals Pay

Most owners are aware that residents are a major marketing influence in that they tend to invite their friends to come live where they do. We go one step further, and deliberately encourage referrals with a gift offer for each referral resulting in a rental. Gift options have a value of about $25, and include gift certificates to local shops and restaurants, as well as desirable items for the home and scrip which can be applied to rent.

In small rental properties where there may not be any need for ongoing rental activity to counter turnover, resident referrals can be particularly helpful. Instead of merely advertising when a moveout notice is received, I have found it effective to notify residents of the opportunity for them to nominate our new tenant. If they are really happy with their home, they'll have your vacancy filled in a few days.

Shop Competition as You Plan Marketing

As you start to detail your marketing, including the advertising message, rent rates, and the presentation of your features, consider everything in relationship to competition in the area. After all, value is a relative thing, and you really can't know what you have unless you know what the alternatives are for typical renters in the area. This is easily accomplished by shopping all of the important competition. Check their ads. Call up and ask questions. Visit and view available units. Go through the entire process, and keep thinking like a real renter. You'll be amazed at how many good ideas you'll get about how to handle your marketing better.

Shop Yourself to Maintain High Standards

Once you have established your own system and methods of handling rental prospects, don't fall into the trap of assuming everything will be done according to plan. Unless you do the on-site contact work yourself, the best thing you can do to create and maintain effectiveness is to have your property shopped and then use the findings to help your employees do their job more effectively.

We do not use professional shoppers; experienced project personnel can spot them much too easily. We simply recruit real people of the type who might in fact rent from us. We ask them to inquire about an apartment by phone, and then just follow through as things develop. After the phone contact and a personal visit, our rental supervisor meets with the shopper to get general impressions and to hold a detailed discussion following a checklist of presentation and closing activities we expect our rental hostess to pursue.

From a number of shopping reports, a pattern will emerge. You will get a general feeling of attitudes and effort which will probably already have been reflected in rental results. More important, specific signals will be received, pointing out effective actions and things that need modification or strengthening.

When shopping reports are discussed with rental hostesses in a positive way, there is no resentment. It must be understood that the purpose is not simply to check up, but to try to help the hostess maintain maximum effectiveness. This is particularly welcome when the hostesses are paid largely through commission, and I think this should always be the case.

Advertising Tips

In marketing a large rental complex, advertising will be a major expense that deserves top management attention. If you are going to do extensive advertising it is advisable to utilize professional creative assistance, usually in the form of an advertising agency. The trick here is to establish the proper, most effective division of responsibilities.

Unfortunately, many advertising people want to have total responsibility, and therefore claim total capability for all aspects of property marketing. My experience indicates this is very rarely true. A competent advertising professional should know how to best present and communicate any given message. However, there is no particular reason to believe the advertising specialist should know what message or what market will work for any given investment property.

The identification of resident profile, and the particular appeals to attract this market should be determined by the owner-manager unless the advertising specialist has really unique experience in real estate. You can abdicate this responsibility, but if you do you lose the opportunity to constantly test the results of your advertising by relating it to on-site traffic.

Monitor Results

In our projects we maintain a very simple system to constantly measure the effectiveness of the media and messages being used. Every inquiry telephone call is registered by date which can then be tied to our specific advertising schedule. As part of the standard conversation, the rental hostess asks, "Where did you hear about us? The response is then record-ed in one of six categories: newspaper advertising, referral, billboards, radio, yellow pages, other.

Our experience indicates that in most cases the most effective ex-penditure for a large project is billboards. Major newspaper space and radio is used only as part of a special major marketing push such as a grand opening. Of course, each local situation is different, so the important thing is to test, track results, and analyze carefully.

Campus Highlands — A Special Marketing Challenge

One of my earliest large properties was a campus complex of 130 units. When I took it over, only 20 units were rented for the next semester! The problem stemmed largely from location. The project was on the out-skirts of the campus area, definitely farther from classes than most hous-ing. Because it was across a bridge from campus, it was psychologically separated as well as geographically.

Because the project had a very low occupancy from its inception, it had suffered from poor maintenance and developed a shoddy, second-class image.

I knew I would have to upgrade the physical condition of the property immediately but my main concern was how to change the total image. I had to make the property desirable as a place for students to live. Since I could not move the building, I had to make it inviting in its present location.

To quickly create a new and exciting image I started with a new name, "Campus Highlands," and a symbol in the form of "Scotty," a Scot-tish Highlander, complete with kilts.

This gave quick visual identification to everything I did in the way of promotion and advertising, and one move just built on another.

No doubt the major marketing coup was the introduction of a mini-bus suitably identified with Scotty, and available for the exclusive use of Highland residents. A driver ran tenants back and forth to school all day, and on weekends we made the rounds of campus bars, hangouts, and athletic events. Now I could advertise as the only apartments that were just a few steps away from every place on campus. In nothing flat, the location problem was not only neutralized, it was turned into a plus!

To get inexpensive attention and build our name, I printed up thou-sands of miniature bumper stickers featuring "Scotty sez..." followed by some risqué remark. It was kind of a student-oriented fortune cookie campaign. Everyone was anxious to read everyone else's "Scotty sez" sticker. They quickly appeared on bicycles, raincoats, notebooks, and throughout the college. Since everyone was asking who Scotty was, the entire student body soon knew about Campus Highlands.

Now that I was getting tenants, I added an amenity that fit their idea of fun. "Scotty's Club" was set up for the residents in an unused basement space as a lounge-recreation area. On Sunday evenings the management threw free beer and pizza parties with special events such as W. C. Fields movies. Pretty soon Scotty's Club was the "in" place on campus. After just one semester, the Highlands was the only apartment complex on campus with a waiting list.

While this was a very special situation, it is a universal example because it dramatically illustrates the most basic of all marketing principles: relate to the needs and desires of your market. Don't look for ideas that will work in all properties — there are none. Keep an open, searching mind. Seek out things you can do to attract and satisfy the best tenants for each specific investment. Then do those things necessary to get them and keep them.

Marketing Turnaround Planning Guide

The following chart presents a concise guide to the analysis of typical marketing problems and the planning of successful marketing activities (see following page):

MARKETING TURNAROUND PLANNING GUIDE

Problem	*Analysis/Planning Tips*
RESEARCH:	
1. Accurate Area Analysis	You will base much of your marketing effort on the evaluation of various economic patterns. What are the economic trends? Is the population up or down? Is there much new building activity going on? What innovations are these new complexes featuring? What is the employment situation? What are the area rental absorption factors?
2. Product Not Competitive	Your product must be competitive with other projects. Analyze their product and their vacancy rates. Capitalize on the efforts of your competition that are working; i.e., special promotions. Decide what superior features your product offers over the competition, and feature these in all advertising and personal contacts.
3. Accurate Market Identification	Analyze your current resident profile and determine if it is desirable. Compile socio-economic and demographic factors of your desired profile. Who are they? Where do they work? What is their income range? Where did they come from? Why should they prefer your complex? What is their life style? From this information, determine your market target and direct all marketing efforts to appeal to this segment.
THE EFFECTIVE CAMPAIGN:	
1. Creative Approach	The graphic approach in logo design, signage, ads, and brochures must fit your desired resident profile. Wild contemporary graphics will not appeal to senior citizens just because it appeals to you. Look for creative sources through whom you can effectively communicate the flavor of your product. Your creative source should have a thorough understanding of the target lifestyle in order to produce an appealing image. Monitor the exposure of your advertising. Is this approach reaching the desired profile? Is it motivating the desired action?

	Problem	*Analysis/Planning Tips*
2.	Media Mix	The exposure tools you choose will determine your results in traffic numbers. This must continually be monitored and experimented with until a high level of response is achieved. It is almost always necessary to combine media tools such as newspaper ads with outdoor billboards or radio. Each visitor should be asked to fill out a traffic card to determine how they heard of your complex, where they came from, etc. Study this information carefully and invest your dollars in the media generating the most consistent results.

ON-SITE MARKETING:

1.	Poorly Located Markets	Models should be located in a place easily found by prospects, preferably close to the site entrance. Attractive signage should lead prospects to the models easily.
2.	Over- or Under-Decorated Models	Models should be decorated for a market one economic notch above the majority of the resident profile.
3.	Sloppy Models	Responsibility for keeping the models spotless at all times should be directly assigned to an employee as part of their job description. During periods of heavy traffic they should be cleaned more than once a day, as required. Set very high appearance standards.
4.	Negative Curb Appeal	The appearance of the site from the highway or internal roadway should always be meticulously maintained. The best signage and landscaping economically feasible is a critical investment.

Problem	Analysis/Planning Tips
5. Poor Closing Rates	Your rental hostess should be closing at least 25% of the traffic. Is insufficient staffing causing prospective renters to wait long periods of time and leave in disgust? Are your rental office hours geared to accommodate heaviest traffic times (i.e., lunch and dinner hours, weekends)? Are rental people paid on straight commission for maximum incentive? Have they been properly trained? Are you competitive price and product-wise? Is an ineffective advertising mix generating traffic beneath or above your desired market target?

LOCATION:

| 1. Negative Proximity to Major Employment | Can this problem be overcome by the organization of resident car pools? Is major employment confined to a specific area? If so, is the establishment of a free or low cost commuter service economically feasible? |

Chapter 15

A Complete Analysis
for a Complex Turnaround

To help round out your understanding of the turnaround planning and activation process, this chapter presents an actual "Problem-Remedy -Result Analysis" as prepared by one of my teams at the time of an actual turnaround purchase of an apartment complex. It literally takes you behind the scenes in a major turnaround.

The project which has been renamed "Honeytree" is a 744-unit rental development located in suburban Detroit. You will note the sim ilarity between this new name and the name of the project discussed in Chapter 18, "Lemontree." There is a reason, and it isn't that I like trees. The two properties are located in the same general area. Since Lemontree is a very successful turnaround with an outstanding image, the second "tree" is simply an effort to hitchhike the image of the new turnaround to the established success.

On the plus side, it has a fine location in an area of growing popularity with a good segment of solid middle-class families. It was reasonably well-designed and built. There is an excellent mix of one to four bedroom apartments and townhouses with a variety of floorplans. There are a number of special interior design touches that will make the units very desirable to women. Good community amenities are available including playgrounds, swimming pool, and clubhouse.

Despite all of the basically sound characteristics, the project is virtually a disaster. It is only seven years old, but it is badly worn and shabby. It is obvious that basic maintenance has simply been ignored to the point that the project has the look of "defeat."

Appearance has no doubt contributed to the lack of occupancy. Marketing had been very disorganized in many respects, so the occupancy trend continued downward. At the time of takeover, vacancy was 29%.

As you will see throughout the analysis, operations were riddled with excessive costs producing ineffective results. The net result had been an horrendous downward spiral ending with extremely serious financial problems.

The key to this turnaround, we believe, is skilled, professional management action in virtually every area. As I am writing this, we are just a few weeks into this particular turnaround, and are already achieving good success indicators. The analysis which follows attempts to provide the initial blueprint for these actions by identifying needs and establishing as many specific actions as possible. You will note in some areas, the "action" recommended is simply further consideration to decide on the right action. At this stage, we are anxious to move rapidly, but only when we are sure of the proper direction.

The document reproduced in this chapter has several uses. It provides the basis for budgeting, for management authorization to proceed, and for the establishment of the MAP which will be used for control. In addition, this analysis has numerous communication values. It is usually shared with the primary lender, particularly if finance is being renegotiated. The analysis is distributed to all on-site supervisors, and is discussed with all staff employees so they are aware of the total scope of the turnaround program.

To provide insight into the full scope of project analysis and planning, this chapter deals with a fairly large development. Obviously, a turnaround analysis for a smaller property, say a four-family building, will be far less complex. Many of the elements covered in this example will not apply. Nevertheless, I urge you to go through the same process, and with the same degree of effort. The attitude and thinking demonstrated by this approach is critical to turnaround success.

PROBLEM – REMEDY – RESULT ANALYSIS FOR HONEYTREE

PHYSICAL

The product has suffered extensive damage through neglect and deferred maintenance. The outstanding deficiencies include the following:

PROBLEM	REMEDY	RESULT
1. Interior Deferred Maintenance a. Worn and shabby carpeting in apartments. b. Deteriorated and torn carpeting in hallways. c. Hallway walls in need of drywall repair and painting. d. Missing appliances and appliances lacking parts. e. Vacant apartments not cleaned or redecorated. f. Leaking roofs. g. Storage compartment area filthy, dingy. Several doors in need of repair. h. Lack of caulking and weather-stripping. **2. Building Exterior Deferred Maintenance** a. Siding delaminated and peeling.	Analyze and budget funds necessary for capital improvements. Raise funds for refurbishing of project. Schedule, implement, and coordinate refurbishing program.	Creation of a viable and competitive product appealing to the market. Increased resident pride. Reduced turnover.

PROBLEM	REMEDY	RESULT
3. Grounds Deferred Maintenance	Prepare cost analysis and budget to correct deficiencies and improve appearance.	Improved curb appeal. Pleasing visual impression...well manicured, plush lawns. Resident pride in project and positive impression on prospects.
a. Deteriorating concrete sidewalks and steps.	Establish schedule and implement.	
b. Sparse landscaping.		
c. Poorly located dumpster pads.		
d. Deteriorated carports.		
e. Broken sprinkler system.		
f. Fences in need of repair.		
g. Disintegrating curbs.		
4. Clubhouse	Prepare cost analysis and budget. Raise appropriate funds for necessary renovations to make the clubhouse the focal point of the Honeytree community.	Clubhouse will function as the social and management focal point. Improved appearance will encourage utilization of facilities and growth of "community feeling." Resident parties will provide additional income. Relocation of management office will improve services and eliminate the need for a separate 12-hour, seven-day clubhouse staff (see details in Operation section).
Badly neglected. Contains the ingredients of an excellent amenity; has been allowed to deteriorate to a regrettable state. Deferred maintenance includes:		
a. Extensive roof repairs.	Move management and rental offices to the clubhouse.	
b. Walls in need of refurbishing and repainting		
c. Worn and shabby carpeting.		
d. Worn and broken furniture.		
e. Broken exercise equipment.		
f. Pool in need of resurfacing.		
g. Lack of pool furniture.		

PROBLEM	REMEDY	RESULT
5. Gatehouse/Entryway The gatehouse is an eyesore and totally ineffective in controlling traffic or preventing crime. The gate itself is broken off, and the gatehouse is seldom manned.	Remove gatehouse. Design and price a suitable entryway including appropriate identification and landscaping. As part of the total security program (see Operations), consider necessity for road bumps to slow traffic through the property.	Improvement in curb appeal, and elimination of a negative reminder of security problems.

MARKETING

PROBLEM	REMEDY	RESULT
1. Lack of Identity No theme. Poor reputation.	(When purchased, this property was named "Deer Creek Park.") Change name to "Honeytree." Develop campaign for grand opening as a "new project." Create visual impact with prominent color-coordinated logo. Honeytree theme to be carried through in minute detail.	Create a fresh start and build desired "up-scale" image. Revitalize interest in the project, generating increased traffic and increased occupancy.
2. No Target Market	Make a major marketing study of surrounding metropolitan areas to evaluate potential targets. Establish resident profile. Implement target marketing through direct mail and contact with personnel departments and employers in the area	Bring in traffic and upgrade resident profile.

PROBLEM	REMEDY	RESULT
3. *Ineffective Media Buying* Analyze dollars wasted due to investment in the wrong media. No outdoor billboards used. Little newspaper advertising.	Analyze area thoroughly with respect to demographics and target market. Utilize proven methods of traffic generation such as outdoor billboards strategically placed in market area and newspaper ads in appropriate publications.	Public awareness and exposure. Increase in number of visitors and rentals. Advertising dollars invested effectively.
4. *Insufficient Rental Hours*	Expand staff and hours to effectively accommodate all potential visitors.	Increased traffic since hours will be geared to consumer needs. Increased rentals.
5. *Competition Ignored* Rental hostesses uninformed regarding competition.	Have rental hostesses shop competition regularly. Record information and draw comparisons.	Rental hostesses will be well-informed regarding competitive market, aiding in their presentation to prospective renters.
6. *On-Site Signage Inadequate and Confusing* No directional signs to administrative/maintenance office or models. The series of "burma-shave" signs are too large and list poor selection of information. No sign is visible from the 275 expressway.	Analyze site for best sign locations. Provide adequate and appealing signs with effective copy and design coordinated with total advertising program.	Exposure to drive-by traffic. Increased visitors and visitor orientation. Eliminate confusion.
7. *Visitor/Site Orientation* Transporting visitors inconvenient.	Provide golf carts decorated in Honeytree theme for rental hostess use in taking prospects on guided tour and inspection of models.	Unique method of transporting visitors, lending extra excitement to rental presentation. Increase mobility and ease of site orientation. Will put rental hostess in control of total presentation.

PROBLEM	REMEDY	RESULT
8. *Too Many Floor Plans* Each apartment type available in several different layouts. The rental office features a large display of all the available styles. This confuses visitors and causes procrastination in making selection.	Do not display all the layout varieties. Interview prospects to determine needs, then show the floor plan that best meets the desires of the individual prospect. Sell specific benefits.	Rental hostess will be able to make strong personalized presentation and prospects will be able to make selection without confusion.
9. *Poor Closing Rate* Renting is considered a secondary function to other operations. No sales training. Lack of interest and enthusiasm in rental office.	Train rental hostesses in professional techniques. Include project indoctrination, competition, resident profile, personality projection, telephone techniques, selling conversation, and closing methods. Base rental hostesses' income on commissions.	By special emphasis on selling the project in terms of benefits to the prospect, and appealing particularly to individual interests, the rental hostesses will be able to achieve much higher closing rates.
10. *Lack of Resident Harmony and Cohesion* Residents do not readily identify with the project as a total community.	Implement programs designed to provide community spirit including: Move-in package providing new residents with move-in gift and pertinent project and area information. • Implementation of an interesting and diversified social program geared to the desires of residents. • Survey letters requesting resident feedback on the project. • Monthly community newsletter. • Referral programs offering a gift to a resident who refers a rental.	Establish an atmosphere conducive to resident interaction and community spirit. Create pride in lifestyle, and encourage friendships within the complex. Reduce turnover. Create positive image within the area.

OPERATIONS

PROBLEM	REMEDY	RESULT
1. Rental Office Location Rental office is now situated in downstairs of three-bedroom townhouse. Used strictly as a reception area. Area not large enough or equipped to accommodate visitors. Rental personnel work upstairs and do not know when someone enters downstairs. Visitors wait a long time before being acknowledged. Parking inadequate to accommodate visitors. Lost income because townhouse used as office instead of being rented.	Move rental office to clubhouse. Provide rental hostesses with desks in rental office organized for presentations and closing activities. Decorate rental office attractively with comfortable seating areas for visitors.	Atmosphere conducive to rentals. Prompt attention to all visitors. Centralized location for clerical work. Ample, convenient parking. Easy for visitors to locate. Positive first impression of amenities.

Additional income by adding one townhouse to rent roll. |
| **2. Poor Communication System** Telephones in rental office and administrative offices are on completely different lines. No intercom between offices. No one assigned to answer phones. Phones answered haphazardly, after ringing many times. Noisy distraction due to people shouting from room to room, or over railing to downstairs to announce phone calls. | Integrate all telephone lines. Install intercom system. Designate receptionist to answer phone promptly and transfer call appropriately. | Efficient operation. Phones answered promptly and caller frustration eliminated. Atmosphere more conducive to rentals and improved service to residents. |

PROBLEM	REMEDY	RESULT
3. Separation of Rental and Management Operations Administrative office and rental office completely separate operations. Resident manager has no responsibility or authority on rental matters. Psychological distinction as "we and they." No sense of unity. Resident manager does not approve applications. Redecorations frequently not completed in time for move-in. Lack of communication.	Place rental office under supervision of qualified resident manager. Instill pride in employees as working in one group for common cause. Have resident manager carefully screen each application and accept or reject based on established guidelines.	Coordinated, efficient operation. Staff cooperation. Upgraded resident profile.
4. Poor Location of Management/Maintenance Office Administrative/maintenance office located in three-bedroom townhouse in unkempt condition. The office has been stripped of parts, is in need of drywall repair, and is filled with maintenance parts. There is a constant stream of maintenance men in and out of the building, even though the small clubhouse is also used as a maintenance building. There is no available parking, so people park in the street, impeding traffic flow. Loss of rental income by using townhouse as office.	Move administrative office to clubhouse and coordinate with rental office. Transfer all maintenance parts to other maintenance office. Redecorate and rent townhouse.	Attractive, functional business office. Ample parking. Maintenance men not congregated in business office. Former office rented and generating income. Eliminate the need to staff clubhouse with separate attendants.

PROBLEM	REMEDY	RESULT
5. High Cost of Furniture *Leasing Arrangement* Furniture in offices and models leased with expensive monthly payments.	Purchase necessary furniture.	Amortization of purchase far less expensive than lease arrangement.
6. Lack of Proper Office *Equipment*	Purchase required typewriters, file cabinets, copier, adding machine, etc.	Personnel equipped with proper tools for efficient operations.
7. Inadequate Administrative *Office Hours* Office open Monday through Friday, 8:30 a.m. to 4:30 p.m. Many residents work and are unable to contact the office during these hours to arrange maintenance service, etc.	Change office hours to seven days a week from 9:00 a.m. to 7:00 p.m.	Hours adjusted to accommodate residents. Improved resident relations, decreased turnover. Efficient maintenance service.
8. Personnel Staffing ineffective and without job descriptions, leading to confusion. Overstaffed in certain areas and understaffed in others. *Example:* A maintenance/ resident manager and a maintenance superintendent. Neither "work" maintenance and both supervise. Maintenance men are assigned "sectors" with no thought to workload.	Analyze all jobs and create detailed job descriptions covering all functions required to operate efficiently. Evaluate existing personnel to decide on retention, release, or reassignment. Bring in experienced personnel in at least the two top supervisory jobs. Hire new people as required and train entire staff to fill positions. Communicate clear job description and define lines of authority.	Work evenly and adequately distributed. Effective and efficient operations created.

PROBLEM	REMEDY	RESULT
9. *Inaccurate Reporting and Record Keeping* Reports and records inaccurate and incomplete; i.e., certain rental statistics were available, but without any verification of accuracy. Much information needed for effective decision making is not recorded.	Implement all Standard Realty systems immediately.	Systems provide detailed cash control and verified information on move-ins, move-outs, delinquency, rental traffic analysis, vacancy trend, etc. These reports are analyzed at both project level and corporate office They monitor important indicators to gauge progress and indicate necessary changes.
10. *Documentation Control* Poor filing system. Forms scattered throughout separate offices. Resident documents not centralized.	Create a centralized filing system.	Efficient operations.
11. *Rental Income Control* Residents slow in paying rent due to seven-day grace period and ten-dollar, one-time late charge policy.	Discontinue grace period. Implement significant late charge on a daily accrual basis. Aggressively enforce new policies after proper communication to present residents. Prepare policy statement to advise new residents of prompt payment requirement at time of move-in.	Motivate residents to pay promptly. Control income on timely basis. Improve cash flow.
12. *Delinquency Procedures* Delinquency procedures totally inefficient and ineffective. Rent mailed to a corporate office lock box. Until the resident manager receives "flash balance sheets" from the corporate office, he has no idea who is delinquent. These computer sheets were slow in coming and inaccurate. Residents who had skipped out months ago remained on the active delinquent list.	Collect rent on site. Maintain accurate delinquency status on a daily basis. Begin calls the day the resident becomes delinquent. Check disconnected phones immediately for possible skips.	Improved collections. Efficient and effective delinquency procedures. Accurate accounting of cash received.

PROBLEM	REMEDY	RESULT
Apartments that are currently occupied show as vacant on the computer reports. Some people who had paid their rent show as delinquent.		
13. Unnecessary Legal Fees		
Expensive and unnecessary legal fees incurred using an attorney to process delinquents through court.	Visit the district court. Get instructions from Court Clerk on requirements for filing. Have resident manager supervise delinquent procedure from date delinquency incurred to eviction.	Tight centralized control on delinquency proceedings. Expedite court process and reduce legal costs.
14. Purchasing		
Excessive spending. Purchasing done at random on-site with no budget guidelines.	Annual budgets, broken down monthly, prepared by resident manager and maintenance supervisors. Implement purchase order system. Purchases over designated dollar amount must have prior consent from corporate property manager. Deviation on any line item over 5% requires written explanation.	Control and supervise spending within budget. On-site management closely in tune with budget.
15. Maintenance Performance		
Hallways very dirty. Lack of maintenance follow-through. Maintenance calls unanswered. Residents unhappy with quality of service.	Restaff maintenance department with skilled personnel. Implement systems service request procedures. Log unit maintenance history. Leave cards in the apartment notifying resident of work performed or necessary delay. Office personnel call residents to spot check their satisfaction with service.	Increased control over maintenance program. Good rapport established with the residents.

PROBLEM	REMEDY	RESULT
16. *Maintenance Staff Appearance* Maintenance men look sloppy in torn blue jeans, etc. Leave disorganized and inefficient impression.	Project "theme" color-coordinated uniforms.	Residents easily identify project staff. Maintenance men project well-dressed, neat appearance.
17. *Maintenance Tools* Insufficient tools on the project. No organized supply of parts or materials.	Purchase tools and supplies. Establish inventory control system for parts and expendables.	Maintenance performed well and promptly. Improved resident relations, decreased turnover. Cost control on maintenance materials.
18. *Maintenance Vehicles* There are no maintenance or snow removal vehicles. Maintenance men walk or use their own vehicles. Snow plowing contracted.	Analyze requirements, budget, and purchase maintenance vehicles.	Time saved for maintenance men. Snow plowing can be done "in house" at considerable savings.
19. *Grounds Supplies* There are no grounds supplies or equipment. Lawn care contracted.	Purchase grounds equipment and supplies. Schedule work using regular maintenance crew.	Well-cared-for lawns, cut costs, happy residents, decreased turnover.
20. *Excessive Use of Outside Contractors* Besides being very expensive, many service requests are at the mercy of outside contractors' schedules. There are no attempts to investigate problems prior to calling a contractor. Maintenance men possess only the most basic skills.	Staff maintenance department with personnel skilled in all areas of maintenance. Discontinue outside services and establish tight schedule system.	Outside contractors eliminated at substantial savings. Increased control over the maintenance program, and better service to residents.

PROBLEM	REMEDY	RESULT
21. Security High incidence of theft. Expensive, contracted security service provides limited and ineffective coverage. The security staff feels no allegiance to the project, and management has no influence on their performance or quality of personnel.	Develop in-house security service to work closely with area police departments. Analyze nature and timing of problems to establish most effective deterrents. Educate residents to take steps to discourage and thwart burglars. Encourage residents to immediately report suspicious actions.	Decreased incidence of crime. Guards' pride in project results in total dedication and loyalty.
22. Pets Although there is a "no pet" policy, many residents have pets. Pets uncontrolled. No attempts made to eliminate or control.	Allow pets. Charge a pet security deposit and additional monthly rent. Enforce strict pet rules.	Additional income. Controlled pets.

V
SELLING

Chapter 16

Selling Is the Time
to Celebrate

Turnarounds Are for Selling

When you're tempted to hold onto a turnaround investment long after it's been turned around, remember that selling is the real source of the big profit. Selling is the moment of victory and the purpose of all your turnaround work.

As I have indicated before, a clean, well-thought-out set of investment objectives is part of the requirement for success. We'll assume for the sake of discussion that your primary purpose is profit. In all seriousness, I realize that a great deal of the satisfaction from business investment is the gratification from a job well done. There is ample measure of this kind of "psychic profit" in turnarounds, but if you are to be a mature and professional investor you will have to know when and how to give up the reins of the project.

In the real estate investment field, nothing is ever static. Your property is an ever-changing entity, almost with a life and personality of its own. During the turnaround process, it is easy to become emotionally involved with a property to the point you feel it should be held forever. It is too great a source of pride to sell. But things change. The property is successfully turned around, and it becomes a routine investment. It requires defensive management to avoid future distress. The creative challenge of moving an underproductive asset to a prize performer is gone. The love affair will surely wither.

In addition to the emotional element, there are several sound business reasons for selling successful turnarounds when the time is right.

First, when you have turned around an investment property, selling is the only way to realize the big profit potential you will have created. You will likely generate cash dollars from your sale adequate to provide additional seed money capital for other turnaround investment ventures. In addition, you may generate as part of your profit dollars, certain debt

199

instrument receivables, which are described in the next chapter. These receivables may be very useful leverage in short term borrowing and future business growth plans. In short, selling is not only the way to realize your big profits, but also it is the best way to grow. By selling and realizing those profits, you have not put yourself out of business, you have put yourself in a position to expand into new challenges that will be more interesting, more exciting, and more profitable.

The second reason to sell is that selling will make use of the "multiples of profit." This is the opportunity to turn the cash flow you have created through turnaround into the true super-money of real estate.

As an example, suppose you purchased a troubled 100-unit apartment building for $1,300,000 with nothing down. At the time of your purchase, the building may have had an actual net before debt of $118,000 per year. Based on the $1,300,000 of debt, typical financing might have created debt service of approximately $143,000 per year. Now let's assume that over a two-year period you have invested $200,000 in the project for planned operating deficiencies, deferred maintenance, and capital improvements. Through your investment and implementation of a well-thought-out turnaround management action plan, you have raised the net before debt to $162,000 per year, an increase of $44,000 per year. You have now got the property in a cash flowing position. You are making a cash flow of $17,000 a year.

O.K., here you are with a very successful improvement, but with a $17,000 cash flow — it will take you almost 12 years to just get your money out of the project! That's an 8½ % return on investment, so you have put in a lot of work just to create the kind of average return you might get from a completely passive investment.

On the other hand, if you turn around and sell the property, and finance the sale, you will likely end up realizing a down payment equal to your $200,000 investment or perhaps even a greater amount, up to say $300,000. In addition, you will probably get a total price of about $2,000,000, thereby realizing a $500,000 receivable.

This paper profit approach to selling turned around properties relates to the principles we discussed in Chapter 7, *The Art of Finance*. The point was made that there is a big difference between the cash price and the price of a deal in which the seller offers easy terms. When you were thinking as a buyer, you had to be willing to pay the premium. Now, as a seller, it's your turn to collect the extra price. This "Magic of Paper" is the subject of the next chapter.

It may be hard to accept the fact that a $17,000 cash flow can sell for as high as $300,000 down payment or that a $160,000 net before debt can sell for a price of $2,000,000. The figures don't match up with the rules of thumb previously discussed, but they are nevertheless accurate. As this chapter unfolds, the mystery will be fully explained. For now, let's accept the fact that selling is the key that unlocks surprisingly high profit for your turnaround effort.

An additional important reason for selling rather than holding a property is simply that you can't do it all. Real estate is an entrepreneurial business and personal control is essential. You must always be conscious of how much growth you can handle without sacrificing the quality of your management. Most active real estate investors are more constrained by the limitations of their own time and control abilities than they are by money or opportunity.

The main point regarding selling is not to be afraid of taking your profit. This may sound funny, but most people tend to be frightened about what may happen if they sell — "What will I do then?" is the typical question. Frequently they wait too long to sell and realize less than they could have, or they simply continue to get a lower return than if they had sold and reinvested the money and their talent in other properties.

Real Estate Is Most Effective as a Small Business

It has been my experience in operating various numbers of apartment units that size in the apartment business generally has an inverse relationship to operating quality. The larger the apartment management company, the less effective they are in doing a good job of managing.

You can prove this by thinking of some of the biggest landlords in the industry. People such as the late William Zeckendorf, or more recently, the re-organization and bankruptcy of the Kasuba empire, are indicative of many owner-manager-investor types who have run into severe difficulties after becoming very big operators. I have carefully studied the operations of a number of large operators who ended up in financial distress. I have also carefully studied the growth of my own company to try to determine optimum size. I found that when we had just 5000 apartment units under management contracts, including affiliate owned properties and properties owned by others, our quality was much lower than it had been when we were handling half as many units.

In fact, the property management business was the least profitable part of our operation in that it was requiring the most effort and time. All of the executives in our organization were spending the majority of their time in property management transactions and problem solving, and the bottom line profit from this area simply could not justify these activities. We therefore cut back to only managing properties that we owned. This allows us to be more effective and to justify the effort by the ultimate profit which will come from the improvement in our properties.

After getting over the desire to become a "giant," I was able to develop a rather unique philosophy of real estate control. Each year, we sell the top end and the bottom end of our portfolio. We turn over properties that have maximized their potential, reap substantial profits, and go on to other properties. We also move out of properties we feel are slow moving in terms of achieving greater value. In this way, we concentrate our efforts only on new challenges and those properties that are moving satisfactorily through the turnaround process. I have found this approach successful in terms of allowing us to keep constant control on the properties, and therefore it is profitable.

In this age of conglomerates and scientific business management, I can understand why successful real estate investors will flirt with the idea of shedding the entrepreneurial image and "going big." I have been down both roads, and I am convinced that real estate is one area where computerized, sophisticated scale is of doubtful value.

We do use computer systems for certain limited functions like payroll, but I do not believe that real estate can be systematized to the extent that has been so successful in manufacturing or fast food operations. It is a crisis-oriented, people-oriented business, and ultimately must depend on people for its decisions and solutions. On-site people must be able to react and either think for themselves or contact someone higher up who is instantly available to apply the instinct, ability, and intuition necessary for rapid-fire decisions.

In the case of my own company, I have learned over a period of years to somewhat merge the entrepreneurial and corporate structure. Our top managers have been selected because they have entrepreneurial characteristics and attitudes. They are highly motivated and capable of independent action. They are compensated through partnership interests in various properties as well as bonuses tied to performance. Each individual has the opportunity to create large earnings essentially in an entrepreneurial style. In this way, we gain the strength of a corporate group while maintaining the power of individual effort.

It is very difficult to say what size is the optimum in real estate operations. It will depend on the organization, the nature and ability of the top manager, and the nature and geographical spread of the properties involved. In my own experience, I have found that managing two to three thousand apartment units has been most effective in our turnaround operations.

Certainly the number will vary considerably in other situations. You should be particularly aware of the effect of geographic expansion. The difficulties of management seem to multiply geometrically as the miles increase.

Timing and the Decision to Sell

The right time to sell is an important value judgement you will learn to feel for different properties. Timing should be keyed to the point when the property either has maximized its potential or is very close. For two reasons it is important not to wait too long and allow the property to become static for a period of time. First, if a property is on its way up, the new buyer will be encouraged to be more optimistic about the ultimate potential of the property. This will affect the price. Secondly, you never know if the property will stay up, so you should "get out when the getting is good." To wait too long and be greedy, may end up with you having to perform a double turnaround that is not profitable.

In deciding whether or not the property is ripe to sell, you must consider many factors. Is the property being used at this time in its highest and best use? Assuming, for instance, it is a rooming house, are you better off to sell it as a rooming house or convert the rooms into small apartments before you sell? Consider whether the rental levels are at their peak for this point in time in the market. It is disadvantageous to sell a property when it is greatly under-rented. It is better to be fully rented at the market than to have to argue to the buyer that there is still room for advancement and the return may be higher in the future.

Another area that you should consider is the general physical appearance. Does the project show well cosmetically? Keep in mind that most buyers will judge the book by its cover. In other words, first impressions and the cleanliness and visual appeal of the property will be all-important in terms of sale appeal. Other considerations are the property's image and reputation with regard to potential buyers. If it has just been turned around, but has not yet been recognized as a success by the local real estate community, you might be selling at a discount because you are selling too soon.

Another consideration will be the present residents. Particularly in the case of a smaller property, make sure your residents will not sabotage a sale offering. In the case of a large property, be wary of possible damage from on-site staff. If you feel you are likely to have unfavorable comments made by current residents or staff to a potential buyer, wait until you have improved the situation. Many buyers will talk to residents before the sale is consummated, and the results of those conversations can make or break the deal.

The final and most-important step in the selling decision process is to review and analyze your turnaround management action plan. How far along are you in your plan? Have you completed all the major items to your satisfaction? How much has the net before debt increased and what is left in terms of potential in the immediate future? In addition, one last area as an external consideration; do you have immediate alternative uses for the funds. That will frequently sway a marginal decision on timing of a sale.

How One Success Leads to Two Opportunities

The second building that I purchased in my career was a six-unit apartment house. This was a building that had originally been a mansion and later a college fraternity. The previous owner had converted the building into six apartment units. During the times of extreme tenant union activities on the campus, this owner decided to dispose of all his holdings in the area. I advantageously picked up this property which required only a moderate amount of physical improvement.

The main improvement I was able to make in terms of maximizing the potential of this under-producing, smaller apartment house related to the operation of the building itself. As I have indicated earlier, real estate is a business that is entrepreneurial in nature and is best kept small for effective and profitable control. The seller of this building was a local attorney who initially hired outside management, then formed his own small management company to manage this property and several others. Since this involved only a portion of his assets, it was not his full time occupation and he was not involved to a great extent in marketing or operations of these buildings. The people he hired, while well-intended, did not have the owner-management instinct that pumps up the bottom line. The properties had been under-rented at amounts much under the market, and several expense areas were higher than they should have been.

By going in and raising rents, I was able to significantly increase the cash flow. Through a property tax appeal, taxes were lowered. Through careful evaluation of other areas the overall expense was reduced. The net before debt on the property increased substantially and the building became a good property for me.

After having the property for a period of 18 months, I was making a $2500 annual cash flow on my original investment of $7000. In addition, I was paying myself 7% of the gross rental as a property management fee for my work and effort. This was a handsome return.

Still, when I was offered $10,000 down on a land contract with an additional $20,000 of profit in equity for my $7,000 investment of a year and one-half earlier, I immediately jumped at the opportunity. The land contract provided for income to me over the next 20 years, like an annuity! Even more exciting, that $10,000 and the ability to use the $20,000 receivable as collateral for short term loans made it possible for me to buy my next two buildings. By turning over one property, I was able to get involved in two properties with more potential for profitable improvement.

Highest and Best Use Is a Function of Timing

The highest and best use of any given property may change from one time to another, and this will have a major bearing on sales value. For instance, it might be better to keep a rooming house as rooms rather than converting it to apartments if there is a shortage of single rooms in a given market. On the other hand, if over a period of time the market demand changes and an abundance of individual private rooms develops, then the highest and best use for that property would be to convert it to apartments.

The point is you should always evaluate the highest and best use in terms of a given point in time. That point in time must also, of course, take into reference the prospective, immediate future. It is important, however, not to minimize the psychological changes and desires of markets which can occur on a rather rapid basis. Make sure you are keeping up with what type of product your market area desires most.

A Case of Critical Timing

An example of timing in the highest and best use is the Rolling Hills project discussed previously in Chapter 8. I worked very hard for over two and a half years to buy this. The entire reason I wanted to buy this property was to convert it into condominiums to be sold to owners on a retail basis. The property, in my opinion, offered a great deal of potential through the condominium sale concept. After extensive negotiations and a deal being off and on many times, I was finally able, with other people, to put together an acquisition of this property. It was a beautiful town-house development situated around three lakes. At first, it was hard to get other people interested in investing and working with me on the condominium concept, but finally they were sold and the deal came together. It seemed like a dream coming true.

As we got ready to begin our condominium sales program, we temporarily operated the property as a rental project. We had filed all our legal documentation with the state and converted it to a condominium, working very hard on the marketing and financing program. Then we began to run into difficulty in terms of interest rates escalating for the individual homeowner loans on the condominiums we would be selling. Financing was getting tighter and tighter, and in my opinion it appeared we might be heading into a slight downturn in market demand based on nationwide recessionary pressures. It is important to remember that the national swings of the economy, which during the last few years have been dramatic cycles of good and bad, can have a lot of effect on specific local property investments. In any event, it appeared to me that the timing for condominiums had dried up, at least temporarily, and the highest and best use would be that of rental apartments.

As it turned out, my partners and I disagreed on whether or not to proceed with the condominium project. This resulted in the investors who I had gotten into the transaction, as well as myself being brought out. For a while the condominium sales effort continued, but the economy simply worked against it. Eventually, the property was taken back to a rental status, and now some years later it is still a rental.

Buy and Sell Against the Stream

As I have indicated before, local real estate tends to swing between over-supply and over-demand. Naturally these cycles have a major influence on the short-term value of real estate investment properties. Values may also be affected by national economic cycles as they affect money supply, interest rates, and the attitudes of investors.

Observation of these cycles has led to the development of my "swim against the stream" theory. Human nature being what it is, buyers become most aggressive when the market is moving up and up. They convince themselves there is no tomorrow, and the growth curve will go up forever. That's when I like to sell.

Conversely, when the market is down and everyone wants out, I prefer to buy. A graphic illustration of a typical economic cycle representing several years makes the point.

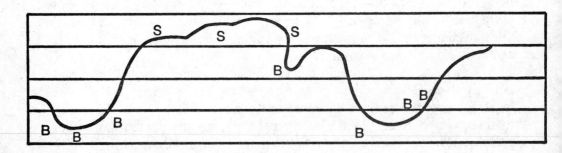

If you continuously observe trends and can avoid the prevailing feelings of the mob, you will inevitably buy and sell better. This does not mean you will pick the tops and bottoms of the cycle; that is wishful thinking. But you can make your moves with timing that will maximize profits. This takes great faith in the fact that the economy is not going straight down the tube when a recession occurs, and that isn't easy. It also means you have to have the perception, patience, and staying power to hold on until the market moves up.

Long Term and Short Term Turnarounds

It should be noted that despite the timing of markets and cycles of the economy, there is a need to review the nature of the property itself in considering the timing for sale. Some turnarounds are capable of being short term in nature, while others will be long term by virtue of the type and amount of work necessary to implement a complete turnaround management action plan.

Another factor that may influence sales timing is the manner in which you have financed your equity. If you have financed your equity in a limited partnership with installments coming in over a period of several years, it is most unlikely that it would be advantageous to sell before the end of the investment installment period. Your investors are generally counting on the tax loss for that period of time and unless a sale is most profitable, they will prefer a relatively long term holding period.

A case in point is Honeytree, the 744-unit apartment development discussed in Chapter 15 which was structured as a limited partnership syndication. The investment input was over a long period of time, and the holding period is anticipated to be 10-15 years. The holding period is based on a combination of how the project was financed both from an equity and debt standpoint and the time it will take to really turn around all the problems and maximize the potential of this property.

Everyone Believes in Tomorrow

Despite all of the rules of thumb and appraisal formulae for establishing real estate values, in the final analysis the market speaks for itself. Real values are established by a coming together of what buyers will pay and what sellers will accept. This is basic to our free enterprise system, and is generally understood.

The thing that is frequently not understood are the influences which shape these free market prices. Most novices believe the base of property value is past performance, with emphasis on the word past. All logic says this should be true, but generally it is not.

If you have ever been involved in the stock market you will understand this situation. Stocks in a certain industry traditionally are worth, let's say, 12 times earnings. Stock XYZ has been earning at the rate of $1.00 per year. Is the price $12 a share? Frequently not. It may just as well be $15 or $18 or $20. Why? Because some analysts or a lot of brokers and buyers are convinced it will soon be earning a $1.25 or $1.50 or $1.65. In other words, the price has discounted future progress, proving once again that "everyone believes in tomorrow."

This syndrome is very often in effect in real estate investment pricing. Frequently the insertion of the future into valuation is fostered by sellers through use of the "pro forma" operating statement. For one reason or another they do not show actual operating figures supported by bank statements, bills, etc. Instead, they provide a very detailed "projection" of income and costs for the year ahead. They may point out that last year had special circumstances which won't be repeated and therefore can't be used for valuation. They assure the prospective buyer the projections are accurate and reliable.

Rather frequently buyers in recent years have tended to accept pro forma figures as the basis for valuation. This has tended to drive prices up relative to their income stream. As a result, it is very difficult to buy good quality real estate at ten times actual net before debt, which has been the historic rule of thumb for years and years. You may buy a property at ten times its pro forma net before debt, but in fact, its pro forma is usually overly optimistic. As a seller, it is essential that you know what the pricing practice is in your particular market.

Why and where this unusual situation ever developed is difficult to say. Since I have been in the real estate business, in both good times and bad, I have found properties being bought in enormous multiples of their actual numbers. Most real estate seems to be sold on inflationary pro formas. Perhaps one reason for this is that by and large for a number of years, inflation has bailed out real estate investors. By this I mean, the buyers' hopes and the brokers' and sellers' stories have come close together after a year or two of economic conditions which help the property's income improve. Certainly another reason is that most buyers are optimists. They want to assume the property will have high numbers in the year ahead. Even if they don't really believe the pro forma, they do believe they can improve whatever the real numbers may be.

My observations indicate that while the average recent real estate investment used to produce 10% cash flow, an accurate figure now is probably close to 6%. That's in the same range as many stock dividends, and nothing to hide. The problem is 95% of buyers still think 10% cash flow is standard. To satisfy their psychic need, they simply buy with a belief in tomorrow.

The importance of this to sellers is that you must relate to the realities of the marketplace when you price your property for sale. It is essential to learn what other similar investments are actually earning. It is essential to determine the real multipliers being used to establish current sale values. Only real knowledge of the buyers' view of value will allow you to price your property at its maximum without pricing it too high to sell.

Tax Impact on the Sales Price of Properties

A complex and often misunderstood area is that of how the tax loss aspects of real estate affect the pricing of real estate properties. The tax shelter aspects of investing in apartment real estate are all-important to the investment incentives of buying real property.

I believe it can be safely said that the tax shelter aspects of real estate investment are essential and are built into the current industry. I personally have misgivings about this situation. Tax incentive in the form of depreciation and other tax write-offs provide a major incentive to capital investment in real estate. Unfortunately this incentive, in spite of tax reform, has at times been abused to the point of damaging the economics of the industry. In fact, some properties are easier to sell for a higher price, justifying higher tax loss write-off than they are for a more economical price and minimal tax write-off! I believe this situation is unfortunate for the industry and am hopeful that gradual tax reform will improve the balance of economics by having rents escalate to a point that can allow for a more normal investment return through cash dollars produced from the property itself.

On the other hand, there have been tremendous attacks on the tax incentives for real estate as being abusive and unfair. While I believe gradual reform is desirable, immediate plugging of what some people call "tax loopholes" would have a devastating effect on the availability and cost of rental housing in this country.

From the standpoint of the turnaround investor, it is essential that tax incentives be thoroughly understood and used in structuring sales transactions. This is detailed in Chapter 17, *The Magic of Paper*.

Preparing an Effective Sales Package

When you are preparing to sell your property, it is a good idea to create a sales presentation package. This should contain the basic information necessary to tell your story and develop interest. Additional information, which is more detailed, should be put together for distribution to serious potential prospects.

The presentation material that can be used to get a party's interest, should include the following:

1. *Description of the property* — This can be a brief section including basic statistics as to the number and size of units, general physical aspects of the property, location, age.

2. *A summary of the offering* — This should include the price, terms, and any unusual aspects of the transaction.

3. *Pictures* — Interior and exterior pictures of the property, particularly if taken from an advantageous viewpoint, can be most effective as a selling aid.

4. *Market data* — Statistical information and graphs and charts of any favorable data showing the type of people who live at the property, where they came from, and so on, can be most helpful.

5. *Historical information* — To the extent that it is helpful, historical information on the property including vacancy factors, what has been done to turn around the property, and why it is doing well and will continue to do so should be included.

6. *Pro forma* — A pro forma based on the current rent roll with any adjustments for rent increases in process should be assembled to show what a normalized 12-month period should be doing. This should be information that is reasonable in nature, but obviously it will be expected to be somewhat on the optimistic side. The information should include an appropriate disclaimer that the figures are estimates to the best belief and knowledge of the individual preparing the information. The information should contain technically and exactly correct expenses as to taxes, insurance, and other similar attainable numbers. Items such as income, maintenance, advertising, and other such numbers which may vary from time to time may be estimates.

7. *Who to contact* — Somewhere in the presentation should be the name and phone number of the appropriate person to contact for further information.

The above outline covers the minimum information which should be made widely available. Usually a serious buyer will also want to see your mortgage and note if the purchase will be subject to those loan instruments and will also want to see a current rent role and vacancy statistics. Having those items available for request will save you time later.

Selling on Your Own vs. Using a Broker

It is difficult to generalize on the best way to sell a specific property. There are some suggestions, however, that can be made for your consideration. If the property is a large real estate transaction (something, for instance, in excess of $100,000), then you certainly should not be paying the full normal commission to a broker. In most cases, a commission would be on a negotiated basis. I have paid commissions of $75,000 to $150,000 on transactions of $10,000,000 or more. This is far less than the traditional percentage, but still a significant amount of money depending on the exact nature and function of a broker's role

In general, I would suggest not formally listing your property. You should be very selective as to who exposes the property and how it is exposed. An investment property can easily become shopworn or over-exposed to the marketplace. If a buyer hears about it in the wrong manner and does not pursue it, it is unlikely that he will pursue it at a later time. For these reasons, I generally prefer dealing only with a select number of brokers on an informal, one-to-one arrangement. Usually I will agree in advance to a percentage or specific fee in the event that their efforts create a sale. They will then be given either a verbal or written, so to speak, open listing. Based on this, if they bring a buyer in who ends up buying the property, they will receive their commission. To protect its reputation, the property is not listed on a multiple listing service.

For a smaller property, under $100,000, the multiple listing service and broker handling similar to that of a single-family home is appropriate and valuable.

The brokers can be useful and in general will help widen your contacts. I have found, however, that generally contacts with people our company has done business with in the past are the best sources. To directly call a number of qualified people and expose the product is the quickest way to find out if they or someone they know might be interested. Real estate investors are a very close-knit group, so exposing property is handled best with an initial, subtle, soft sell. Many people like to think they are being exposed first or in an early grouping to an insider type deal. A one-to-one, personal exposure to a potential buyer by either the middleman or the seller directly is the best way to get somebody interested in property.

Generally, I negotiate with one person at a time. I try to avoid professional conflicts which can tend to disturb potential purchasers. I go out of my way to honor verbal commitments and make sure that a bidding situation is not created on a property intentionally.

On-Site Management Incentives While Selling

One of the big problems many large projects have is that of the resident manager or other personnel saying adverse things on the Q.T. to potential purchasers. The resident manager is in an awkward position during a sale. On the one hand, if he is loyal to the present owner, he may end up coming out of the transaction without a job. The property may be sold, and he may be sitting there without any real future. If the resident manager cooperates with a prospective new owner, it may be to his advantage, since this could be the source of continuing employment.

The on-site people can make or break any sale. What they do or don't say may materially affect a buyer's interest and final commitment to the transaction. If you have any concern, you should always make sure that the right people are on-site. In fact, your people should be loyal to you and trained in how to behave in a prospective sales situation.

My company generally provides assurances to our people at the higher middle management levels that their employment is secure no matter what happens to the particular property. We indicate to the lower echelon, that we will find jobs for them within our company if they choose not to stay with the new company at the project. We always live up to our word to the employees, and we never try to hide a potential sale. It is almost impossible to hide the fact that a property is up for sale, and it is much better to talk candidly and in a forthright manner with your employees rather than have them hear rumors and end up asking questions or forming beliefs based on half-truths.

In addition to merely assuring security, I provide cash bonus incentives if the project is successfully sold within a certain period of time. For instance, recently we had a 12 million dollar transaction. I made a deal with our resident manager that if the project was successfully sold, which would be in part the result of his efforts to keep the project in top A-1 condition, he would receive a $2500 year-end bonus. In addition, the maintenance superintendent of that project was made the same bonus offer of $2500. For a total of $5000 in bonuses, the project was kept in outstanding saleable condition. Further, employees were kept in line by the on-site supervisory personnel and became a catalyst rather than a detriment to the sale. The sale did consummate, and it was most profitable for everyone involved.

Chapter 17

The Magic of Paper

Back in Chapter 7, *The Art of Finance*, we examined the opportunities available from a buyer's point of view to use creative approaches to financing real estate investments. Now, let's look at the same subject from the seller's viewpoint.

Certainly the simplest approach would be to let the buyer worry about finance. This would pretty much limit deals to cash down to an existing mortgage, or cash with new debt financing arranged by the buyer. While these seem to be attractive approaches, they are not necessarily the most realistic, popular, or advantageous for either the buyer or seller.

More often than not, the buyer will need or want financing that can best be worked out with the participation of the seller. In turn, the buyer will be willing to negotiate a higher price and other conditions favorable to the seller.

This kind of sale creates "paper": a second mortgage, a land contract, or other debt instrument which becomes an asset of the seller. There really is magic in paper because it allows creative financial structures that are limited virtually only by your imagination and ingenuity. The only confinement is that of very reasonable laws regarding debt, instruments, and real estate transfer. What I have enjoyed so much about structuring unique paper transactions in selling properties is that this, like other areas of negotiation, can often be a non-zero sum situation. In other words, you can structure the financing of the sale so that it is not only beneficial to you, as the seller, but also beneficial for the purchaser. You are not, therefore, in a direct adversary position where one party must win and the other party lose.

Selling on Leverage

Throughout this book I have indicated that the buyer should look for reasonable leverage in purchases. Fortunately, selling with leverage for the buyer usually makes good sense to the owner. Basically this involves taking a portion of your seller's equity in the property in cash at closing and deferring, in one manner or another, the balance of the equity you have in the property based on the sale price. One of the reasons, in fact, to sell on a leveraged basis is simply that the amount of profit and the amount of "seller's equity" can often be much greater if you are offering favorable terms to the purchaser. In a typical situation, the best price you might be able to get for a particular property in a cash sale would be let's say $100,000; if you offered it with a 10% down payment, the price might well jump to $120,000 or $130,000.

A second major reason to sell on leverage is that it provides much greater exposure and opportunity to sell your property. Except in times when substantial new financing is available to refinance properties, it is difficult to find investors who will pay enough cash down to provide for cash transactions of anywhere near the price you might like to receive. In fact, a third reason to sell on leverage, is that some deals simply cannot be made any other way.

While I believe in selling successful projects, I have seen many very marginal real estate investments successfully sold at a time when they were in such financial difficulty as to be in default and possibly in foreclosure. The only way they sold was by providing such flexible terms that the purchaser was able to justify the transaction. As we will discuss later in this chapter, there are certain tax implications that give purchasers incentive to buy even marginal properties if the terms are right.

There are certain disadvantages which must be considered when you are reviewing the merits of selling a property on a leveraged basis. A continuing relationship is created with the property and the purchaser. In the event the purchaser becomes unhappy with the property, he may attempt to offset alleged representations or warranties in the sales agreement, and you may face problems and even have to go to court to collect payments. This won't happen often, but in general you have to recognize there is an ongoing transaction cost to dealing with paper receivables.

Obviously, there is a lot to be said for the old bird-in-hand theory. The time value of money must be considered carefully. However, when you are trying to evaluate the cost of not having the money immediately in any given situation, you must evaluate it in light of the entire situation. Consider the tax aspects which will be discussed later in this chapter. Consider the borrowing power of the receivable being created. Most of all, consider what amount of cash could actually be attained in a cash sale, and then decide whether the trade-off is worthwhile.

Too often a seller will be negotiating a transaction on a highly leveraged sale basis and then decide that he wants cash for the property and is only willing to discount for a normal or reasonable type return on what would have been his sale price based on high leverage. The two things generally don't equate. A sale price on a cash basis is often much lower. Therefore the seller in this situation frequently ends up continuing to own his property simply because his greed and desire to have-his-cake-and-eat-it-too has overcome more logical judgement.

Establish a realistic position on your desires and your price spread between cash and leveraged sale before you get into negotiation. Too often, I have seen sellers trap themselves by starting to negotiate a highly leveraged sale at a high price, then decide they want cash. The entire negotiation falls apart if they are unable emotionally to accept a deeply discounted price in return for a cash transaction.

427 Glendaloch Place — A Typical Leverage Sale with Big Profits

As discussed in Chapter 13 on operations, 427 Glendaloch Place was the first building I ever purchased. After having made substantial improvements in the income in the property through physical and operational improvements, the rooming house consisted of 11 rooms plus a small apartment. It was running quite smoothly and my cash flow was approximately $5370 per year.

While having the cash flow was nice and helpful in paying off other debts I had established, it seemed time to move on. I had owned the property about two years at this time, and due to my expansion into other properties, I was certainly in need of cash. In addition to needing cash, it seemed important to show lenders the true results of at least one property. The only way to establish the true results was to have an example of a property that had gone through the entire improvement process and finally been sold at a profit. With that in mind, I began to consider methods of selling my first rooming house.

After a fair amount of study, it became apparent that while a cash sale would be possible, it would be much less profitable than a sale on terms. In this case, a sale on terms would not only attain a much higher price but, in fact, would also establish borrowing power and ongoing cash flow from the receivable.

After having settled a lawsuit for $1400 that I won against the original seller, I had in the property $2600 of my original $4000 down payment, plus about $1000 of improvement money and a lot of hard work. I had received back approximately $1800 in cash flow over the period of the two years I owned the property. Therefore, netting it out, I still had about $1600 invested. The land contract to the people I had bought the property from called for a 7% interest rate and payments of $200 a month. At that time, I still owed a little over $21,500. I decided to expose the property for sale through real estate brokers without giving an exclusive listing. I put the property up for sale for $52,000 or almost 4.5 times the gross rent. I asked a $4000 down payment.

I felt that the gross rent multiplier could be somewhat higher than when I originally purchased the property, due to the improved nature of the property. Its profitability, its tenants, and the entire appearance were greatly enhanced since my original acquisition. I also felt that by offering it with a $4000 down payment, which was less than 10% down, I would be able to attract a reliable purchaser based on the high leverage available. At the same time, I asked for a $500-per-month land contract payment at a 9½% rate. Interest had gone up since I purchased at 7%.

After the property was exposed for a period of time, it turned out that a friend was interested in a direct purchase from me. This was of great assistance since even though by this time I was a real estate broker, and would have been entitled to half of the commission, simply paying 3% would have greatly decreased my net proceeds from the sale. Instead, I sold for a total price of $49,000 with $2500 down. This very low down payment was more than the amount I still had invested in the property, and the balance of $46,500 was in the form of a land contract. The land contract called for payments to me of $450 per month at 9½% interest. This was an 18-year amortization. My underlying loan was also a land contract and had about 15 more years of payment. I was not only making a 9½% interest rate on the creation of "paper," but also I was getting the benefit of the difference between the 7% rate I was paying out on approximately $21,500 and the 9½% rate I was receiving on the receivable.

In addition, payments that I was receiving were $450, while the payments that I was making were $200 per month. On an annual basis, I was continuing to get a $3000 cash flow, even after I had sold the property and gotten back all of my money in less than two years. This $3000 cash flow would continue for 14 years. Then, after my underlying land contract was paid off, I would keep the entire $5400 per year payment for four more years after which the entire loan would be paid off. As you can see, I had created a very good receivable. Unlike the way I have suggested you should buy, this receivable was secured both by the property itself and a complete right of personal liability against the purchaser.

As you can see in this example, the creation of paper can be a most profitable way to sell a property. In this particular example, selling the property in this manner delivered a tremendous profit over a long period of time. Selling for cash would have yielded a much smaller profit. The purchaser in this case also benefited since the higher price was justified by the increased income created by the turnaround. The income stream that the purchaser was buying was a new and different product than I had bought some two years earlier. In fact, the income stream combined with the tax advantages of the higher price produced an excellent return for the purchaser.

Let the Seller Beware

Because of the continuing relationship created by leveraged sales, it is very important that the purchaser be selected with great care. You are, after all, loaning money to the purchaser, and there really isn't any "magic" in paper if you never collect. Some loans will require collection effort, and any sale that is not for cash does involve a certain degree of risk. Your risk can be minimized significantly by a business-like approach in your selection of purchasers to whom you are willing to extend credit. To be of any protection to you, this screening process must occur prior to entering into the sales agreement.

In considering a particular purchaser, you should be concerned with all aspects of the individual's financial and personal background. Start with a check at your local credit bureau. A simple credit report will give you basic information. Also, check into the individual's reputation. If you are pushed to finalization of the sales agreement, make it subject to satisfactory review and acceptance of an individual's financial statement. Request a completely detailed financial statement and then specifically review the status of both assets and liabilities, particularly non-real estate assets. Does the buyer appear to be heavily in debt or in a well balanced position? Is there sufficient cash income to support the apparent standard of living as well as debt obligations?

Perhaps the most important consideration is the person's moral character and background. Trust your own impressions but only after you do thorough research on reputation. Particularly when selling smaller properties, many buyers may not be financially well-heeled, so to speak, but may indeed be very fine credit risks. This should be decided on their background, attitude, and moral fiber. My rule is that desire to pay counts equally with ability to pay. In short, check out how the person does business and then make your decision; but always realize there is a degree of risk. You obviously will reduce this risk by having good legal documentation to make sure the building is security for performance of your debt receivable.

Working with Underlying Debts Structuring the Sale

When you are considering selling a property, one of the first things to do is consider your underlying debts. You should review the mortgage and any other current debt financing and ask yourself if there is any way you can advantageously refinance prior to a sale.

You might find you can increase your first mortgage financing, and thereby provide a significant amount of cash to yourself before you sell the property. This will also create a smaller margin between your first mortgage and selling price. With any given down payment, this smaller margin will minimize the amount of finance you might have to offer through a second mortgage or land contract. Very often, if you refinance, you may end up getting a slightly higher price from a new buyer because you will be able to offer greater leverage.

When considering the underlying debt structure, always review your mortgage constant. This is simply the ratio of your annual mortgage payment in the current year to the total outstanding debt at the time. You generally want to have as low a constant as possible. The lower the constant, the more the cash flow available after payment of your debt service. If, for example, you have a home improvement loan, a first mortgage, and a second mortgage, and the total of the payments on the three loans added up to $12,000 per year on a total debt of $60,000, you would have a constant of 20. A 20 constant would be considered a very high ratio of payment to debt and would indicate that refinancing should be considered to arrange lower total payments.

In fact, any time your constant is over 12 you should look into the possibility of new underlying financing prior to a sale. In this example, if you were to go out and obtain a new first mortgage for $60,000, paying off the three other loans, you could probably end up with payments of about $6000 per year, instead of the $12,000 payment. Your constant would now be 10. You obviously would be paying off less principal per year, but your cash flow would be increased by $6000.

Another approach to attempt in this situation, which would probably be more favorable if you were considering sale, would be to find a new first mortgage for a greater amount than the present loans. The "greater amount" would be determined by how much debt the property could support. If the property were easily covering the $12,000 debt service, you could very likely borrow $100,000 or more and continue to pay the same debt service. This would put at least $40,000 in your pocket before you even started to negotiate the sale of the property.

An Example of a Highly Creative Sale

Sunshine Apartments was a turnaround property that is an example of good and bad practices. This project violated many of the now cardinal rules of our turnaround process. Its location was marginal, and the physical product was not well-built. The property had low per unit purchase price, but there was good reason why the particular bank sold the property to us for such a low price. The property had only a 30% to 40% occupancy over five or six years since its completion. The bank had actually foreclosed on the property when it was halfway built. During a time of heavy construction strikes, the bank had finally finished the property with non-union labor. They had to have armed guards protect the labor while building the property. The unfortunate result was a project that was not well-built and suffered from construction defects.

In spite of the latent defects and bad location, we did substantially turn the property around through aggressive marketing. While we learned lessons that later led to some of the cardinal rules included in this book, we were at least able to boast after one heck of a lot of hard work, not only a high occupancy, but in fact 100% occupancy with a waiting list!

With that under our belts, we attempted to find a method of re-financing and paying off part of the debt we had structured on short term notes. Again, this property taught us a lesson. This purchase was prior to the establishment of my cardinal rule against personal liability.

Because of the need to put cash into the project to effect a turn-around, the property was purchased with no cash down for a total of $1,000,000. The bank-seller provided an $850,000 first mortgage loan, which was non-recourse; in other words, it carried no personal liability. A second mortgage for $150,000 was a personal liability note. Both loans were short term as we anticipated getting permanent finance as soon as we could show improved performance. The first mortgage was due in two years, with 8% interest only payments. The second mortgage was due in one year and was a 7% interest only loan.

At the end of the first year when the second mortgage was due in full, we had not yet found a source of long term financing. The fact that the project was an inner city type property with 100% minority occu-pancy created much greater financing difficulty than I had ever antici-pated. Because this was one of my earlier large acquisitions, I had very significant limits on my personal financial ability to support any trans-action with personal funding. My limited cash was already highly lever-aged and simply unavailable. I began to realize that I was in a position of not only being foreclosed, but of being sued for $150,000. If a judge-ment was obtained against me, my liquidity would not have been suffi-cient to come anywhere near paying even a reasonable portion of this debt, and I would be in deep financial difficulty.

Instead, what I did was to honestly and openly explain my plight to the bank. They were understanding and helpful but kept a fair degree of pressure upon me to resolve the situation quickly. I continued to pay the interest on the second loan and the regular first mortgage payments. In addition, over the next nine months, I paid $10,000 off on the $150,000 loan while I looked for a way to solve my problem through a sale. Within that nine-month period, I found a group of doctors who had put together an investment fund operated by a real estate syndicator-manager for whom I had great respect. This particular individual was very sophis-ticated and knowledgeable about property, so I felt we might work out a mutually advantageous deal.

We began to negotiate to sell the property to this group on as high a leverage basis as possible. My primary objective at this time was simply to get out from under the personal liability that was hanging over my head. Of course I was interested in obtaining some kind of profitable position as well. We analyzed the needs of the doctors' group carefully and found that they were in a position of having high income but not a great deal of immediately available cash. Their credit was excellent, certainly far greater than my own. In addition, they had a piece of land that was worth approximately $200,000 and was free and clear of any debt. The land at that time was doing them no good, since it had been bought for a project the group had now abandoned.

We finally ended up with a complex transaction that involved a property exchange, wherein we ended up with the land but gave the bank a mortgage on the land as additional security for the performance of the bank's second mortgage on Southview. I sold the apartment development to the investment group for a price amounting to $1,575,000 less the value of the land as a property exchange. After a series of complex accounting adjustments, I ended up with a significant profit deferred as a ten-year receivable which accrues interest. At the end of ten years, this amount due from the doctors' group will have grown to more than $700,000. That will be extremely collectable, since it is personally guaranteed by the doctors individually and the real estate developer who is a well-to-do individual in his own right.

The bank also came out quite well, since we arranged to have the debt restructured putting both of the mortgages on a long term basis, with the doctors agreeing not only to be liable on the $150,000, but on the first mortgage as well.

The doctors' group ended up in a very favorable position, since they had converted a piece of land that was otherwise useless to them into a portion of an apartment development that would provide excellent tax benefits and future cash flow potential. This was the kind of investment they had been looking for, and it had the extra value of not requiring a significant cash down payment. In the final analysis, a non-zero sum negotiation was created by using high leverage, the good credit of the group of doctors, and creative structuring to end up with a transaction that benefited all of the parties involved.

Why a Paper Deal Can Improve Tax Implications

One very important reason for selling on high leverage, with the seller taking back financing, is the favorable tax implications created for both the seller and buyer.

From your standpoint as the seller, if you receive less than 29% of the purchase price in the first year, and have two or more installments on a contract, you may be in a position to treat the transactions as an "installment sale." This has substantial advantages in that for tax purposes the gain on sale is spread over the period of the installment contract. This gives you a much better opportunity to plan your personal tax situation and defer realization of gain or income to lower tax bracket years.

Here is a simplified explanation of how this can work. If you have a property with an adjusted tax basis of $10,000 that you have just sold for

$15,000, you have a net gain of $5,000, or one-third of the total price. If you receive a $1500 down payment, you would take one-third, or only $500, as a gain on your taxes that year. The balance of your gain would be deferred until received.

You would take your ordinary gain based on determining how much of your gain related to items that would be recaptured as ordinary taxable income first, and take your capital gain second. In other words, let's assume that you had $1000 of accelerated depreciation that you had written off while owning the property. You would have earlier received tax advantages for that $1000 of accelerated depreciation; now at sale the accelerated depreciation would represent ordinary gain, rather than capital gain, which is taxed at a lower rate. This ordinary gain would be first recaptured as gains received in the installments, then leaving the balance of the $5000 or $4000 to be treated as capital gain.

The interesting thing to note is that an installment sale can actually defer a substantial tax liability on sale. Let's go back to our example and now let's make the assumption that there is a $12,000 mortgage owing on the property. Your adjusted tax basis is below that of your mortgage — namely, $10,000 at the time of sale. Had the property been a cash sale, you would have received $15,000 in proceeds, paid off the $12,000 mortgage, and had $3000 left. However, the sale would still have triggered a $1000 ordinary gain and a $4000 capital gain. Assuming you are in the 40% tax bracket, you would in essence be paying $400 tax on the $1000 of gain, and $800, or one-half of your normal tax rate, on the $4000 of gain. Your total tax liability would be $1200, which would come out of your total received proceeds of $3000. This would leave you net proceeds of only $1800.

By taking the installment method, you defer the bulk of your tax liability and only pay tax on money as received, on the basis of one-third of the dollars received in each installment, including the down payment. The bulk of your $1200 of tax will be deferred until the final payment when you are no longer subject to the mortgage underlying the property.

It is also important to the seller that the purchaser has enough favorable tax implications in a transaction to not only make him interested in the property, but to make him willing to pay a high price for the property. In fact, tax incentives are so favorable to real estate, that in a very real sense it sometimes makes it financially advantageous for a buyer to overpay for what would otherwise be the economic market value of a particular property. The higher the price, and the more interest that is charged, the more tax loss or write-off the buyer will receive in any given time period.

Since an owner is able to apply tax loss from a given real estate investment against other income, this loss can be very valuable. The loss can be used by an individual owner or limited partner investor to reduce personal income tax.

As an example, suppose you have a property that you are interested in selling, and you negotiate to sell it to a buyer for $800,000 cash; subject to your $600,000 existing first mortgage, you end up with $200,000 cash for your project. The buyer ends up with a property having a debt service, let's say, of $80,000 per year. The buyer will also receive an overall depreciation of perhaps 5% or $40,000 per year. In the 50% tax bracket, that $40,000 per year is worth $20,000 in immediate cash tax saving, or about 10% of the buyer's down payment.

Now let's take the same situation, but you increase the price to $1,000,000; and instead of having the buyer pay a $200,000 down payment, let's say you agree to lower the down payment to $100,000 as an additional incentive. Now your total profit is $400,000: $100,000 in cash at closing, and $300,000 in a paper receivable. The buyer now owes $900,000 on the property. Assuming the property is one that is likely to go up in value, you can assume the property will be able to pay its debt. You might negotiate a slightly higher payment of, say, $90,000 per year. The underlying mortgage will be paid from this amount and you will receive some cash flow. In the future, you will receive the $300,000 owed to you, plus interest either through a balloon or natural amortization of the loan, depending on how you set up the deal.

From the buyer's standpoint, he now is depreciating $1,000,000, which at our same depreciation basis of 5% per year will provide $50,000 in depreciation. Again, if the buyer is in the 50% income tax bracket, this will be worth $25,000 in immediate cash tax saving. This $25,000 tax savings results in a 25% return on the $100,000 down payment investment. This obviously is a much better return for the buyer than if he had paid $200,000 down on a cash basis. In the long run, the seller will come out with an additional $200,000 plus interest. The buyer will come out with a higher return per dollar invested as down payment. Over a period of time, the transaction will be much more advantageous to the buyer than if he had paid a lower price but with more cash equity required. In fact, both the seller and buyer are winners! Obviously, the tax implications of each transaction should be gone over by a tax attorney or accountant. This is a complicated area and each case must be reviewed separately.

Financing Security Forms

There are many ways of establishing installment sales and creating paper receivables. These methods usually involve an obligation or debt, which may be in the form of a promissory note, and there is usually an instrument that establishes the property itself as security for the debt or promissory note. This security instrument is usually a mortgage, land contract, or similar instrument. Security forms vary from state to state, particularly when they involve the seller taking back financing. In all matters of this type, it is obviously important that you consult your attorney as to the best method within your state and the particular facts of your situation.

Some financing forms to consider are the following:

1. *Land contracts* — A land contract or similar instrument, which may be called a contract for deed or deed trust, is basically an instrument where title is held by the seller, but the beneficial rights of ownership are transferred to the buyer. The buyer holds a contract wherein the seller agrees to deliver title after the buyer has performed all obligations under the contract. This agreement will give the beneficial rights of ownership but not the legal title to the purchasing party. The key result is that in many states it is somewhat easier to foreclose or forfeit a land contract or contract for deed than a mortgage.

2. *Second mortgages* — A second mortgage is a subordinated mortgage loan which the seller can extend to the buyer as part of the consideration he is paying to acquire the property. It must be written so that should the first mortgage go into default, you as seller will have a right to make the first mortgage payments and begin foreclosure. This could put you in a position where you are paying the payments on the first mortgage simply to protect your subordinate or secondary lien position, but do not have possession of the property.

3. *Wrap-around* — A wrap-around, as we have discussed earlier, is basically financing where the seller is paying the first mortgage and receiving a single payment from the buyer, which may or may not be an amount different than the first mortgage and may have a different interest rate. The wrap-around has somewhat more control and better advantages than a second mortgage.

4. *Purchase money mortgage* — A purchase money mortgage is simply a method of a seller extending financing and taking back a mortgage from a buyer. It differs somewhat in form from a standard second mortgage instrument. It may, in fact, be an instrument used on a free and clear property, wherein the seller is taking financing rather than the purchaser mortgaging on a cash purchase basis.

Irrespective of the legal financing form, the key consideration is what is best for your purposes in securing your loan obligation. Your attorney is your best source of advice in this area.

Legal Aspects

When you're selling on terms, you must be very cautious. Obviously, the entire transaction is of no benefit if you only receive the down payment and subsequently end up in litigation or with an uncreditworthy loan. Assuming you have checked out your buyer carefully, your next step to protect yourself is to review with your attorney the legal aspects of your transaction, and make sure your documents contain certain key clauses for your benefit.

You must have adequate protection against "milking" of the property. In other words, if the purchaser is letting the property run down, you must be able to act for your protection, including instituting a foreclosure if necessary. The mere fact that payments are made on a timely basis does not guarantee that your security is in good condition in the event payments in the future are not made. You should have a right to receive reports on the property. You should have a right to inspect the property on a periodic basis. And you should have certain rights to uphold standards of good maintenance and repair, and insure that the purchaser is not committing what is called "waste" in the legal sense.

In addition to protection of your security, you should consider other clauses which might or might not be acceptable to your purchaser. You should try to negotiate a clause making your entire loan indebtedness due and payable in full if and when the purchaser to whom you have sold the property resells the property. This will give you an opportunity to at least evaluate the new buyer, and at the same time consider whether or not to up the interest rate or change other terms of your loan. Another similar clause that you should make every effort to obtain is that of a balloon in your mortgage. A balloon is simply a call or acceleration of the amount left owing at a given point in time. In other words, you might offer a 25-year mortgage amortization schedule but with a balloon at the end of ten years. This would mean that at the end of ten years, the entire amount of indebtedness not yet amortized would be due and payable in full, and the buyer at that point would likely have to refinance.

Another legal consideration is that of making your paper marketable. Discuss with your attorney any and all ways to put your paper or debt in a form that can be used as security and/or used as a loan document that can actually be sold to a third party. The concept of making the note itself negotiable should be considered by your tax advisor. In general, a negotiable instrument is the same thing as receiving a cash sale, and you would likely not qualify for installment sale treatment. It would, therefore, probably not be in your interest to make your note negotiable. However, you should consider any and all suggestions by your attorney to make the note and security instruments more marketable.

Discounting for Cash

Another part of the magic of paper is that paper doesn't necessarily have to wait until it is paid off in order to be cashed out. If you have properly documented debt and security instruments, and a good, credit-worthy buyer, your paper may in fact be very marketable. There are various individuals 'and companies that regularly buy second mortgages, land contracts, and purchase money mortgages. It is therefore not necessary for you to wait the entire term of a land contract, for instance, to receive your balance. You may turn around and sell the right to receive the payments to a third party.

You will almost surely not receive the face amount of your debt obligation. It will be "discounted" depending upon the interest rate versus the market at the time, the type of buyer, the type of property, and so on. Basically, the party interested in buying the debt obligation is interested in the quality of the future flow of dollars as well as the number of dollars. The individual or entity buying the land contract will expect to obtain a yield that in their business judgment is commensurate with the risk of the paper as they see it.

The activity in the market to buy paper changes from one time to another depending on the money supply and demand and a particular lender's interest in various types of investment at the time. Savings and Loan associations have been known to buy land contracts and purchase money mortgages. Individuals buy second mortgages and land contracts. Mortgage companies buy second mortgages, land contracts, and purchase money mortgages. There are mortgage companies that specialize in doing wrap-around loans. One source of finding these entities is simply to start by calling your local savings and loans who are likely to have the lowest discount rate or the best return for you if they are interested. Another source is to put a small ad in your local real estate classified section offering a land contract or second mortgage for sale.

Very often you will find that by creating paper, then letting it "season" or prove its reliability for a year or so, you will be able to sell it at a discount and still net a greater cash total than if you had sold the property originally for cash. If you are able to get a relatively high interest rate on your receivable, and if the paper market is favorable, you should be able to cash-out without too deep a discount. Because your leverage sale will usually bring you a considerably higher total price, you will generally end up well ahead of a cash sale.

VI

PUTTING IT
ALL TOGETHER

Chapter 18

How We Turned a "Lemon"
into Pure Gold —
The Anatomy of
a $25,000,000 Turnaround

How It All Began

It was January 1. I was on my way to the airport for one week in San Juan. We had just completed the syndication of a ten million dollar transaction. We had purchased the property August 1 and turnaround efforts had been very successful. The syndication of outside investor money to help capitalize the partnership was completed, and with a great sense of satisfaction I was off for my annual one-week vacation.

Before I had even signed the last document completing the syndication, I was wondering about what to do next that would be bigger and better. I began to think about what deals I had heard about that might be available and fit the abilities of our company.

Now on the way to the airport with my executive vice president, our first line of communication was potential acquisitions. Suddenly I recalled that Knob-on-the-Lake, a huge apartment complex located on the I-94 expressway, was up for sale. We had not looked into it in the past, but it was widely known that the project had serious financial difficulty and the owner had actively been trying to sell it. There had been ads in the *Wall Street Journal* and local papers as well. Yes, Knob-on-the-Lake, that would be our next project!

I anticipated they might initially want more money than the project would be worth and there would be any number of other problems. However, in my mind, the logic for the deal making sense, was there. If the seller was really interested in selling and had financial problems, the chances of us making a deal would be very good. After all, I could afford to be reasonable in negotiation and my company had the ability to take on something of this magnitude.

It was settled, and while I was gone, per instruction, my executive vice president began contacting the appropriate people. Some general information was gathered while I was gone. When I returned, I found our first meeting on the new project was scheduled for 10:00 a.m. of that day.

A few hours later we left to meet the owner and the exclusive sales agent/broker. My first impression as we drove through the project was a feeling of awe. I was amazed at how large the development was. It seemed like an entire town spread out before me. We arrived early and the manager, the son-in-law of the owner, was giving us a tour through the models. It became apparent immediately that the project was extremely well-built. It also was apparent to me that the project was not being marketed to its fullest extent. There was a world of difference between passing by on the expressway and actually coming in and experiencing the environment of the golf course, the lake, and well-built apartments themselves.

Finally, the owner and broker came in. What was to be a long and unforgettable odyssey was underway. The broker was a friendly, smiling Irishman, probably in his late forties. The principal owner was a 79-year-old gentleman who had been a long-time builder in the greater Detroit market. That first meeting was so disarming. I remember the broker, my executive vice president, the builder-owner, and myself driving through the project in the owner's Lincoln Continental. We then went to Howard Johnson's, had some coffee, and discussed the project in general. The owner seemed a mellow, quiet, kindly gentleman; almost a man in a world of his own. He seemed extremely easygoing and pleasant. My first impressions were that negotiation with him would be a cakewalk.

Later, I was to learn that this disarming first impression reflected only the shadow of what turned out to be one of the most interesting but difficult men with whom I have ever had the pleasure of negotiating.

The Village of Knob-on-the-Lake

To the south, lying adjacent to a major east-west artery coming out of the hub of Detroit, lies the 136-acre apartment community originally called Knob-on-the-Lake. The project is situated about 30 miles from downtown Detroit. Fifteen miles farther west on the I-94 expressway is Ann Arbor, the home of the University of Michigan. The location represented the distant extremity of what many would call a desolate area of cornfields, occasional factories, and pockets of small residential neighborhoods lying in the exurbia of the Detroit market.

While the location wasn't convenient to very much employment, it did have several natural attributes to offer its prospective residents. The 136 acres of slightly rolling land included substantial winding frontage on a beautiful, 8-mile long lake. The lake provided beauty and excellent swimming, boating, and fishing. It had recently been part of a state-wide reclamation program and had been completely cleaned out and stocked with fish. The land was originally an apple orchard and had been well-used in the overall site plan and construction by the builder-developer.

Knob-on-the-Lake was planned as a 1600-unit project, but only 1145 were built. Some of the buildings bordered the lake, while the project's 70-acre, PGA-rated, nine-hole golf course provided beautiful, open, green spaces throughout the central areas of the development. The developer added that the natural beauty of the site had been enhanced with outstanding landscaping — shade trees, lush lawns, and brilliant flower-beds. The apartments were all constructed with large balconies and an orientation toward the exterior living concept.

In addition to the golf course, swimming, boating, and fishing, the project offered more conventional amenities, such as tennis courts and swimming pool, as well as large clubhouse facilities. The units themselves were large and well-designed. There were a total of 543 one-bedroom and 602 two-bedroom units. The one bedrooms ranged from 685 square feet to 740 square feet. The two bedrooms ranged from 875 square feet to 940 square feet.

The developer-builder, in an extremely progressive move for apartments at the time, provided each apartment with very high quality shag carpeting, central air conditioning, dishwashers, carports included in the rent, and electric heat, also included in the rent, controlled on a room-by-room basis. Many of the apartments also included such unusual amenities as fireplaces, and individual washers and dryers within the unit.

At the time of our acquisition, the financial situation was incredible. The project's occupancy had hovered around 58%. The rental rates being obtained were much lower than those originally projected for mortgages. In addition, a number of the expense areas had gone higher than originally projected. The development had created a $173,000 cash deficit per month. There were approximately $2,000,000 past due in mortgage payments, $1,200,000 of unpaid subcontractors' bills from the construction itself, and another $350,000 worth of overdue operating expenses. The local electric company was owed in excess of $200,000 and was seriously considering shutting off the power to the entire project.

The Village of Knob-on-the-Lake is a beautiful physical creation and should be regarded as a monument to the pride and desire of its builder-developer. It sprawled gracefully through the land; more a way of life than just bricks and mortar. On the other hand, the market was not ready in that time and that place for that product. Because the market would not support it, the project became a physical disaster as well as a financial impossibility. The downward cycle set in and could not be controlled. By the time I made my first visit, the deterioration had seriously affected the owner, the residents of the project, and in many ways the surrounding community itself. This was a project which I knew was ripe for a turn-around.

Why the Best Laid Plans Ran Afoul

To simply say the market wasn't ready and didn't support the needed rents is an over-simplification, to say the least. There were several things that contributed to this otherwise well-conceived project becoming a financial disaster. Many of these factors which could not be solved in the short run, could at least be dealt with by an aggressive turnaround plan including a complete financial restructuring of the transaction. Since it was now obvious that the initial financing had been ill-conceived, it would have to be replaced by a more realistic arrangement.

Some of the problems that this development had during its initial four and one-half years of operation prior to our takeover included:

1. *Original market feasibility was unrealistic* — The projections used for the mortgage applications had unrealistically high rental rates. Further, the expenses were underestimated, both in terms of their aggregate total and in terms of the percentage of expense to total gross income projected to be collected. It is not unusual to find "optimistic" projections used in a mortgage package. It is also not unusual that during times of high liquidity, loans are made based on these optimistic assumptions. In fact, many times, these assumptions end up fairly accurate due to inflation during the long construction period. In this case, the unrealistic projections were not, so to speak, "bailed out" by inflation during construction.

2. *Location too early* — Building 1145 units over a four and one-half year time span in this location was simply too much too fast for the area. While the market potential for this area appeared to have good long term prospects, it certainly represented the extremity of apartment living from the high employment centers. Another significant problem regarding the location included an extensive expressway construction project which lasted for some three years, causing various inconveniences to the residents of the project. Expressway detours and construction problems were most detrimental to the location during the early rent-up period.

3. *General economic problems* — During construction of the third and fourth phases of the project, the local and national economic conditions were in a serious recession. This was also a time quite adversely affected by the beginnings of the serious energy crisis. Gasoline prices were going up at a very fast pace, and the idea of potential gasoline rationing concerned many potential residents. Since this project was farther from areas of employment than many other rental apartment developments, it was the first type of housing to suffer from both the recession and the energy crisis.

4. *Overbuilt market* — The general Detroit area had been seriously overbuilt. As is typical in the housing industry in recent years, sup-

ply and demand seem to go in cycles. We move from times of extreme housing shortage with lack of adequate construction to keep pace with new family formations, to times of dramatic oversupply. Unfortunately, when the units on Knob-on-the-Lake were being built, other people in the greater Detroit market and even some in the immediate vicinity of Knob-on-the-Lake had similar ideas. The temporary overbuilding that occurred caused an excess of competition and a soft rental market for a period of time.

5. *Management and marketing* — The original owner of Knob-on-the-Lake self-managed the project. In hindsight, his policies and decisions seem typical of many similar situations. When rent-up originally started, the resident selection standards were quite high. As the project ran into financial difficulty, they ran various "giveaway" programs to attract any possible prospects. This ended up giving way to an element of resident that would not have otherwise qualified. The delinquency rate went up, the good residents moved out, security became more of a problem, and the condition of the hallways and other common areas became worse and worse.

At the same time, the management in an effort to stay solvent, cut back on necessary services. The downward cycle began to speed up and things got worse for the residents and the project itself. Mortgage payments became very delinquent, other bills were paid very slowly if at all, and the property developed a very bad reputation.

Certainly there was no one problem that caused the downfall of this fine development. In fact, this is charactertistic of most properties that get into financial distress. There are usually a multitude of factors working together. That is why it is so important to not trust a surface analysis of any turnaround situation.

Can All the King's Men Put Humpty Dumpty Back Together Again?

As I tried to decide whether to take on this turnaround, I found very positive factors hidden among the horrors. The major problems that had devastated the financial condition were curable. The property had the basic ingredients of a successful turnaround: financial distress, good construction, and what we believed would in the longer term be a good location.

In addition, I saw several bonus characteristics. First of all, the owner had to get out because foreclosure was imminent. Secondly, the property was overbuilt and contained many amenities. While these did not command commensurate rental value at the present time, over the long haul they would be very important assets to the property. Finally, there would be a big bonus in the market improving over time.

I believed that if I could only buy time from the various creditors, in the long term, the property could produce adequate revenues to service the debt against the development. To say such a thing is quite easy. However, it seemed to be an almost impossible feat. The property was losing so much money it was difficult to visualize the property ever breaking even. After a great deal of analysis and soul-searching, I still believed that deferral of mortgage payments and other debts for a period of time would provide the opportunity to assert ourselves in the marketplace and eventually raise rents by providing a superior product.

To attempt to purchase the property subject to satisfactory negotiation with the several lenders involved, plus all of the construction and operating creditors, would have been a virtual impossibility. Before the many agreements required could have been reached, the project would surely have been in bankruptcy.

Therefore, I decided to take what appeared to many observers to be a very sizable calculated risk. Probably it was, but it seemed the best way to achieve our goal, and a realistic approach. I reasoned that if we could get into possession and quickly start to gain credibility, the various creditors would coalesce in support of our effort. They would be faced by the choice of cooperating with us, or risking the confusion and chaos of bankruptcy proceedings complicated by several lenders foreclosing individually on various phases of the project and trying to operate as separate entities. I called this line of thinking the "possession/confusion theory."

Logic said the best thing for all the lenders and creditors would be for them to ride with an honest, capable turnaround expert. I felt that with only modest risk in a financial sense we could establish the control of possession and be in a position to offer creditors the benefit of expert management tied to the motivation of ownership. This became the objective of the negotiation.

How We Closed the Deal, or Did We?

As I have pointed out earlier, the project had so many problems and creditors and claimants of all kinds, it was very difficult to structure a purchase. The basic problem was that it seemed to be an almost impossible task to get the ownership title in a condition that would not be subject to many claims of foreclosure that would have priority to the ownership interest we would be purchasing. These problems might normally be enough to turn anyone off in a deal that would involve millions of dollars of debt and an extensive concentration of time and effort. To me, however, this was part of the excitement and the challenge.

On the other hand, it did seem reasonable to expect that the seller would be so anxious to get rid of his headaches that any kind of deal would be acceptable. A lesser man would have frankly declared bankruptcy, but the owner of "Knob" was not the kind of guy who would throw in the

sponge and call it quits under pressure. While I had been disarmed by our
initial meeting, he quickly showed his colors in early negotiations. He was
a tough, proud, tenacious, stubborn man who quickly made me forget he
was 79 years old. This gentleman had built a beautiful project but was in
part a victim of unforeseen tough times. I came to respect and learn a great
deal from this fine elder businessman.

Throughout the months of January and February, the intensive day
and night sessions wore more heavily on the rest of us. It was from my
elder teacher that I learned many things about the true art and style of
negotiation. While he was in a completely untenable position, and without any leverage whatsoever, he managed to hang on and keep fighting
for his "rights" and his needs and desires. Despite his weak position, the
seller was determined to get as much out of the property as he could.
Dodging creditors and lawsuits, we continued to negotiate in secret for
eight to ten hours a day with a string of attorneys and other close
associates.

It was February 18 when we finally entered into our first sales agreement which was a document of roughly 40 pages. This was the result of
many hours of disagreement between one of the youngest and one of the
oldest members of the real estate fraternity.

The transaction itself was closed March 1. I should say the transaction
was closed only in a sense, because the deal was predicated on a continuing bond between seller and buyer. Mutual trust was to be a necessary
part of the future if we were to keep the property together for me as purchaser, and realize financial salvation for the seller. During the process of
negotiating, we had simply "agreed to agree" on many areas, but had not
been able to create sufficient definition to take out the vagueness and
finalize the transaction with specifics in a normal way. In essence, the seller gave us protection on the downside, and we promised him monetary
rewards for his investment of effort and money, but to be paid only after
the turnaround was accomplished.

My major concerns during the initial negotiations were those of downside protection. In that regard, we were most successful in negotiating
financial protection so our losses would have been significantly under
$100,000 if the entire property was foreclosed after our purchase. On the
other hand, the potential profit to my companies and myself in just a few
years could be well in excess of $1,000,000. In the long range, profits
could be several million dollars.

My second major objective in early negotiations was to establish a
working format and to gain the maximum leverage possible to achieve
favorable future definition of vague areas in the agreement. This too was
successful in many ways. Since the seller was essentially conveying a 25
million dollar property for somewhat ill-defined promises of future payment, there had to be a great deal of faith and psychologically based acceptance involved. This deal could not have been put together with a man

of less experience with people or less confidence in his own judgement. One interesting note is that toward the end of the negotiations, but prior to signing the sales agreement, another serious potential buyer appeared. This buyer had negotiated for some time before I became involved, but the contact was broken off when the seller felt bad faith was shown in various ways. About the time we were planning to move for a close, this other prospective buyer made a new offer which seemed better than mine in all respects and included $500,000 immediate money to the seller. The funds were actually escrowed in an account at a local bank. When we later heard of this, we were quite surprised to find the seller completing our transaction. The seller had turned down $500,000 cash in hand because he had more faith in my integrity and my plan to make the property successful.

The transaction we structured was necessarily complex. In fact, the final documents completely fill three 4-inch wide black binders. From the beginning, I regarded this transaction as a long hurdle course. Each time we would get over one hurdle, there would be still more to come. The potential rewards were good, our opinion was that we could do it, and the determination was unfaltering on both sides.

The Possession/Confusion Theory at Work

Naturally, the closing of the purchase was just the beginning of our real negotiation. Now I had to face lenders and creditors with $3,550,000 worth of past due debt. There was so much confusion and chaos among all of the various creditor interests and all the pieces of the huge puzzle that I believed the situation could be used to our advantage.

By my people keeping their confidence and composure when everyone else was running around in circles looking for easy answers to potential financial disasters, we were able to convince many people to cooperate. There were subcontractors who could literally have been bankrupt by the unpaid claims of the project. In fact, some of the contractors were severely damaged and possibly put out of business by problems before our involvement. It was clear that any one individual creditor or mortgage lender suing to receive their claim would only end up in a very lengthy court proceeding that would likely produce bankruptcy.

We tried to get everyone to realize that if a receiver was put in control of the real estate, rather than an interested owner-manager with turnaround expertise, everyone would be disadvantaged. We explained that the real estate did have the potential to become a viable, productive asset that could begin to pay off the claimants over a period of time. We were confident and believed 100% that our efforts could maximize the position of everyone who had a potential interest in the project. While we would have to negotiate in a somewhat adversary position, our interest was of course to compromise and negotiate debt where possible. We were realistic and fair. We had the leverage of basic logic, confusion, and being the titleholder in possession, and we counted on these thin threads to hold the entire transaction together.

There were those creditors who did not go along with us and a number of lawsuits were filed. In fact, at one point there were 16 lawsuits pending. As I am writing this, two years later, we are down to only two lawsuits, both of which are of little consequence. All lawsuits were settled in due time in our favor. Most people think of leverage in a financial sense. I believe the greatest leverage in a real estate transaction or in any other transaction can come from non-debt type leverage, particularly leverage of negotiating position. I have a strong belief that possession is nine-tenths of the law and one of the great forms of leverage. If you are in possession of the project, an adversary has to legally dislodge you. Too many people have the fear of foreclosure action. As long as there is good communication, logic, and fairness, you will probably be able to negotiate satisfactory results. The primary thing I needed in this transaction was "time," and by being in possession, and particularly with the added confusion of separate financing for the various phases of the project and the number of creditors involved, I was able to negotiate the time needed to make the deal work.

The First Line of Attack — Getting a Handle on the Monster

Although we believed I could buy time and negotiate ourselves into a position of credibility that would help us achieve financial workouts, I realized that once we took possession, we had to work fast. Our first line of attack was to review our test Management Action Plan while also taking care of a few absolute essentials. We needed to get the routine operational control underway as fast as possible. We began by integrating key personnel from our organization into the 50-person staff inherited with the project. We immediately took control of tenant accounting, maintenance, purchasing, and other key operations by installing our systems.

The next step was to interview all personnel on an individual basis. We ended up keeping a surprisingly large number of personnel. In spite of having to cut their salaries, many of these individuals became very loyal and outstanding employees of my company.

A great deal of effort and care went into establishing records in the non-operational areas of the project. We verified all our previous understandings and assumptions about creditors. We immediately called each lender and creditor and set up meetings to describe our situation to them. We began to develop our rapport with a fair and honest statement of what we felt we could and could not do for them. No false promises were made.

Having opened up the lines of communication with creditors and having taken over the operations, we were ready to get into the meat. The most important thing we needed to do in setting up a revision of our test Management Action Plan was to find out about our market. We started a twofold approach. First, we began keeping detailed traffic records on all prospects who walked in the door. We found out where they came from, who they were, why they were interested, and why they did or did not decide to rent at our project. Next, we surveyed by both personal interview and written survey, every one of our residents. This proved many of our earlier assumptions and changed others which helped make our MAP more realistic.

How We Established Rapport with Creditors and Local Government

The keynote of our program was honesty; open, candid, expressing all facts in a professional and businesslike manner. Since our central theory revolved around the fact we were the best possible solution to this complicated problem, it was obviously incumbent upon us to show the various interested parties why this was the case. I personally made trips to the West Coast and other areas of the country to visit with lenders who were involved.

Initial contacts with these individuals had two purposes. First, to establish how bad the project was and what really was going on. Second, to establish ourselves as credible, forthright, and capable of solving these problems. The lenders knew enough of the problems that they believed no one was capable of solving them and a foreclosure and loss would probably be their best answer. Our challenge was to convince these people to give us a stay of execution, so to speak, and watch what we could do with the project for a period of time before they made their legal actions irreversible. One of the lenders did file suit, but after a period of time agreed to wait and watch.

My strategy was simple. Do the best job possible and make sure that the right people knew what was being done. In line with this objective, soon after our takeover, we completed a preliminary report for lenders and important creditors which was 187 pages in length. It covered all of the reasons the project was in trouble, and preliminary thoughts and a position on how to turn the development around. Subsequent reports and communication with the lenders occurred on no less than a weekly basis, and included letters, phone calls, and personal contacts. This continued for a long period of time until the property began to stabilize.

One of the early things I believed to be important to our prospective success was to establish a good rapport with local government officials. Unfortunately, the past owner had not always been able to deliver his well-intended plans and there was some community apprehension and concern about the project. We scheduled meetings with township officials and found a very interested and honest political atmosphere. Our candor was refreshing to the local officials and the rapport began to build.

Since then, there has been excellent cooperation with mutual benefits. Our project represents a major part of the population and tax base of the township, so we are very important to each other. At one point, as I was making an emotional plea before the township board for further tax reduction, after being granted a sizeable reduction through earlier assessor reviews, the township supervisor proclaimed to the local board members, "What Mr. Hall is saying is like what Mr. Wilson, the Chairman of General Motors, said during World War II to the President, 'What's good for General Motors, is good for the U.S.A.'" This was half in jest, but in fact, I believe there is a lot of truth in the idea that what is good for the project is good for the township. Had we not been successful in filling up the project with desirable residents and making it financially viable, the township could have had an unattractive area with unhappy local residents complaining to building code officials. The township's cooperation on our tax appeal and other matters has been gratifying. We have been able to reciprocate by providing community access to our golf course facility, the use of our clubhouse for events, and other cooperation that has helped the area. We have further maintained our value as a tax base for the township by working together for our mutual benefit.

Establishing Management Action Plan Priorities

Having begun efforts in the area of lender-creditor communication and having had a chance to more completely analyze on-site problems at the project, we were ready to begin implementation of our Management Action Plan. Our programs, by necessity, had to address many areas at the same time.

Primary emphasis was given to existing residents. Because the occupancy was not great, our desire to keep the rent-paying residents we had could not have been stronger. Through the resident survey we found that security was a serious problem and a key cause of move-outs. In addition to the survey of existing residents, we did an extensive phone survey and mail contact with past move-outs to try to analyze reasons for the turnover. These surveys verified security, maintenance, erratic high rent increases, and inconsistent management policies as being major contributors to the high turnover and low occupancy.

Major emphasis was placed on development of social programs, improved security, and timely quality maintenance. Every improvement helped make the existing residents happier, and bit by bit we made progress in this area.

Our full attention also needed to be turned to marketing to increase occupancy. In essence, we needed to attack three fronts, all as high priority items at the same time: first, we needed to deal with the creditor-lender problem; secondly, we needed to make the existing residents happier and more satisfied; and thirdly, we needed to get greater traffic into the project and rent to more of the traffic so that our occupancy and collected rent dollars could increase.

Recruiting the Biggest and Best Sales Team — Our Employees, Residents, and the Public at Large

Within 90 days of takeover with many of the routine systems under control, we began to market more aggressively. Our theory has always been that in a turnaround don't tell people what you are going to do, until you have done something. Once you have begun to perform, you can begin to tell the people what you have done and what you will do in the future. It is better to have a loud whispering campaign than to make a big splash and sink.

We began with the assumption that our most important salesmen were our employees. That included everyone from resident manager to hall cleaners. We gained the credibility and confidence of our employees by developing a sense of pride and perfection in their work.

As major promotional developments started, we held frequent employee meetings so everyone on the team was fully briefed in advance. Ideas were solicited from every employee, and soon we had a real team feeling. The employees were well aware of the financial difficulties, so everyone was determined to help get more residents and keep those we had. We were all pulling together to make it work.

Through large resident parties, a newsmagazine which we started distributing to residents monthly, and frequent informal letters, we began to point out to residents the many service improvements and physical improvements being made at the project. It was as though somebody was running a political campaign and everyone was talking about the election. More and more people were coming into the office just to compliment the staff on the fine job being done.

The next step was to get the public working for us. This, of course, would be more difficult. One thing we always do in large projects is offer a selection of gifts, which cost us about $25, to residents who make a referral resulting in a rental. This referral program combined with the growing momentum of resident interest in our programs did begin to get outsiders involved.

A Knob-on-the-Lake Becomes a Sweet "Lemon"

While rentals were beginning to increase and the residents were talking up how great a place it was to live, the project still seemed tarnished by its past reputation. In fact, the name "Knob-on-the-Lake" seemed to work against us in many ways. It was too long for good graphic presentation, and it produced an identity problem with several other area developments that had names "in the woods" or "in the hills."

Recognizing these facts, and desiring to sink or swim on our own image, we decided after four months of effort that a new name with a completely new image would be necessary. After all, what we were really doing was taking the basic shelter offered by the buildings we had acquired and converting this into a concept of total living. The value turnaround we needed could only happen if we truly met all the social and housing needs of our residents. We were becoming a self-contained community in exurbia that còuld be a total escape from the day-to-day aspects of the big city and the working life after a mere 30- to 45-minute drive from work. We were giving all of the advantages of an expensive weekend resort, yet in a convenient location and at a price affordable by many people in middle level jobs. This story had to be told as a new "happening," not just a warm-up of an existing unsuccessful property.

To select a new name and frame the new image, we set up a brainstorming group consisting of myself and six other members of my company's marketing action team. After several days of long hours, we were getting a little punchy and started building absurd name ideas just to let off steam. I got to thinking about how many of my real estate friends had been saying, "Well you really bought a lemon this time," so suddenly I blurted out, "I've got it. Let's call it The Lemon!"

Everyone laughed, but in the tradition of brainstorming, they started hitchhiking positive thoughts. Someone suggested "Lemontree" with the rationale that it had more class than lemon alone, and it would visualize tropical relaxation. Pretty soon we were all joking about the things that could be done with a crazy name like Lemontree.

That was a Friday. At the end of the day we took a straw vote and Lemontree was selected for more consideration! Everyone was to think about it over the weekend. I heard later there were a lot of second thoughts and some half-serious phone conversations centering on whether Craig Hall was diabolically testing the sanity of his executive group.

Nevertheless, the die was cast on Monday morning. There were plenty of underlying reservations, but overall the group felt the boldness of the name would work. Thirty-five days later, Lemontree hit the market with the largest coordinated public relations, advertising, and on-site promotion campaign ever put behind a property in the Detroit area.

The preparation was handled with absolute security because we felt the shock value had to be preserved. Professional planners, writers, and artists worked around the clock, with the master plan coordinated by our internal marketing staff. A short term budget of $40,000 was established for the creative work and media exposure during a 60-day blitz period. Since the new name was to be announced on June 6, the next months would be ideal for rent-up, and I believe in buying attention when it will do the most good.

We first announced the concept and program, including showing billboard, posters, and detailed plans to our employees a week ahead of public exposure. I must admit, they were less than enthusiastic at first. Perhaps they shared the beliefs of others that their leader had flipped his wig over the new name.

Our next line of communication was to the residents. We had a huge birthday party for the birth of Lemontree. During the previous week, over 30 signs including large billboards were being painted during the day with burlap stretched over them at night. These were unveiled at daybreak, June 6. A newsmagazine was also delivered to each apartment that morning proclaiming the birthday of Lemontree and detailing the festivities. This had been preceded by several direct mail pieces indicating that a super-change was coming.

The center of activities was the renovated clubhouse with a huge canopy all done in bright yellow with dark green lettering spelling out Lemontree at the end. A long, green-carpeted walkway now spread before the entrance to the community building, and the interior foyer and hallway were decorated with 25 real lemontrees. Every employee from that day on wore good-looking, custom-made, yellow-and-green clothing. Not uniforms per se, but a reflection of the lemontree fun spirit. Girls have their choice of yellow-and-green slacks, skirts, blouses, and jackets. Men in management have yellow slacks and green blazers. Maintenance men have yellow coveralls.

So the Lemontree service brigade was born. Our rental hostesses and office girls became known as the Lemon Lassies. Our maintenance men quickly became known as the Lemon-aides. An entire lemon vocabulary came into use, and the spirit of the Lemontree team soared.

That Saturday was full of enjoyment for all. The day began with games and festival events for the children of the project. Throughout the day, the large tent which spread over one of the parking lots was full of events celebrating our birthday. That evening a hot dog, hamburger, and barbecued chicken resident party served over 750 people. This was capped with live music and dancing. The reputation of Lemontree had begun with a big bang.

Exactly one week from the party, we scheduled the public announcement as the beginning of a six-week long grand opening. But prior to that, we had a Wednesday afternoon press party which included a cocktail hour, a sitdown luncheon, inspection of the project, and an afternoon of golf. Press packets with complete facts and photos were supplied, and I gave a short speech to introduce the concepts of Lemontree and what we were planning. The reaction was great. There were 17 newspaper stories throughout the Detroit area. The event was treated as news, as well as generating coverage in the business section of some papers, the real estate section of others, and even got good editorial comment.

The grand opening came off unbelievably well. Over the two days of the first weekend many festivities occurred. We served hot dogs, cotton candy, and popcorn to over 3000 people attracted by heavy advertising on radio and in newspapers. Not only did all of our residents come back for grand opening events, but they brought friends as well. Key creditors and lenders were invited to observe, and they did with smiles. We had clowns, games, activities, a water ski show, a balloon ascension, cutting of the large lemontree cake, bands of all types including rock and bluegrass music, radio stations transmitting from mobile units, and fun for everyone. Hundreds of people toured the models. Lemontree was on the map and on its way!

Building Momentum — Excitement as the Results Begin to Show

The sweet smell of lemons was in the air. It was unbelievable to see the overnight change in a project that everyone had called a lemon. In our worst week during the next six months, we rented more apartments than the best week in any of the four-and-one-half-year previous history of the project. Rentals were unbelievable. Traffic tripled, then quadrupled. Occupancy began to climb much faster than our projections. The momentum built on the hard work of the many fine employees was beginning to pay off.

It is really true that success breeds success, and we were all wallowing in the enjoyment of seeing the fruit of our efforts begin to bear lemons. By midsummer of the first year, occupancy was up to 70% and rising. Occupancy is extremely difficult when you have a property that is 40% to 50% vacant after four to five years. This usually indicates a high turnover, so you not only have to rent to fill up, but you have to re-rent significant numbers of old units just to stay even. It is therefore a much harder job than simply renting up a new project. In spite of all obstacles, however, the ink on our graph was moving upward at a gratifying rate. During the fall season, we continued to improve and by winter our occupancy was in the high 80 percentile. In fact, we peaked out in less than 1½ years at 98% occupancy!

Lenders Begin to Become Believers

At first, as we changed the name to Lemontree, I believe the typewriters began to go fast and furious on the foreclosure papers. While the rapport and openness had been good some of the lenders thought it crazy to be changing the name to something as wild and way out as Lemontree, particularly when it offered no description of the type of project. In fact, one of the lenders wrote me two very nasty letters indicating that I couldn't change the name. Fortunately these letters came to my attention two weeks after the campaign was underway and there certainly could have been no turning back. Equally fortunately for that lender, I have also been known to be a person of strong convictions who will take the risk of doing what I believe is right.

Negotiations for a workout program that would help solve some of
the financial difficulties of the project on a long range basis continued
throughout the first year of our ownership. Interim agreements were made
to allow a continuation while negotiations progressed during the first six
months, but other progress was slow in coming. At the end of the first
year, we still did not have a single workout agreement in a formal state
on any of the six mortgages. The rental success and proof that I was in fact
ahead of projections earlier given to lenders began to build strong credi
bility that would carry us through to successful interim and long term
agreements. I believe it is always better to be conservative in projections
and beat your estimates than to give a lender an overly optimistic picture.
In fact, the lenders believed our projections were not attainable. As a result, my results brought us a large part of the distance toward final resolu-
tion of the loan problems.

Capitalizing a Lemon — How We Raised $3,300,000 to Help Hold the Deal Together

While it was not known exactly how much money we would need or
how we would raise it, we initially formed a limited partnership when
we acquired the property. After six months it became apparent we would
require substantial increases in the anticipated funding in order to carry
out all of our long range programs for the property. After considerable
evaluation, we decided it was necessary to raise $3,300,000. It is impor-
tant to understand that even with the tremendous occupancy increase, the
project was still losing money and would for some years. Raising the funds
would not be easy.

The decision was to admit additional limited partners to the partnership. We put together an offering prospectus and got the necessary
clearances by filing our offering memorandum with the State Securities
Bureau. The offering memorandum turned out to be a document of more
than 200 pages. It covered all aspects of the project from origination to
current time, discussed how the partnership was set up, and what the
various investment risks were for new partners.

In a very real sense, the offering memorandum was an absurd document. We were offering people an opportunity to invest over six years in
installment payments, a minimum of $66,000 in a project that was in de-
fault and could be foreclosed at any time. Investors each had to put up
$24,000 per unit as a down payment, but they were also personally liable
for their future installments. Their gain, if the deal worked, would be
major tax loss during the ownership period and eventual capital appreciation if the project became very successful and increased in value.

When the final limited partnership was sold, we had the problem
of wanting to put the checks through December books so that they would

be in the proper year as far as banking records. The executive vice president of the bank we were dealing with personally offered to reopen the bank well after closing on December 31 so we could transact business. Late the evening of December 31 we entered the bank, which had even kept its Computer Department operative so our business could be recorded. We deposited over $1,000,000, well after what most people considered the closing time for the bank's operations of that year. The syndication was done, on schedule, but barely.

Setbacks — a Huge Fire and More

With our year-end syndication under our belt, we proceeded to push aggressive programs to improve the project. Our continuous marketing campaign was making the name Lemontree a household word in the Detroit market. Our occupancy and reputation continued to grow.

Perhaps we were beginning to have a slight case of "postpartum blues." Employees can't stay at a peak level of emotion and momentum all of the time. Keeping everybody "up" is not easy, but we tried to with social events, parties, contests, and other rewards for employees. Indeed, the winter doldrums and the hard times of worrying about the syndication had put somewhat of a lull in our growing campaign to establish ourselves as number one in the local rental market.

On January 14 at about 11:45 p.m. as I was approaching the expressway area of Lemontree on my way to my home, which was 15 miles beyond Lemontree, I noticed the entire sky had a reddish-yellow tone that lit up the night's darkness with a blazing glare. At first the person with me (who lived at Lemontree) and I both began to make jokes in what I now recall to be a sick sense of humor, thinking perhaps someone was burning down the competition. Quickly we came to realize that not only' was it a huge, horrible fire, but it *was* Lemontree.

Throughout the night and into the wee hours of the morning, I watched $1,000,000 worth of real estate, an entire building of 34 apartment units, reduced to rubble as walls caved in from the high-intensity heat. I recall the flames having a blue, Bunsen-burner type color in places. Newspaper reporters and television cameras swarmed through the project. Perhaps because of our constant promotion, the fire drew more attention than most.

Throughout the night, which was cold, windy, and snow-filled, I kept going back and forth to the community building where employees were helping the homeless and confused residents arrange temporary shelter in nearby motels. Thankfully no one had been seriously injured, but sadness and tragedy was all about us. I remember standing knee-deep in snow on the golf course, with tears in my eyes, staring at the buildings as they burned. My mind was filled with concern for the residents who had been displaced by the fire and thoughts of the sad, ironic setback this could create.

The project had had two earlier fires — one during construction and one shortly after the second phase had been completed. This being the third large fire, it created untrue rumors about the construction and safety of the project. Newspapers ran headlines and stories about this for days, and we made the 6:00 p.m. and 11:00 p.m. T.V. news for several days.

Unfortunately, the fire department made several mistakes, and had frozen fire hydrants to contend with. So, a fire which should not have run out of control became a serious disaster. Since this time, with the cooperation of the township, improvements have been made in fire protection, and we strongly believe that any future fires would not get out of control as this one did.

Indeed the setback of the fire hit the morale and confidence of the employees, residents, and the public alike. We simply had one thing to do and that was rebuild. We not only had to rebuild the construction of the demolished rubble, but rebuild our morale as well. We did everything possible for the residents who had been displaced by the fire. We made the best public statements possible and attempted to explain the fire properly to the media. We then proceeded to go full speed ahead to rebuild the units which had been destroyed and rebuild ourselves. It was the only thing to do We couldn't let a fire stop all that had been accomplished.

Trade Creditors Settle

During most of the second year of ownership, a primary financial achievement was in the area of trade claimants. Through a complicated series of legal maneuvers, the sellers' attorney became the primary negotiator for trade settlements.

The primary motivation for settlement appeared to be twofold. First, claimants were not sure the property could make it so they wanted to get something now rather than wait and find out there was nothing. Second, the time it takes for any plaintiff in a court action can be devastating to a small business. When you are trying to collect a just debt, our legal system sometimes seems unfair and unfortunate.

The mortgage negotiations began to progress better during the second year. To understand this situation, keep in mind there were four first mortgages, one on each phase of construction. In addition, there was a second and third mortgage on Phase I. Finally, a little over one and one-half years following the acquisition and over a year after the change of the name to Lemontree, we made the first negotiated settlement.

Eventually, during the second year, we were to settle with all of the first mortgage lenders. Some of the settlements involved a year-to-year review and annual renegotiation on certain points. Still others involved a long-term restructuring process. The net effect was an arrangement that allows the project sufficient cash flow to remain solvent, in return for adjustments which justified the cooperation of the mortgagees.

None of the deals came easily, and it was only after breaking down the original obstacles to real negotiation that deals were finally struck for mutual benefit. In fact, one of the mortgagees used to come in almost every two or three weeks and spend a couple of days with us. I would end up spending a great deal of time, including late night sessions, discussing the project. The personal rapport and relationship which came about after a couple of years of friendly negotiation resolved all differences between the parties. In fact, I am hopeful that some very favorable long term relationships were established.

Lemontree Thrives

In general, as we continue our stabilization process at Lemontree, the use of specific events and social programs as well as other services and amenities usual to apartments is helping us keep our residents. While words like "leisure" and "total community living" have become clichés and are overused in advertising, we are striving harder and harder to deliver them to our Lemontree residents.

Instead of cutting back on image activities after the rent-up, we have steadily increased our efforts. We have added a fleet of five minibuses for transportation to special events, have held frequent contests to build community spirit, and in fact have a continuous schedule of community activities. The effect of this has been most gratifying.

Residents Give a Vote of Confidence as Rents Go Up

As with any financial venture, it is imperative to not forget the objective — profit. While this was a long term venture and the turnaround stabilization was anticipated, we knew it would take six to seven years before the property would break even at the debt service originally scheduled. Nevertheless, we have to stay on track every month in order to meet projections. The key, of course, is income and expenses. The collected income is the real figure to watch. With normal good management, expenses seem to stay in line. However, collected income is the key.

Collected income is determined primarily by occupancy and rental rate. It was important to us that we obtain the maximum net rent increases (rental increases over and above expense increases) that we could possibly achieve in as short a time as possible. From the beginning, we had projected the need for $45 of net rental increase for the project to break even at 95% occupancy. It is very difficult to hold a 95% occupancy in a large development, and obviously a rent increase over expenses of $45 takes a number of years to implement, if in fact it is feasible at all.

During our second year of operations, we had three large rent raises. The very desirable lake units were raised a total of $60 to $75 during that period. The golf-side units increased $30 to $45 per unit. These increases were necessary for several reasons. The lion's share covered inflationary increases in basic expenses. One particular element was the skyrocketing cost of electric heat which we supply as part of the rent. A smaller portion of the increases paid for the improved services being rendered to residents. Finally, an average of $17.50 per month per unit was actual net increase. This was a sizable step toward the $45 required to break even, so we were making progress.

As could be expected, the rent increases did have an adverse effect on occupancy. Almost immediately we lost some of the high percentage we had achieved. As we came into the winter months, following a late fall rent raise, occupancy dropped slightly more than 5%. Interestingly enough, however, because of the rent increases, income went up in spite of occupancy going down. What was most pleasing was to notice the number of residents renewing leases in spite of the increases. They had become believers and were convinced that in spite of the rent increase, Lemontree was a way of life for them.

Journey of 1000 Miles Is on Track

With our rent increase working well, this turnaround is definitely on the way to success. The lender workouts have been accomplished, trade creditors satisfied, operating bills settled, and residents pleased with services. To say the project is now financially successful is almost an understatement, even though it is still not at breakeven on what original debt payment would have called for before our negotiated lower payments. The progress toward bringing the property into a stabilized turnaround has been much better and faster than we had expected. There are a great number of people who deserve to have pride and gratification from this success.

This turnaround was and remains a long term undertaking. The odds against final achievement of a profitable cash flow based on original projections were quite high at one point. The odds of success today are on our side. We will not and cannot let down our guard. The challenge of this turnaround is to keep it on track. Of the proverbial journey of 1000 miles, we have many miles yet to go, but the lonely miles, the most uncertain miles, are behind us.

Chapter 19

Turning the Corner

During the first three years of my career in real estate, the dominant theme was financial uncertainty. Looking back, I can see clearly I was undercapitalized, underexperienced, and overextended. I was short of everything except desire, and that somehow kept me going no matter how hopeless my finances seemed from time to time.

I had a running joke with my secretary. Whenever things seemed to look like something good would happen, I'd say, "See, we're finally turning the corner." Then another unexpected problem would occur and I'd be back on the roller coaster of uncertainty, financial pressure, and personal stress.

Eventually I did turn the corner financially. Bank accounts became substantial. Properties proliferated. Recognition was extended from all sides — social, business, and civic. "Friends" literally sprouted like mushrooms.

In the traditional sense, I knew I had turned the corner, but for some reason I was not full of satisfaction. The joy of success was missing, and for a while I couldn't understand this. Finally, it dawned on me. The "corner" I had been trying to turn was the wrong corner! Financial success was what I had been chasing, but it wasn't really what I needed.

As my work continued and the turnaround techniques crystallized, I finally discovered that at least for me, winning was in the doing. Success is not monetary results as much as it is the process of turning troubled properties into assets serving residents, investors, and the entire community. It is the gratification of seeing a smooth operation replace chaos. It is the thrill of motivating a group of disparate individuals to work as a productive team. It is the helping of people to help themselves become more complete individuals, living life with purpose, and maximizing their own potential. It is the power of problem solving. It is the challenge of creating something from nothing and making a benefit to fellow mankind.

Obviously many businesses cannot be anything more than a vocation for profit. This is not true of the turnaround business. It is a way of life which demands everything you have, but it pays back with the satisfaction of producing benefit for everyone.

If this book has opened your eyes to the potential in turnarounds, I invite you to follow through. There is always room in this business for someone who is determined to succeed and willing to work to make it happen. I challenge you to go out and make yourself some good luck!